A GENERATION
OF LEAVES

A Ukrainian Journey
1923-1948

Ivan Kochan

Edited by Christine Kochan Foster

&

Mark Collins Jenkins

ISBN: 9798378088164 (Paperback)
ISBN: 9798386495275 (Hardback)

Cover design: Adam Hay
Typesetting/Interior: Stewart A. Williams

Library of Congress Control Number: 2018675309

Printed in the United States of America

Like a generation of leaves, just so is a generation of men. The wind scatters some leaves on the ground, but the flourishing forest Grows others, and the season of spring comes; Just so one generation of men grows and another ceases.

HOMER, THE ILIAD

CONTENTS

PROLOGUE 1
The Daughter's Tale
PART ONE

CHAPTER ONE 7
The Lost World of Tudorkovychi

CHAPTER TWO 18
Winter Tales

CHAPTER THREE 33
Seedtime and Harvest

CHAPTER FOUR 44
A View from the Carpathians

CHAPTER FIVE 62
Blitzkrieg!

CHAPTER SIX 85
Strewn Roses

CHAPTER SEVEN 97
Barbarossa

CHAPTER EIGHT 109
Nur Für Deutsche

CHAPTER NINE 125
In the Shadow of Death

CHAPTER TEN 136
Larissa

CHAPTER ELEVEN. 149
What Song the Partisans Sang

CHAPTER TWELVE. 164
Trains in the Night

CHAPTER THIRTEEN. 177
Dust and Ashes

CHAPTER FOURTEEN. 191
The Cossack's Gift

CHAPTER FIFTEEN 204
The Displaced Ones

CHAPTER SIXTEEN 219
Only That and Nothing More

CHAPTER SEVENTEEN 228
Somewhere in America

EPILOGUE 244
The Daughter's Tale
PART TWO

FAMILY PHOTOS. 251

ACKNOWLEDGEMENTS. 255

The Daughter's Tale

— PART ONE —

I knew the door would be unlocked because it's easier that way. He expects me almost every afternoon at this time and he waits in his easy chair. The garden path is familiar, the heavy gate, the porch swing, the fragrant climbing jasmine, the white line painted on the only step so it can easily be seen. Lately he is in a better mood and welcomes me with a smile.

His eyes are often closed, dreaming of younger days and other lives. Today I sit closer on his footstool so I can get a better look at him, see how he's feeling. The woolen beanie on his head and three layers of shirts plus a vest keep him warm, even though the summer sun is bright and the breeze has fallen. Once again, his outfit is a crazy-quilt mixture of stripes and plaids. Clothes were once important to him. He was even a dapper dresser.

He still has a good face, round, not very wrinkled, clear skin. That kind smile and those tired eyes, one bright blue, the other clouded and fading away. It hasn't been easy for him to lose so much of his sight.

Ivan is ninety years old.

Today's world is not his world. Everything is too fast, too loud, or not loud enough. "Speak more slowly," he says to me. "Come to see me, but not if you can't stay." While I was working, I would try to pop in and see him after work or on a lunch break, but faced with both kids and work I couldn't always stay and live this slower time with him. If I only came for an hour, it would often anger him—and he was always quick to show that to me.

Lately, however, it seems to be increasingly important to work less and visit more, spending the time it takes getting to understand this man. This man who I have known my entire life but don't really know like I think I should.

He now leans forward, looks at me closely, pats my back, and says, "You look good, you are a pretty girl!" It's been a very long time since I was a girl, but he sees me the way I see my own grown children.

"How do you feel, Daddy?" I ask. He very proudly announces that he feels good and suggests we go upstairs and do some work. I follow, holding his back gently as he climbs the steps to assure myself that he is indeed moving forward. Ivan is still strong but increasingly unsteady on his feet. He's a big man and I couldn't possibly catch him if he were to fall.

The first order of business is to pay the bills. He holds the invoices, the checkbook, tells me what to write and to whom. Then he checks my work. This method painfully prolongs the process but is the only method he allows. His prescription drug orders are much the same; he directs me while I am on the phone to fulfill the order through an automated attendant that cannot understand Ivan's heavy accent. At such times he gets very frustrated with me, even with my very presence, my inability to understand his concerns, his lack of control. I get it and try to swing with his moods.

After the busywork we change chairs and return to our work on the computer. As he reclines and closes his eyes, we resume the task of recalling his life. He picks up exactly where he left off the previous day and I repeat it back to him as I type. I often check the names of battles, treaties, and dates, my cellphone confirming most details. He just sits there, smiling patiently, knowing his memory is correct because he had lived it.

Ivan dropped back into the past effortlessly and always landed lightly on his feet in a movie-set world of the 1930s and 1940s. He had that kind of cinematic memory. That surprised me, but I was being surprised often during these hours spent with him. The whys and the wherefores of decisions I had once thought dubious were now becoming obvious to me. Much of his story was surprisingly charming; some of it verged on terrifying.

My father was an interesting man. He was a doctor, a scientist, a naturalist, a wood carver, and a poet. He had strong opinions and was quick to raise his voice. He frequently disciplined my older brothers and sentenced them to hard labor in our backyard. I was more my mother's ward and when I misbehaved, it was she who received the discipline. "Why does she not speak Ukrainian? Why doesn't she eat more? Why are her skirts so short?" When I was little, I lived in fear of him. Today I think maybe he was a little afraid of me as well.

After my mother died in the 1990s, our relationship flipped right-side up. I became his "go to" person, whether the problem was his blood pressure or his sticky garage door. He did remarry—he always had an eye for pretty ladies—but that did not impact our increasingly close bond. As he entered his eighties we were practically inseparable—whenever work or children allowed me free time, that is. More and more he wanted me to take him to his endless eye appointments and to the Ukrainian store in Sacramento. We sang old folk songs in the car along the way. Sometimes he recited poetry, or we talked about family, and we continued to work on the memoirs.

The memoirs really brought us together. Ivan enjoyed the attention, and I enjoyed the stories. His demeanor softened with the years. He raised his voice less and opened his mind to other ways of thinking. He began to see me and really listen to me. My father, I realized, was the gift my mother bequeathed me when she died.

When I was little, whenever we didn't go to church on Sundays, we had Ukrainian lessons in the living room where no one ever sat unless there were guests. My mother didn't participate in this ritual, so it was only my two brothers and me. My father was determined that we knew who we were, and that meant learning Ukrainian history and learning how to speak the Ukrainian language. We had to conjugate verbs and memorize endless pages of Taras Shevchenko, the Ukrainian Shakespeare. We understood the language well enough; but we were also American suburban kids and as we grew up, we were less and less inclined to speak it. When our parents spoke to us in their native tongue, we mostly answered in English. Sometimes these Sunday meetings didn't end so well; sometimes I cried simply from the tension, but mostly we were bored. Ivan had a difficult job trying to make his American children understand the importance of our family's history.

He was a good father, though. Family, he said, was the most important thing and Ivan was always the protector of his family. We went on the standard family vacations in the 1960s station wagon like everyone else. He took us fishing, rock collecting, and exploring—he loved all the natural beauty of his adopted country. Through him we all learned how best to appreciate the great American outdoors. Sunday nights were storytelling time, and he would follow up my mother's goodnight kiss with a story for me while perched on the edge of my bed. The tale usually involved sheep and a wolf that dipped its paws into flour—one that surely came straight out of old Ukraine.

Ivan and my mother were at their best playing hosts at dinners or cocktail parties. My father was always relaxed and funny with his guests and my mother was a sight to behold: lovely, tall, and elegant. Wherever we were—California, Texas, Ohio—the home they created showed off their mutual talents and interests, especially my mother's gardening and my father's woodworking. Ivan's woodcarvings, large and small, intricate and fluid, reflected the beauty and pain of the culture of his homeland. They stood mute in the background, though, whenever he had his graduate students over for beer and conversation. Although he had a heavy accent, English being his fourth or fifth language, he was a wonderful storyteller and prided himself on being a good teacher, immunology being his specialty. My parents were also avid bridge players, and their fellow devotees were more often than not gathering in our living room.

Dr. and Mrs. Ivan Kochan enjoyed being married and living the American Dream together. They deserved to—they had lost nearly everything during the Second World War.

The shadow of the war, though, only fell over our living room when our Ukrainian friends visited. Oh, those were lively times! But too often the vodka bottles were emptied, and the talk turned to Ukrainian politics. The air sometimes crackled with tension because old disagreements still simmered just beneath the surface. In the partisan-haunted forests of the 1940s, people had been killed for lesser reason than repeating silly arguments around our coffee table. Even my father and my uncle, who had shared so many tribulations together, had their quarrels—always followed by long and stubborn silences.

Ivan and I began working on his memoirs in the late 1990s, after the breakup of the Soviet Union and the establishment, for the first time in living memory, of a free and independent Republic of Ukraine. I was a young mother then and I couldn't join my father when he finally returned to the village he thought he'd never see again. But you can't go home again, he said, adding nothing more.

So I bought him a cassette recorder and asked him to return home in memory. Cassettes piled up and were stacked in boxes. Eventually the cassette deck was replaced by Ivan's first and only home computer, to which my oldest son installed a Cyrillic keyboard so my father could type letters. For more than a decade these memoirs were written and rewritten, the memoirs of a man whose first quarter-century of life uniquely refracted both the titanic war surrounding him and the struggle for freedom of a proud people too often overlooked by history.

Only by working with him on the memoirs did I begin to understand the urgency with which he tried teaching his kids all those matters uniquely Ukrainian. That urgency was bred in the bone. In 2015, two years before he died, the Russians seized the Crimea from Ukraine. He seemed saddened but not surprised.

I asked him if he thought the Russians might be satisfied with the Crimea, never a part of traditional Ukraine until Khrushchev bequeathed it to the republic in the 1950s.

"No," he said.

I asked why.

"They'll be back," he said matter-of-factly. "They always come back."

"Where are you going, Ivasyu?" asked my grandfather Semen Kochan, using his affectionate name for me, instead of my name Ivan.

"I am going to find the place where the sun sets down to sleep for the night," I replied while walking with my dog, Sirko, on the path leading from our orchard to the pastures behind the barn.

"Oh! Then you plan to make a long journey," said Didoon, or grandfather. "Maybe it would be better to wait until tomorrow morning; a cool evening is coming, you are tired from playing with Sirko, and Babunya Marina will worry when you don't come for supper," said my smiling Didoon while giving water for the night to Chorny, his favorite horse. Chorny made satisfied noises with his nose and his black skin glistened in the light of the setting sun.

"Didoon Semen," I announced, "I will go to find the sun's resting place tomorrow. Sirko is hungry and needs a rest."

CHAPTER ONE

The Lost World of Tudorkovychi

To a child growing up in the magical world of my Ukrainian village, the sun really did seem to rise from a cradle of branches and sink to sleep in a bed of leafy treetops. After all, only a mile and a half away, the mighty River Buh marked the place where the East began, while the smaller Variazhanka, even closer, traced the border with the West. Both streams were lined for miles on end with tall elms, poplars, and willows, all waving majestically whenever a summer thunderstorm approached.

That's how it seemed to one particular child, anyway, one who always had a strong imagination; because that little story about a quest to find the sun's resting place is about the earliest fragment I can excavate from the many-layered bank of memories I've accumulated throughout a long and varied life.

Trees marked the approaches to the North as well. From horizon to horizon, rising sheer out of the nearby fields, a wall of trees marked the edge of what we could only call The Forest. Despite more than a thousand years of Christianity in Ukraine, whenever we entered The Forest, to pick mushrooms or hazelnuts or simply to cut a fir for Christmas, some deep layer in our Slavic souls snapped awake; for beneath those ancient oaks and gnarled hornbeams all was still hallowed and haunted. Mischievous sprites and pixies lurked behind the hazel bushes and beneath the mushroom caps. Legendary bandits, now an improbable several centuries old, might snatch us and carry us off to their hidden lairs. And where the River Variazhanka swung in from the west and met the Buh, cleaving through The Forest, the still pools beside the swampy edges were, our mothers assured us, inhabited by female *rusalka,* just waiting to pull young boys under the surface and keep them forever in labyrinthine underwater grottoes.

When autumn twilights fell, you could hear the deep sonorous hooting of eagle owls somewhere in The Forest. Oracular ravens dwelt there, too. In winter the endless ranks and files of trees lay shrouded in a white blanket of secrecy. Come spring and early summer, when the full moon rose you could see from the village the roe deer grazing in the nearby fields and, more exasperatingly, the wild boar rooting up the potato crop. The boar was the only dangerous creatures in those leafy glens—at least until battalions of two-legged monsters arrived. But that would come later.

Only when I grew older did I realize The Forest, *our* Forest, was just one component in an immense band of interlinked woodlands stretching hundreds of miles from someplace called Warsaw in the west to another and more magical place, for Ukrainians, called Kiev in the East. So north, east, and west were wilderness, and had remained so, seemingly, since the first Germanic and Slavic tribes entered them many thousands of years ago.

But when I was a child, if you climbed a tall oak and looked to the south—well, a very different scene would meet the eye.

There, stretching farther and farther in an ever-expanding triangle with its apex at our oak, were the limitless smiling fields and meadows, sprinkled with hamlets and villages, of old Halichina, the Ukrainian province more widely known in Austro-Hungarian times as Austrian Galicia, one of the three crownlands of that Empire. If we were like the ravens circling and cawing high above, we could see this beautiful country rolling onwards, past that loveliest of Austria-Hungary's provincial capitals, Lviv, and up the slopes of the wooded Carpathian Mountains, along which the base of that triangle ran, some 125 miles away.

This vast sweep of countryside is agricultural land to feast the eyes upon. No sandy grit underlies it like it does The Forest, for the subsoil here is the legendary chernozem, the rich black humus six to ten feet deep in places. It was so deep you never found a rock in the fields of Halichina.

Looking down from out perch in the oak tree to the scene at our feet, that younger version of me is pointing out a storybook village of white-washed, thatched-roof houses, all fronting a red-brick main street, all the chimneys trailing wreaths of smoke, and he is telling you this place, with its lanes and footpaths and far-flung fields just south of The Forest, was my first home, my much-loved but long-lost Tudorkovychi.

I was born in Tudorkovychi on August 20, 1923; but that date could just as easily have been 1823 or 1723, for the village seemed suspended in time and only brushed, albeit unhappily, by the twentieth century. It was a middle-sized village with around a hundred houses and its red-brick main street, called *burok*, ran from north to south through its midst, passing the church before joining a dirt highway angling from south-east to northwest, from our county town and nearest railroad juncture, Sokal, about seven miles away on the Buh, to Hrubieszow, some twenty-five miles beyond the belt of forested country. During the spring and autumn rainy seasons, that dirt highway became a muddy, potholed mess, especially for heavily loaded horse-drawn wagons. But you could walk dry-shod down Tudorkovychi's brick-paved burok.

Not that we entertained many visitors in those days, the dirt highway being our bypass. The occasional tinker or merchant passed through, and if he needed to repair any of his iron fittings he could stop by the blacksmith's forge in the center of the village. There I used to hang out, fascinated by the deep red glow of hot iron. When I grew a little bigger the shop's owner, a man named Korolchuk, permitted me to pump the harmonica-like bellows, making the coal burn so hot the iron turned orange and became more pliable. The smithies could make anything for you, but they spent most of their day fashioning two staple items. One was horseshoes; they could hammer them out in their sleep. The other was iron rims for wagon wheels. Circular and spoked, wheels of every imaginable size leaned against the shop walls. Most of them had damaged iron rims and were awaiting new ones, for tight-fitting rims were what held wooden wheel-frames together. Ukraine at this time ran on horsepower—horsepower and wagon wheels.

The only other regular visitors were theater troupes and itinerant musicians. When they arrived, they filed into a large brick building near the blacksmith's forge. This was Chitalnya, a kind of one-stop community center dedicated to the activities of "Prosvita"—"Enlightenment"—a Ukraine-wide cultural and educational organization, founded in Galicia in the nineteenth century, that played a very influential role in village life at this time. In that building was a co-operative store where villagers could buy such daily necessities as sugar, salt, kerosene, and yeast, paid for with either money or chicken eggs valued according to size. Next to the store was an auditorium for those concerts and theatrical performances. Its stage was also used for village festivities, dances, political debates, and every other conceivable assembly. Portraits of famous Ukrainian poets and statesmen hung from its walls, but one corner in particular displayed a large canvas depicting a broken cannon over the inscription: "For Those Who Died Fighting for a Free Ukraine." I remember this vividly because underneath it was a list of names—one of which belonged to my uncle and namesake, Ivan Kochan, who at the age of sixteen had joined my father in that fight but had never returned home.

Adjacent to the auditorium was a small room that served as the village library. This was the proper *chital'nya* or "reading room" so stocked with books, magazines, pamphlets, and other educational materials on Ukrainian history and the Ukrainian language, supplied primarily by Prosvita, that we came to call the whole complex Chitalnya. Here old men might gather to discuss politics, one longing for the good old days of the Austro-Hungarian Empire, another grumbling about now being shoved into the new Second Republic of Poland, while yet a third corrected him by claiming he should call it instead "Occupied Ukraine."

But whether argument, dramatic performance, or festival of traditional song, Chitalnya's central importance to the village cultural life was further underscored by the adjacent building: The village school, complete with an apartment for its one teacher.

All of that—blacksmith's forge, Chitalnya, schoolhouse—was part of "downtown" Tudorkovychi, so to speak. We might even have boasted a municipal park, for the stream bisecting "downtown" was not only spanned by a substantial wooden bridge but was also flanked by long, pleasant, grassy swales. Unfortunately, those swales had been colonized by the village geese, and take but one step onto the grass and the ganders would come at you, hard and fast—a terrifying experience for children.

The Industrial Revolution had also reached Tudorkovychi. No automobiles yet, that I can remember; but steer your team down the burok, past the church on the south of town, turn left on the dirt highway as if you were going to the train station in Sokal, and on your left you'd pass a steam mill that made flour from our grain. The local housewives baked fragrant rye and wheat breads that were so delicious I can still taste those loaves today. Turn your team around, clop north up the burok toward The Forest, and you'd find the local distillery for making horilka, or Ukrainian vodka; and near that a small poppyseed oil factory, which extracted a savory and non-narcotic cooking oil from the seeds of the opium poppy. Poppyseed oil was a staple in the village diet; during Lent, it was the universal substitute for butter or pork fat. The dry, biscuit-like byproduct, called *makookh*, was fed to the pigs to fatten them up. What the pigs didn't eat went to us children. It was kind of tasteless. But it filled an empty stomach.

Tudorkovychi was overwhelmingly a Ukrainian village. Of the twelve hundred or so residents on the 1930 census, there were only forty Poles and ten Jews. The rest of us were Ukrainians, almost all communicants of the Greek Catholic Church. You won't find many of those outside of Ukrainian-speaking areas with roots in Halichina, or Austrian Galicia. Ukrainians living beneath the heel of the Tsar had their Greek Catholic churches ruthlessly razed to the ground in favor of Greek Orthodox ones. Here is the difference: In the seventeenth century, the Roman Catholic Poles ruling the old Polish-Lithuanian Commonwealth then stretching from the Baltic to the Black Sea finally compromised with us, the Ukrainian minority. If we acknowledged Papal supremacy, we got to keep our cherished Byzantine Greek rite. St. George's Cathedral in Lviv then became our mother church. That's the simplified version, but it will suffice.

Tudorkovychi was a wealthy village surrounded by good soil, a good supply of lumber, and industrious farmers. Grandparents, parents, and children lived together as one family in one house containing four or five rooms and surrounded by flower and vegetable gardens. Those were the domains of the women, all of whom, from the very oldest to very youngest, wore the traditional headscarf sometimes called babushka in the West. Barns and stables, the domains of the men, stood just outside the gardens. Every roof on every structure was thatched, the cylindrical shape of a threshed wheat blade being an ideal insulator, keeping the house warm in winter and cool in summer. Hence the gigantic mounds of straw seen towering behind most of the barns.

The all-important well, lined with cement, was always located close to the house. You drank your water from your well and you excreted it in your equally important outhouse. There was no indoor plumbing and no electricity. In summer, you could always keep a stoppered earthenware jug of water cool by attaching a rope to it and hanging it down in the well. Most villagers also had free-standing brick cellars, set deep in the chernozem and covered with a layer of insulating soil and the heavy door insulated with straw mats. Sour milk, a ubiquitous staple of the Ukrainian diet, stayed cold and pleasantly refreshing in these cellars.

Spiders, for some reason, liked them, too. When we were young, my cousin and I used to catch these spiders and, being boys, remove their legs. We found no explanation for why the legs continued to jerk after being separated from the spider's body.

At our northern latitude, summer days were long, and twilight lingered most of the night. The reverse was true in winter; the sky always seemed dark. You saw either the moon riding high in the velvet sky or a billion stars dancing around the Milky Way. Inside the house, the only light, besides the flickering reflections of the hearth fires, came from the fitful glow of kerosene lamps. Bedrooms were usually cold, especially in winter. But there were usually enough brothers and sisters around that many could pile in a few beds. Families were important in Ukraine. And since many generations lived beneath one roof, every child knew everybody on both his maternal and paternal sides—every child but me, it seemed.

As far as I knew, I was an only child without parents.

Throughout my earliest years, I lived with my paternal grandparents, Semen and Marina Kochan. They were constantly reassuring me I *did* have a mother and a father like other children. But seeing is believing, and I never saw any parents.

I did see a number of uncles around, all of them older than me. Even though I was never neglected because Babunya Marina was always re-minding those uncles of my existence, I often felt lonely. Nobody knew just what to do with little Ivan.

When I reached an age when I could comprehend more, the ex-planation shifted. My father, I was now told, was an important man, something called a Posol, or representative, to something else called a Sejm, or parliament, in that faraway place called Warsaw, and my moth-er was with him. Soon I learned his name, Volodimir Kochan, but had no face to match it with. Then I discovered he was the eldest of Didoon Semen's seven sons, all of whom had reddish-blond hair and most of whom were tall and rangy men. That was some help in now imagining what he might look like.

Yet I knew nothing whatsoever of my mother and her family. Of course, I couldn't know that in the deeply religious world of old rural Ukraine not only was divorce unthinkable but so was even the idea of marital separation. Being too young to understand that, I would have been deaf to the whispering behind my back, whispers telling how my mother had left my father and returned home to her parents, who were living on a farm only a stone's throw away from ours. Apparently, she had been there for quite some time.

Somehow those whispers must have reached even my small ears, be-cause I remember that when I turned five years old, I resolved to go meet her.

I can't recall how I knew the way. But I marched down to the bridge and turned up the grassy swale toward the back of a certain farm some-one must have pointed out to me. I don't even remember the details of that first encounter because I was so traumatized by the hissing and pecking ganders hurtling toward me that the only thing I recall is, when leaving to return home, my mother's voice telling me next time to car-ry a stick: "Listen to me, Ivasyu, you are bigger and stronger than the gander and when you hit him once with the stick, he will run away!" Alexandra Kindrat, for that was her maiden name, was a farm girl from sole to crown.

I was a proud little boy for finally introducing myself to my mother and I would never let that relationship fray again. I know now what she saw in me, that tall, slender child with the round face and hair with a yellowish tint in its curls: She saw a shy boy who nevertheless had braved the geese to come and meet his mother.

I ventured into the grassy valley many times thereafter, always to the consternation of the resident geese. I tried sneaking around them, but the ganders were vigilant and inevitably one of them saw me as soon as I entered his territory. If he extended his long neck with his sharp yellow beak, then I knew he would rush hissing and clacking and chase me over the banks of the creek. Then he'd return to his harem, spread his wings, giggle maniacally, and dance his little victory jig.

Yet each time *I* had won, because I was back in my mother's house, visiting with her and my three-year old brother, Yaropolk, whom we always called Yarko. I was also meeting a new set of grandparents, Kindrat and Maria Dula, as well as one of my new aunts, Stefonka, whose son and my first cousin, Mitonko, would become the lad who helped me pull those legs off those spiders.

I had found my other family—and it couldn't have been more different.

My two families, I now clearly saw, were a study in contrasts. Semen Kochan and Kindrat Dula, for instance, were both close to fifty years old when I was a child. But in every other respect they were opposites.

Didoon Kindrat, my mother's father, was a character straight out of Ukrainian folklore. He was an impressive man—tall, well-built, and very strong. His was a round face with a bushy gray mustache and his head was encircled with a long white pageboy haircut. In good company, he liked to drink strong alcohol, to smoke homegrown tobacco, and to sing Ukrainian songs—songs that brought tears to your eyes but always restored your flagging soul. He had a deep, resonant voice and his friends said in his younger years, it even carried as far as the neighboring villages.

The one idiosyncrasy his wife and daughters found abhorrent was his habit, while handling a juicy piece of meat, of passing his greasy fingers through his hair to keep it shiny and untangled.

Didoon Semen, my father's father, was much more reticent. He, too, was tall, but he was clean-shaven and always wore his hair trimmed short. He was not particularly sociable, seldom spoke, and surely never broke out in song. Semen once smoked heavily, but when I was young, he had quit that habit due to fits of uncontrolled coughing. By that time he could never tolerate tobacco smoke or smokers anywhere near him. Nor was he the most efficient farmer. The twenty acres he had purchased from the Stechishin family only grew progressively smaller, as we liked to put it, as he sold off one parcel after another. What he really cherished was horses, a love picked up from years of service in the Austro-Hungarian cavalry.

Didoon Kindrat, on the other hand, only owned about five acres. But his people were deeply rooted in this corner of Ukraine, and he was an excellent farmer, loving his family, his animals, and his soil almost equally. He not only talked to us grandchildren; he also held conversations with his pigs, the storks nesting on his roof, even with the trees in his orchard. Kindrat was an uneducated man from whom I learned much about life. He taught me how to hold a broom to sweep more efficiently, how best to grip a rake, how to spade or how to use a scythe to cut clover for hay. From him I learned to be more thorough in my everyday tasks and to appreciate a job well done. He always told me, "I know you will not be a farmer but even a doctor has to know how to do ordinary things properly!"

Whereas Didoon Semen did not like priests and rarely went to church, Didoon Kindrat was a devoutly religious man. I can still hear the prayers he softly murmured every evening when making his bed. He endured severe pain in his back without complaint and, several years before his death, he walked bent over double. He treated his varicose leg ulcers just like he treated those on his horses: he burned them with creosol. He loved his domestic animals and considered that they, as he himself, had a purpose to fulfill in life.

Didoon Kindrat was married to Maria, my mother's mother, who was a tiny woman. I remember her most clearly carrying large loads of leaves cut from the harvested sugar beets, leaves she used to feed the pigs. She piled the leaves onto a linen sheet, tied two diagonal corners, and carried the bundle on her back by holding onto the other two corners. Beneath that load she was invisible. One could see only her skinny legs walking beneath an enormous pile of leaves. My own mother was cut from the same cloth; she resembled my grandmother in so many ways, physically and temperamentally.

My father's mother, Marina, unlike Didoon Semen, ran the affairs of her household very efficiently. Hers was a demanding job because she had to feed and care for all those boys, my uncles. Yet I never heard her complain. The first compliment I ever gave a woman was to her. When I was six years old, she and I were sitting at the window through which rays of the setting sun illuminated her hair and made it shine like gold. Gazing at that, I told her she had the prettiest hair in the whole world. She kissed me and I saw tears in her eyes. Ukrainian farm women, I realized, lived hard lives and seldom had the opportunity to express their feelings.

The one opportunity that did give them solace, however, was afforded by the church.

Our church, although standing to the south of the burok, was the beating heart of village life. There I was baptized by the Greek Catholic priest, Father Osmak, whose granddaughter became my playmate. Although in communion with the See of Rome, the Greek Catholic Church permits its priests to marry and have families. There was no more respected a figure than the priest in an old Ukrainian village. Whenever it was sunny and warm, Father Osmak would stroll on the church lawn while reading his breviary. Every woman who happened to walk past would greet him, then bend and kiss his priestly ring.

Villagers both old and young went to mass every Sunday morning and attended all church celebrations and festivities throughout the year. No musical instruments were ever used in our church; instead, a choir composed of young people sang a High Mass that lasted nearly three hours. There were no benches to sit upon and I disliked standing for such a long time. The adults, however, had learned how to rock from one foot to the other in immemorial rhythm with the ancient mass. The church building, however, had been newly built, the former one having burned to the ground.

Ours was a rich parish. Father Osmak not only had a rectory, attached to the new church, in which to live, he also had the rights to over a hundred cultivable acres belonging to his benefice. The villagers gladly sowed and harvested them for him, for nothing was so abiding in old Ukrainian life as the intertwined rhythms of the church year, the agricultural calendar, and the cycle of the seasons. One year nearly resembled another. The generations of men and women danced accordingly, with little disruption but one—a succession of violent and cataclysmic storms sown not by God but by men.

Ukraine means "borderland." That name might have been coined around Tudorkovychi, for in 1914 it had been the northernmost Ukrainian village in the entire sprawling Austro-Hungarian Empire. It was the apex of the Galician triangle whose base ran along the Carpathians. For the lands just east of the River Buh and just north and west of the Variazhanka—the lands where the sun woke and where he went to rest—had then belonged to an old, old enemy: Russia.

And the reason our old and much beloved church had burned to the ground? It had been struck by a Russian artillery shell.

CHAPTER TWO

Winter Tales

Wars and rumors of war remained very distant during my childhood. Taking their place, at least in remembrance, were the gargantuan rhythms of the passing seasons, the majestic wheeling of sun and stars and their most intimate association with those of us living so close to the good Ukrainian earth. Perhaps surprisingly, of all the seasons my memories of winter remain the most sparkling and serene.

Whenever the first frost approached, we insulated house and stables. We laid bundles of fresh wheat straw upon the roofs and stacked them against the outside walls, securing them with long wooden sticks that reached from ground to eaves. We even piled straw bundles beneath each window; if temperatures really plunged, we could plug the window jambs, too. We closed all but two of our rooms. The smaller one was heated by the cook stove, its iron surface featuring cut-outs to accommodate large pots. Behind it was a hearth made of heat-resistant bricks, which Babunya Marina used to bake bread and smoke hams and *kovbasa*, or sausage. In this small room was a large bed for my grandparents. Across the hall was a larger room with a wood-burning stove, a small sitting area, and two double beds shared by my uncles and me.

Wherever we snuggled on wintry nights, however, we all slept beneath thick goose down comforters on mattresses stuffed with long blades of wheat straw, changed whenever they lost their softness.

The stables were also insulated with bundles of straw. That kept the animals warm even in the most severe weather. They were watered twice daily and fed a mixture of thinly cut sugar beets mixed with straw. The stables were also cleaned daily, the manure being piled outside. In early spring it would be spread over the fields as a fertilizer.

One magical dawn, invariably in late November, we'd all awaken to find the stark fields and orchards transformed into a sparkling wonderland by the season's first snowfall. My friends and I would roll the wet snow into cylindrical blocks and build a snowman with them, using charred wood for eyes and a long carrot for a nose. While walking in the fields we recognized the footprints of various animals and birds and by following them we discovered their lairs. We also had snowball wars. The boys with the longest arms usually won because they could throw the balls farther and more forcefully. Other boys would lie down in the snow and make impressions of themselves. Still others had sleds on which we'd skim down steep slopes. You could also attach them by rope to the sleigh of a passing farmer and catch a ride the easy way—but you had to do so with a quick-release knot. The farmer, having noticed his uninvited passenger, might turn his horse whip on you; but if he did, it was usually more in jest than in annoyance.

The sleigh was the ubiquitous vehicle of the Ukrainian winter. One sunny but cold day, Didoon Semen decided our horses needed some exercise. Since he also wanted to buy items for the farm in Sokal, he harnessed two horses to the sleigh and volunteered to take me along for the ride.

On the seat Didoon placed a bale of tightly pressed straw for comfort. We covered our legs with woolen blankets. The sleigh was light and quiet, running on two twelve-foot-long wooden runners. The snow was dry and the horses were trotting energetically, guided only by a wooden tug to which the reins were fixed and steered by Didoon. The horses had small bells attached to their manes that jingled and warned people about our impending approach.

We left the village heading south, passing the church and cemetery and flour mill before gliding through the hamlet of Voislavychi. We covered the remaining five or six miles without much difficulty. The only challenge we encountered was in the western suburbs of Sokal, near the railroad station, where the wind had removed the snow but had left a thin layer of ice atop a brick road. The horses had no difficulty running on the ice because horseshoes were equipped with spikes, ensuring them a firm grip. Our sled however was not so stable! We slid from one side of the road to the other until Didoon could slow the horses and safely approach the wooden bridge over the River Buh.

While we were still sitting in the sleigh, before we even crossed the bridge, Jewish merchants approached us. They were hoping to buy fat chickens for an upcoming Sabbath feast and were stopping every sleigh and wagon coming into town for market day. Any chickens they found they examined by hand, feeling for the telltale fat beneath the skin. The chickens did not like this and complained noisily. Nor did the Ukrainian farmers who owned the chickens appreciate being bargained with in Polish, a language they did not understand and moreover did not care to understand. Yet Jews who had lived for generations among Ukrainians had never learned the Ukrainian tongue - something that always puzzled me.

After crossing the bridge, we entered old Sokal, as opposed to its newer, eighteenth-century suburb with the train station. To the right was the market square over which loomed the tall tower of the synagogue. Wagons and sleighs of every description filled that space, having churned the unpaved surface into mud-colored slush. That square was ringed by the small shops of Jewish merchants, already thronged by the country people exchanging farm products for manufactured goods. We, however, drove further into the center of town and parked our sleigh in the yard of the Ukrainian store called Narodny Soyuz, the People's Cooperative, where my grandfather usually sold his farm products. We gave some hay to the horses, covered their backs with blankets, and went to my father's apartment.

I didn't know my father had an apartment here. Nor did I understand, at that young age, that as a Posol he was representing the Sokal district in the Polish Parliament. All we did in his apartment was pick up his dirty linen to be washed back at home. I might not have remembered all this, but the suits and underwear had this pungent reek, neither human nor animal, like nothing I had ever smelled before.

Afterwards we shopped in several Ukrainian stores, in one of which the shop supervisor and a friend of my father's, Volodimir Velichko, gave me a small bag of hard candies, which Didoon and I enjoyed on our sleigh ride back home. Of course, as I was savoring them, I did not know the meaning of those soiled clothes behind me. My father, I later discovered, had been arrested for defending our Ukrainian churches against the attempts of our Polish overlords to impose their Roman Catholicism on those of us who practiced Greek Catholicism. That very day he was being held in Sokal before being transferred to a prison in Lviv. The smell lingering about his clothes, I later learned, was carbolic acid, or phenol, which the prison authorities were using as a disinfectant.

Another memorable sleigh journey still brings a smile to my face. One of our mischievous pre-Christian sprites seemed to have confused Didoon Kindrat when we were returning home one winter evening after visiting some members of his family.

It was a trip of about six miles from the village of Uhryniv to Tudorkovychi and we expected to be home before dark. Since the road was covered with several inches of fresh snow, Didoon Kindrat decided to leave the women to spend the night in Uhryniv and take us boys and men home to help care for the animals. My cousin Mitonko and I slid into the back of the sleigh, covering ourselves with heavy sheepskin coats while Mitonko's stepfather, Mikhalko, and Didoon Kindrat climbed into the front.

Our journey, alas, was delayed by that "last glass of horilka for the road," which ensured that a moonless, frostbitten night was fast falling, catching us in the midst of snow-covered fields about two miles from home. Soon us backseat passengers realized Kindrat had lost his way. We were riding over a series of low hillocks and we knew there were no hillocks on the road from Uhryniv to Tudorkovychi. To prevent ourselves being jostled out of the sleigh we wedged ourselves between the two seats. Even the horses decided there was something wrong with the driver and would not go any farther.

Finally, Kindrat and Mikhalko reluctantly admitted they were lost. Discussing what to do next, Mikhalko decided to scout ahead and went off staggering through the snow. Both of them were drunk and the whole situation seemed hilarious to Mitonko and me. We laughed so hard our stomach muscles hurt. We knew our drivers considered their situation more serious than it really was. But we could not explain how Didoon Kindrat found these hills on our way to Tudorkovychi! Sooner or later, however, we did find the road and eventually arrived safely home.

The next day we returned to Uhryniv to fetch the rest of our family. No hillocks along the way. But we did notice sleigh tracks in the potato field, the one in which the tubers were gathered in fifty-foot-long, six-foot-high mounds and covered in straw and soil for the winter. Didoon Kindrat had inadvertently wandered off the road. But he was now claiming he had been misled by a mischievous ghost and not by several glasses of horilka! It was surprising the sleigh did not turn over when climbing such rises.

Winter was the season that left the deepest imprint on my memory. For one thing, farmers had more free time to visit with family and friends, to attend lectures or performances in Chitalnya, or to catch up on books and magazines. Sundays were enforced days of rest anyway; you couldn't even shop on Sundays or religious holidays. Furthermore, it was during winter and early spring that the church's ritual year was at its busiest.

Advent, the beginning of the church year in November or December, meant nothing to us children. We were focused instead on St. Nicholas Day, and weeks before its arrival we reminded each other to behave well and be helpful to our parents because the festival of St. Nicholas was approaching. The good bishop, they taught us, would give the most desirable gifts only to those children who were helpful and polite throughout the entire year.

The feast of St. Nicholas is celebrated in the middle of December in the Julian calendar and on that morning, everyone assembled in Chitalnya and waited for the arrival of the blessed saint. He appeared onstage via the building's back door, wearing a bishop's mitre and stole, accompanied by angels dressed in white and sporting wings made of goose feathers. That Godly ensemble, however, was followed by a devil, garbed all in black and sporting horns on his head and a tail protruding from his rear. Instead of the beautifully wrapped gifts carried by the angels, he held bundles of willow sticks and was eager to distribute them to both children and adults.

St. Nicholas addressed the children, reminding them to be truthful, polite, and helpful at all times. Each child then came onstage and was given a gift by the angels while the archangel read aloud from a book the story of that child's good deeds over the past year. Meanwhile, the devil was waiting impatiently for his turn. The child would step from St. Nicholas and be confronted by the devil, who pulled out a willow stick while reciting a catalog of the youngster's trespasses, which sometimes were embarrassing indeed. The devil then told the now abashed child to give the stick to his parents for use in delivering punishment.

In 1928, when I was five, I was lucky! I received several gifts from the angels and no stick from the devil! The next year, however, I received not only two sticks but was also publicly humiliated when the devil related the story of my stealing some coins from one of my uncles. The devil knew I had not been punished for this theft, as I should have been; and he then piled misery on woe by claiming my grandfather and uncle should punish me forthwith! I was quite embarrassed, but duly delivered the sticks to Didoon Semen and Uncle Sidorko. They never did punish me, instead giving me a lecture about the sin of stealing; and my hurt feelings quickly recuperated with gifts of candies, chocolates, and warm mittens.

After St. Nicholas and the devil finished their "work" with the children, they turned to the adults. Now the devil was in high stride: He revealed things some people thought nobody else knew. Although there was much laughter in the hall, there was also a seething anger when intimate secrets or unpleasant trespasses were brought to light. In a small village, nobody escapes a public shaming.

In the Julian calendar Christmas fell on the seventh day of January. The first Christmas I remember fondly was in 1929, when I was six. I celebrated the feast not with my father's family but rather with my mother in the house of Kindrat Dula.

The most important celebration during a Ukrainian Christmas takes place on Christmas Eve, when the family gathers around a meatless Saints' Supper, featuring many traditional dishes. Several days earlier, Mitonko and I had accompanied his stepfather, Mikhalko, on a journey into The Forest to select a Christmas tree. Mikhalko cut a fir and we pulled it home on our sled. It was our job to dress the tree. My brother, Yarko, was three years old and although he tried, he could not help us. First, we encircled the fir from top to bottom with a paper chain we had already made from colored strips and glue consisting of flour and water. On the topmost branch we fastened a golden star commemorating the one which led the three kings to the newly born Jesus. On the lower branches, we hung apples, sugar cookies, and candies wrapped in colorful paper. Finally, we hung glistening bulbs, saved from previous Christmases, from any unadorned twigs. On some of them we even put "snow" made from thinly cut white paper.

On Christmas Eve, Didoon Kindrat placed hay both on and beneath the dining room table. This commemorated the hay in the stable where Jesus was born. The tabletop hay was in turn covered by a white tablecloth on which my mother then placed three large candles while Aunt Stefonka arranged festive dishes and silver spoons and forks. Every five minutes Mitonko and I ran outside to determine whether the first star had appeared in the frosty evening sky; once we saw it, that would be the time to begin the supper. While waiting for the star, we passed the time beneath the table simulating the noises of domestic animals. Didoon Kindrat had told us that by doing so we would ensure another good year for our livestock.

At last, we saw the first star and it was time to start the Saints' Supper. Everyone sported scrubbed faces, freshly combed hair, and festive clothing. We took our places at the table, the candles were lit, Didoon Kindrat said a prayer, and finally announced to everyone the birth of the baby Jesus.

The Saints' Supper traditionally opens with the father of the family offering every member a spoonful of *kutya* while at the same time wishing him or her good health and prosperity in the name of the newborn Jesus. *Kutya* was a Ukrainian dish of immemorial antiquity, made of cooked grains of wheat mixed with honey, ground poppy seeds, walnuts, raisins, and sometimes dried apricots or other fruit.

The first course was usually a hot soup, called *borshch*, enriched with dried *Boletus* mushrooms fried in oil. These mushrooms were very aromatic and tasty. We also ate marinated herrings with rye bread which the adults washed down with several glasses of horilka. Then there was fish prepared in aspic with slices of cooked carrots or baked in tomato sauce. After several fish dishes, we ate *vareniki*, some filled with sauerkraut, others with potato and cheese. After being boiled they had been fried with onion slices. And there was always a dish of *holubtsi*, cabbage rolls filled with mushrooms and rice and served with tomato-flavored sour cream gravy.

For dessert we ate compote made with dried fruits, followed by *pampushky*, similar to doughnuts, filled with fruit and sprinkled with sugar. The supper was finally concluded with more *kutya* blessed by Didoon Kindrat, who filled his spoon with it, threw it to the ceiling, and from whatever stuck he predicted the size of next year's crop. An extra bowl of *kutya* was then left on the table overnight for family members who had departed from this world.

After supper, the family went to admire the Christmas tree in the next room. Mitonko, Yarko, and I then sang various carols to each family member and for this we received five or ten *groszy*, or Polish coins. Many groups of boys and girls would then go house-to-house, greeting each family and singing Christmas carols. Some wore costume, disguised as animals, priests, Cossacks, or merchants. There was often one person dressed as our old friend the devil, as well. Alongside the singing of carols these young people also gave entertaining performances.

That night in 1929, Mitonko and I could not sleep because we wanted to see our deceased ancestors consume *kutya*. We thought it might be at midnight when spirits awaken to disturb people. Several examinations, however, showed no decrease in the *kutya* so after midnight we decided to go to sleep. The next day we were told the *kutya* had indeed been eaten by the souls of our ancestors and, moreover, the dish had been washed clean by them, as well. We liked that! It was good for us to know that our ghostly ancestors still appreciated cleanliness, even washing their utensils after eating.

On Christmas morning, the villagers went to church to celebrate the birth of Christ and hear more Christmas carols. Throughout the day, families tramped through the snow to visit each other and admire the beautiful trees standing in every house. The second day of Christmas was generally reserved for visiting relatives living in other villages. During the evening of the second day, the village artists presented a play on the stage of Chitalnya. It was always standing-room-only on such occasions because they enlivened the otherwise snowbound monotony of village life.

Two weeks after Christmas there was another colorful festival called Yordan, which commemorated the baptism of Christ in the River Jordan by John the Baptist. To celebrate that event, we would all gather at the church, form up in procession, and then walk solemnly down a lane between snowy fields to Starhorod, a village about two miles to the east on the banks of the River Buh.

The procession was led by a man carrying a large golden cross. A priest dressed in colorful robes followed him; behind the priest, young boys and girls carried church banners, which were embroidered or painted with pictures of various saints. Behind them walked the church choir singing Christmas carols. At the end of the procession were people who carried various bottles and mugs to be filled with blessed water.

It was a beautiful sight to see this colorful procession moving slowly through a blanket of white snow. Older people wore long embroidered coats made from white sheepskins. Younger men were in boots and riding breeches; their coats had black velvet collars, cuffs, and hems from behind which peeked embroidered shirts bound under the chin with red ribbons. Their heads were capped with either rabbit-skin caps or Cossack hats, called "krimka," made from skins of black-fleeced Caucasian lambs. Women's headscarves were similarly made of black wool, and the younger girls wore red or black skirts ornamented at the bottom with colorful bands. In front of the skirts, they sported embroidered aprons.

Upon reaching the banks of the Buh, we saw, standing before us, a six-foot high cross carved out of the ice blanketing the river. A hole in front of the cross revealed the water flowing beneath the frozen surface. After a short service, Father Hardibala blessed the water and people filled their bottles and vessels with the sanctified fluid.

Didoon Kindrat stored some of his water in case he needed to treat future illness, using the rest to bless the house and the stables. Mitonko and I assisted him, chalking crosses on the doors of stables and barns while he sprinkled the water on each of his animals. Didoon then told us that on *this* day, and *this* day only, animals blessed with holy water could speak at night to each other. Naturally enough, Mitonko and I just had to hear what they had to say. Throughout the evening we kept creeping into the stables; but despite the sounds of heavy and continuous chewing no words were ever heard. Disappointed, we went to bed.

Back at Didoon Semen's farm, one cold morning, after washing myself with icy water in the corridor that divided the heated from the unheated part of the house, I dressed and entered the kitchen. Babunya Marina was busily preparing breakfast and asking me to say my morning prayer before she would serve me my buckwheat sweetened with milk and a boiled egg, which I afterwards ate with a slice of buttered bread.

As I seemed to be in a hurry, Babunya asked me what were my plans for the day? I told her I had to discuss with Didoon the issue of my pid-kovy—metal blades that attach to the bottom of boots—which I needed for skating on the ice. She shot me a skeptical look but didn't say anything.

After excusing myself, I found Didoon in the stable speaking to his horses. I greeted him with a cheery good morning and reminded him of his promise to buy me a pair of pidkovy. Didoon pretended he did not hear me and scolded an unruly black gelding, which refused to be harnessed to a team with other horses. I interrupted, suggesting the horse probably needed shoes to keep pace with the others and that I needed pidkovy so I could skate with the other boys.

There was a pond on the property of our neighbor that was covered with an even sheet of ice. Many boys were already skating on it and enjoying the pleasant glide across the frozen surface. I liked the clean beauty of the two parallel lines they left behind them. Didoon was telling me I was too young for such an activity and I might hurt myself falling on the hard ice. I replied that I was already six years old and it was time for me to learn this beautiful exercise.

After much negotiation, Didoon gave me thirty *groszy* and, dashing into the village store, I bought a pair of shiny pidkovy, which fit snugly to the soles of my boots. Sidorko, one of my favorite uncles, then fastened them with several short nails and I was ready to try. When nobody was at our small pond to watch my first attempts, I ran to gain some speed, tilted my feet to the right and slid across the ice—but not on the pidkovy; rather on my back! After more unsuccessful trials, my back was hurting and I decided I needed some instruction from an experienced skater.

I asked Petro to teach me. Petro was the youngest of my uncles and was only a few years older than I was. He advised me to keep my legs somewhat apart and to lead with my right one throughout the glide. This advice did help somewhat but not all that much. After many more falls I managed to skate for short distances. The lesson? I learned that observations suggesting the simplicity of some exercises are frequently misleading. To achieve beauty and apparent ease in art or sport requires training, determination, and endurance.

Petro taught me many things. When I was a child, we had two dogs on Didoon Semen's farm. One was my dog, Sirko, and the other was the much older Brisko, who snoozed away the winter afternoons curled up in one of the cozy tunnels worming through the house-sized stack of straw that stood behind the barn. Unless we disturbed him with our games of hide-and-seek, that's where Brisko remained until dark, when he and Sirko came into the house to join the family at supper time.

Once inside, Brisko would greet everybody in his dog-way, but he always ignored Sirko. After eating his meal, he just lay down close to Didoon Semen and listened for a while with closed eyes to our conversation. Didoon had raised him from puppyhood, and he once had been a powerful dog who helped Semen by pulling a small wagon loaded with farm tools, wood, or vegetables. Come nightfall, he'd then go sit on a large tree stump at the gate of the farm to protect the property against any potential predator, four-legged or two-legged. The villagers still believed he was on that stump every night, when in reality he'd long before crept off to his warm and good-smelling place in the stables, where he slept until morning.

But with Brisko in the stables and Sirko in the barn or out protecting the orchard from the hares, there was no dog to guard that huge stack of straw from other hungry hares on the prowl. So Petro took on that task.

One evening, he asked me to come watch. Leaving Sirko in the house, we crept noiselessly to the third barn and through a crack in the planking we looked toward the stack of straw. There we saw the wire loops, attached to stakes driven into the ground, that Petro had placed earlier that day. We also saw several hares playing in the moonlight.

It was a beautiful sight; the hares seemed so happy and there was such harmony, even cheerfulness in their behavior, that I wished Petro would not catch any of them. Petro hoped, however, that play would make one of the animals careless enough that a wire loop would snag its leg. The hares, however, deftly avoided any loop visible in the reflected light of the moon. Their number only grew, and as they pirouetted and played, they uttered high-pitched shrieks of seeming delight.

Suddenly, as if on command, they all bounded off. One of them had probably sniffed our presence. But to me it had all seemed so magical, a Dance of the Hares from some exquisite ballet.

Eventually Petro did snare a careless youngster. It had shiny gray fur and was trembling from fear. I touched it with my hand and felt its rapidly beating heart. Everybody in the house then admired its beauty and nobody volunteered to kill it. We even sighed with relief when Babunya asked Petro to let the hare go. There was not enough meat on that young hare to feed anyone properly, she said, instead promising to make a stew from the meat of a large chicken. Babunya's chicken stew with sour cream gravy being a dish one of everyone's favorites. Petro went duly outside and released the hare. I was very glad to see it bound away to freedom in the snow-covered fields.

The end of March was approaching but the ground was still covered in deep snow. By late afternoon there was frost in the air and it formed white strings along the hairs in the noses of old people and animals. I was sitting near the window in Didoon Semen's house waiting for Uncle Sidorko, who had promised to take me to a play in Chitalnya. He was a tall blond-haired man who was always reading a book or a newspaper or a magazine. He was largely self-taught but he had a passion for education and would eventually be the ad-hoc director of Chitalnya. Whenever he was around, he was always very nice to me.

While I waited, the frost was painting beautiful flowers on the windowpanes, and I was dissolving them with my hot breath to better see what was happening in our yard. The sun was setting with a reddish hue forecasting another very cold night. From my uncles I had learned the sun doesn't go to bed at all; it is the Earth that rotates around the sun and the spinning of our world causes night and day. But looking at the setting sun through my window, I was not convinced about this rotation of the Earth. Nor did I believe old stories that the world is supported by huge pillars or rested on the shoulders of Hercules. It seemed to me, studying the sun as it melted into a sea of crimson and gold, that the sun was doing all the moving, even deliberately hiding behind the tree-lined border of our fields.

Didoon Semen walked from stable to stable, supplying hay to the animals to help them withstand the rigors of the coming night. He let out our four horses so they could have a drink of water from the wooden trough adjacent to the well. The well was about twenty feet deep and three feet wide; it was lined with cement cylinders and, being so deep, its water never froze during the winter.

The horses were happy to be out of the stable; they ran several times around the grounds, and then drank some more water. It was during his years in the Austro-Hungarian cavalry that Didoon had acquired his love of beautiful horses. One of our geldings was shiny black and the Polish army had wanted to buy it for 1,000 zlotys, but Didoon would not sell. I once asked him if he had such a shiny black horse while in the cavalry. He replied that black was associated with sadness and death and therefore troopers preferred horses of a different color.

My dog Sirko tried to help Didoon persuade the horses to go back into the stable. Yet the horses were enjoying their momentary freedom and continued to frolic in the invigorating evening air. Eventually they returned, but only after Didoon lured them with cubes of sugar. The horses knew their places in the stable and rarely did they kick or bite.

After the stable doors were locked for the night, Didoon and Sirko came into the house, bringing with them a wave of cold air. Sirko was allowed to spend the chilly evenings in the warm kitchen, but after we went to bed he slept someplace in the barn or chased hares out of our orchard, where they chewed the bark off young fruit trees, damaging them. The hares preferred to eat hay, but had now grown wary of Petro's schemes to keep them at bay.

Dusk was descending and still there was no sight of Sidorko. Babunya Marina remained unperturbed, persuading me to eat some supper before going to Chitalnya. The performance would be a long one and she was concerned I might become hungry in the midst of it. So she served my grandfather and me mashed potatoes sprinkled with *skvarky*, fried salt pork; we drank sour milk and ate bread dipped in poppyseed oil.

Finally, I heard the unmistakable crackling sound in the dry snow made by Sidorko's approaching boots. After eating his supper, he dressed me warmly and wrapped my feet in square flannel sheets before helping me pull on my own knee-high boots. Although I was even wearing an overcoat, Babunya insisted on wrapping my head in a woolen babushka. She simply ignored Didoon when he teased her for dressing me like a girl. Since time was short, Sidorko decided to carry me on his back to a Chitalnya already filled with people. Before we went in, he removed the babushka from my head. He did not want my friends to see me dressed like a girl.

The hall was illuminated by only one kerosene lamp hanging from the ceiling. The feeble light was further dissipated by the clouds of home-grown tobacco smoke that burned my eyes. Nevertheless, I found my friends up toward the front, close to the stage, and when the curtain opened, we all had to kneel so the people behind us could see the play. We had to be especially good that night because all the village elders occupied the front row and they most certainly would not tolerate noisy and unruly behavior.

The drama we watched that long-ago night had to do with the child-hood of Ukrainian poet Taras Shevchenko. You could not grow up in Ukraine at that time without knowing Shevchenko lore. He was to us what Pushkin was to Russians or Shakespeare to the British. Shevchenko was the Ukrainian prophet because in his verse he reminded us of our storied history and instilled a reverence for our proud heritage. In one of his poems, he even encouraged Ukrainians to pray to God to send them a man like George Washington to help throw off the yoke of foreign domination and lead them to a successful fight for freedom.

After the performance, Petro found me in the hall and together we went home. The night was very cold with a full moon high in the sky. The snow was sparkling on the roofs of the houses and the crunching of it under feet echoed down the lanes. Faraway dogs were barking, some even howling like wolves. Floating in the distance we also caught the singing of boys and the laughter of girls.

Finally, we came to our house, drank warm milk, and ate *pireeh*, baked rolls stuffed with buckwheat. Babunya always coated the crust of *pireeh* with soft pig-fat and garlic that made them very tasty. After saying our prayers, we went to bed in the "big" room. I slept with Petro on one double bed and Sidorko slept on the other one. The room was cold but we covered ourselves with goose down comforters and soon fell fast asleep.

CHAPTER THREE

Seedtime and Harvest

Around the middle of April, the clouds disappeared from the sky and a warming sun began melting the snow, first from the roofs and roads and finally from the fields and pastures. Our creek ran brimful with meltwater and its bordering willows began to bloom. Although both village and farm lanes became slippery with mud, sleighs were nevertheless put up and wagons rolled out. Crows built their nests on tall poplar trees while larks sang high in the clearing skies, their cheerful songs floating down upon the dark and patient earth.

While farmers prepared their equipment for work in the fields, my friends and I went to grassy pastures to collect the sorrel growing wild on the hillsides. The herb was an excellent substitute for beets in borscht. Sorrel borscht, mixed with sour cream and eaten with black bread overspread with fresh butter, is a famous Ukrainian delicacy.

Another telltale sign of early spring was the arrival of the storks. During the first days of spring in 1930, my cousin Mitonko and I were waiting for the pair of storks that had their nest atop Didoon Kindrat's barn. About three feet in diameter, the nest was made of twisted twigs and lined with moss. Each spring it grew bigger and bigger as the birds added to it. For all we knew, the same pair of storks had been using it for years.

One sunny day the female touched down on the nest. But there was no sign of the male. She and everybody in our family were waiting for him and, when he was finally spotted circling down, there was much joy in the house—matched by an equally joyous clickety-clack on the barn. Both storks stood on the edge of their large nest and extended their necks up and down, greeting each other and making much noise with their long red beaks. They were announcing their arrival to everybody in the neighborhood. After half an hour of this happy reunion, they started organizing the nest and looking for delicious frogs in the creek.

Kindrat did not miss this opportunity to give Mitonko and me a lesson. "You should know our storks are welcome visitors. They come to us every year by flying from faraway Africa and therefore, you should treat them as our guests." Clickety-clack, clack, clack. "They are good animals," he continued, "but when disturbed, they can be very angry and might even punish bad people. An angry stork can find a live ember, take it with its long beak, fly to his nest, and burn it up—and when the fire spreads, it also burns down the building of the inhospitable people."

Didoon Kindrat instructed us that we should never chase storks away or throw pieces of dried dirt at them. Occasionally, there was talk among the children that storks are good because they bring babies to parents. But I preferred to believe Didoon Kindrat, who told me babies are born more like our farm animals were.

We liked storks because they were very majestic birds and despite their large size, they walked very gracefully and with much dignity. It was an unforgettable sight to see the storks stalking behind a farmer undertaking his spring plowing. The plow was pulled by two horses and although the reins hung around the farmer's neck, he never used them because his horses knew the routine and would respond to his voice alone. He held onto the plow handles more for steadiness than for direction. As the plow cut the black chernozem it left deep furrows of freshly tilled soil so rich in organic matter it glistened in the sun with various colors.

A few feet behind the farmer stalked the white storks on their long red legs. Behind the storks was a procession made up of smaller birds, starting with ravens and sliding down the scale to crows and robins before finally ending with small larks and sparrows. Each bird picked its own favored food from the upturned furrows and kept its place in this strange but beautiful procession.

Spring in the Ukrainian mind is closely associated with the celebration of Easter. When I was growing up the feast always fell in April, after the plowing was finished and the buried seed had burst into delicately green shoots of grain, symbol of resurrection. Many customs in our celebration of Easter, such as the veneration of eggs, stem from pre-Christian times and survived even the years of atheistic Communism, which was never able to eradicate the deep-seated faith in the Ukrainian heart. It sprang right back when a new sun emerged from behind the clouds.

As Easter Sunday approached the women and girls set eagerly to work preparing the *pisanky* and *krashanky*, the ritualized eggs symbolic of the season. The *krashanky* were simply colored eggs that could be eaten during the festivities. But the *pysanky* belonged to a different order altogether. They are eggs intricately painted or "written" by hand using beeswax over layers of progressively darker dyes. Each one took hours to complete and were not intended to be eaten. That and most other preparations were finished by Wednesday night of Holy Week and placed in baskets to await the feast.

Maundy Thursday was devoted to ritual cleansing, and on Good Friday, the old-timers entered church on their knees and, during their prayers, expressed their veneration for Jesus by bowing until their foreheads touched the floor. Many people refused fatty or even milk-based food and some did not eat anything until Easter dinner. Didoon Kindrat was one of those who drank only water throughout Good Friday and Holy Saturday, fasting the entire time.

Meanwhile, on Saturday and Sunday morning the housewives finished filling the covered baskets with items to be blessed in church: a traditional bread called babka, homemade sausages, smoked ham, butter, and those pysanky and krashanky. Each housewife covered her basket with a pretty embroidered towel and, early on Sunday morning, her husband carried it to church. The baskets were left outside, and after mass the priest blessed the food and sprinkled it with holy water.

Easter morning also followed a prescribed ritual. Didoon Kindrat would gather the family and boom out, "Christ is risen!" and we'd all respond, "He is risen indeed!" Then we would rock on our feet in church for a few hours before finally breaking the fast with the Easter feast—cheese, pastries, and eggs, always eggs at Easter, Ukrainian sausage, and horseradish sauce—and many a glass of horilka I saw being downed.

Girls gave pysanky to their favored boyfriends or as tokens of good will or remembrance. They were also placed in stables to improve fertility, in fields to stimulate the growth of crops, and in homes to work the same magic with families. The joy of Easter in Ukraine was a celebration of life—a bursting of sheer vitality out of the dark soil, out of the long and very cold winter.

The weeks between April and October in old rural Ukraine were given over entirely to the ritualized rhythms of seedtime and harvest, at least for the farmers and their brothers and sons. But work in the fields was heavy, laborious, and often dangerous, and fatal or crippling accidents were common. Children were generally onlookers, not workers or participants, outside of ferrying food and water to the men and older boys.

Our farmers grew not only the wheat that made Ukraine the breadbasket of Europe; they also planted barley and rye in varying proportions. They sowed potatoes in the sandier soil close to The Forest. One of the continent's leading sugar beet belts ran right across Ukraine all the way to Kiev. But the beets exhausted the soil and needed to be rotated with peas or beans. Then there were hayfields, orchards, and acres of forage crops like clover, all needing weeding and tending. When the farmer wasn't driving the plow, he was swinging the scythe. Then he'd plod home and take care of horses and cows. His wife kept the chickens, watched over the pigs, and nurtured the kitchen gardens. Rural life in old Ukraine demanded hard work from every adult.

Unfortunately, of all Didoon Semen's six surviving sons, only Petro proved to be a reliable farmer. Most of his brothers pitched in from time to time, but I didn't think my still-mysterious father ever did. My mother, on the other hand, was a born farmwoman.

So Sirko and I were often free to rove as we pleased if we didn't go too far. I'm sure a watchful eye was always upon us.

Toward the end of spring, with the crops planted and starting to grow, the June beetles would emerge in the lengthening twilights. They'd swarm in such numbers they'd weigh down the branches of trees and shrubs. Since they might damage our orchard, one of my jobs was to rid our fruit trees of them. During chilly mornings many hungry chickens waited impatiently for me at the door of our house. They would follow me into the orchard with much noise and enthusiasm. I shook the limbs of the plum trees and the beetles, immobilized by the nightly chill, would fall to the ground like ripe fruit. The chickens then consumed them quickly and in large quantities.

Occasionally, I collected some of these bugs in a small box and took them with me to school. I placed the scratchy bugs behind the collars of girls whom I liked but who did not pay any attention to me. That made them turn their eyes my way, but the results were rather disappointing. Some boys tied June beetles with thin strings to small sticks and "enjoyed" the buzzing the bugs made while flying in circles around the sticks. That quickly bored me, and I preferred to feed them to our chickens or to place them behind the collars of pretty girls.

From the members of my family, I learned about the good and bad qualities of various flowers and plants. Some of them were edible, or had a pleasant fragrance and taste, while others were poisonous and dangerous even to the touch. I grew to know each kind by sight, taste, and potential medicinal use.

There was krovavnik, or lovage, a tall perennial often used in salads and believed to have aphrodisiac properties but whose juice was also a blood coagulant. There was khreen, or horseradish, whose root not only provides the famous condiment but whose leaves, applied superficially to the forehead, can also reduce a headache. Kropiva, or common nettle, has a well-known sting that reduces the pain and enables the movement of arthritis-stricken joints. The poppy, *Papaver somniferum*, with its beautiful flower and intricate head, not only produced those delicious poppy seeds but also the well-known balm that reduces pain and, additionally, induces sleep in a crying infant. And being Ukrainians and hence Slavs, we were all intimately familiar with the many delicious mushrooms and fungi found in The Forest.

Villagers struck with arthritis might also use bee sting venom to reduce the pain and swelling in their joints. Others might use leeches to remove "bad blood" from infections, "bleeding" being an ancient and sometimes derided medical practice. But it is possible the removal of hemoglobin from red blood cells via bleeding reduces the availability of iron needed by the infecting bacteria, thus slowing if not halting the spread of infection.

We frequently forget that most of our most beneficial medications originated from plants. When I was a young boy, people were living with nature and using its gifts for their benefit. The willow trees down by the creek belonged to a genus that for thousands of years had provided people with bark preparations that soothed pain and inflammation. When synthesized in the nineteenth century, the active properties provided the world's most famous anti-clotting analgesic, aspirin.

I grew interested in medicinal plants because from a young age I always wanted to be a doctor, a healer. When I was still small, a local farmer suffered an eye injury which partially blinded him—or should have partially blinded him, but soon afterwards, for no apparent reason, he lost sight in his good eye, too. The man went completely blind and there was no explanation for it. I felt so sorry for him that I resolved to grow up and one day be able to treat such maladies, to help people and not hurt them. It turned out this unfortunate man might have had a rare disorder called Sympathetic ophthalmia, something not well understood but probably related to an autoimmune reaction.

As spring turned to summer the days grew longer, the light staying in the sky until 10:00 p.m., and the mornings sometimes started with a thunderstorm.

In the middle of June, when the wheat in the fields was already high and the farmers were making room in their barns for the storage of the new crop, Didoon Semen welcomed the arrival of Uncle Miron, who was attending business school in Lviv during the rest of the year. Didoon had hoped that during his vacation, Miron would help with the upcoming harvest; but Miron was more inclined to read books and play his violin. Of all my six uncles, Miron was physically the smallest. But I didn't like him all that much because his jokes were always personal and had an unpleasant sting in them. Part of the farm belonged to my father, too, but even when he was not in prison, he was never around.

Nevertheless, Semen did ask Miron to do some light work around the farm. Sirko and I were usually observers but, occasionally, even I pitched in. I liked to help with the farm work because it made me feel like I was a valued member of the clan. I particularly liked hanging around the chickens, especially once they started laying eggs. My motives here were entirely selfish. I liked to eat the eggs—raw. One day, while sitting near the grain-storage building that stood about fourteen inches above the ground, I noticed the chickens laid some of their eggs beneath it. Sirko was sitting next to me and must have read my thoughts because he squeezed his body under the building and came back with an egg, holding it gently in his mouth, and gave it to me. I praised him and encouraged him to repeat this useful act. In a short time, I had about twenty-five eggs. Some of them were spoiled but many were edible, and I had a feast.Some eggs I gave to Miron for his hair treatment. Somebody had told him washing the hair with egg yolks would prevent balding, for Miron had started losing his hair at an early age. After that, however, my generosity with eggs was sharply curtailed. An egg with a poorly formed shell happened to break in Sirko's mouth and he tasted the yolk—and from that moment on he never brought me another one.

When the summer sun dried and warmed the soil, I asked Babunya Marina to allow me to walk barefooted. In my boyhood days I loved feeling the warm soil beneath my feet. My friends and I liked to walk barefooted over the warm powdery dirt road and then cool our feet in the waters of the creek.

I was also frequently asked to take baskets of dinner and jugs of cold water to my family members working in the fields. Since I liked being helpful and enjoyed doing useful work, I filled jugs and bottles with cold water hoisted up from the well. After carrying it out to my thirsty and hungry relatives I would sit and eat with them. It seemed to me that food tasted better when it was eaten in the field.

Summers were also times when the villagers were constantly fighting with hordes of houseflies. The stables and piles of manure around them were breeding places for the pests, and they invaded every crevice in every house and gave no peace to its inhabitants. They were constantly buzzing around our heads or falling into soups and drinks during meals. People invented various methods to keep houses free of the flies, which not only spread infectious agents but also interfered with rest. Since screens were not available, housewives hung linen curtains in the doorways. But the flies streamed in whenever someone entered. Strips of flypaper, impregnated with sweet but adhesive glue, hung from the ceiling in every room. Some women even placed poisonous mushrooms in a dish made attractive to flies with sweetened water. If anything annoyed a housewife more than flies it was children constantly going and coming through the doorways, parting the fly-curtains and letting the hordes spill in!

In August 1930, I finished my sixth year of life. Since I was tall for my age, the older boys sometimes permitted me to play with them. As summer turned to autumn, we would invade orchards to sample apples, pears, or plums. It seemed to us the orchards of our neighbors always had tastier fruits than ours did. The owners chased us out but never intended to catch us because they had done the same thing when they were our age.

On sunny days, we would go into The Forest and collect hazelnuts, the wild hazel bushes usually producing a good crop every year. We opened the nuts we collected with sharp pocketknives. I was permitted to carry a small one given to me by Uncle Sidorko. But the knife I really wanted was called "cyhanik" (gypsy-like); they were sold by an old Jewish tinker who visited the village every month to buy scrap iron and tattered fabrics for recycling. When he next came around I had some old horseshoes I had found in the workshop next to the barn, and these I exchanged for that particular knife. When Didoon Semen learned about my deal, he became upset because I had not told him about it. He said the Jew had cheated me and he would have a word with him. But he never did.

Yet my problems with knives were not over. The older boys had even better knives than the cyhanik, knives that sported both long and short blades plus mother-of-pearl handles. Since I was almost their age, I felt I should possess such a knife, too. But they were prohibitively expensive.

Then I had a bad idea. I took money from Sidorko's desk drawer.

As the treasurer of Chitalnya. Sidorko had hundreds of twenty-five-groszy coins stashed in his drawer. Surely, he would not miss four coins!

I showed the coins to my friends, and they admired my riches; soon the whole village knew Ivan was a rich boy. Sidorko eventually heard about his rich nephew, and I had to return the money to him. In exchange I received a reprimand and a long lecture about the sin of stealing. Didoon was even more upset and told me he would tell my father; fortunately, he never remembered. That was the episode that led to my infamy on St. Nicholas Day, when the devil gave me two willow switches in Chitalnya. My theft of Sidorko's money became a family joke: "If you need money, ask Ivan how to get it!"

The wheat was always harvested in late June and early July. Barley and rye were cut in the autumn. All were labor-intensive activities. As the days became shorter and it rained more frequently, I could no longer walk barefooted. The roads became muddy and slippery. The farmers were threshing bundles of wheat and you could hear the continuous pounding of the thresher all over the fields.

Potatoes were the last crop harvested. About two or three weeks after they flowered, they would dry out and the leaves could be shorn off, piled in a field near The Forest, and burned. My friends and I would watch, and when the flame died down and became embers, we'd bake a few potatoes. We were convinced potatoes baked in the remains of the fire with the hot soil around them were much tastier than potatoes baked in ovens. When the spuds were ready to eat, we spread them on the ground to cool and enjoyed our feast, even though the crusts would leave our faces gray and sooty. After eating enough potatoes, we exercised by trying to catch a ride on the cows in a nearby field but they did not like acting as horses. Domestic cows were good-natured animals and they never used their horns and after eating enough grass, they preferred to be left in peace.

When the weather turned cold in early November, it was hog-killing time. Didoon Kindrat prided himself on his expertise in slaughtering them. He used a "shayka," an iron rod about half an inch thick and a foot long that was sharp on one end. With this deadly instrument he pierced the pig's heart. Mikhalko was his assistant, and his job was to hit the pig so hard over the head it fell unconscious, making the task much easier. But sometimes Mikhalko missed his aim—and then the whole family ended up chasing the pig.

After the slaughter, Kindrat worked day and night making kovbasa, a sausage smoked in the secondary part of the oven located behind the one used for baking bread. He also made a blood sausage made from the hog's lifeblood mixed with various fillings. The leftover pig fat he salted and packed into a barrel. After aging for several weeks, this fat was soft as butter and could be eaten raw with rye bread, or used for cooking and for making skvarky, those delicious pork cracklings. The hams were first marinated, then smoked, and finally hung in a storage room where they partially dried. Whenever a piece of ham was needed, say for Borsch or for flavoring Sauerkraut, all one had to do was go into that room and slice it straight off the ham.

But the autumn ritual I remember most poignantly was always an unforgettable spectacle: the preparation of the storks for their flight to Africa.

Gathered in the creek valley behind the village were hundreds of storks that had separated themselves into several groups. The birds looked mysterious in their inactivity. They were quiet and appeared to be very solemn in their deliberations. As they stood around, a single "messenger" or "facilitator" stork ran back-and-forth between the groups as if informing each one about a decision that had been reached. I'll never forget this picture of the deliberating storks. It seemed the assembled birds were planning their trip and their order of flight, perhaps electing leaders for their long journey. When night fell, they did not return to their nests; they kept standing motionless in those tight circles.

The next morning, I went to see whether the storks were still conferring, but the valley was empty. They had all left. The storks living on the roof of Didoon Kindrat's barn were also gone. I missed them and everybody in our family was sad about their departure. In our thoughts, we wished them a safe and happy journey to their warm winter home in Africa.

Over the next few days, I saw more groups of storks flying over the village. These groups flew in a V formation, with one side longer than the other. I asked my grandfather, "Didonniu! Why does the leader in the front of the group retire to the short side while another takes his place from the longer side?"

"Oooh, this is very interesting to observe how these birds distribute the effort of their flight to the whole group!" answered Didoon. "The first bird of the V has the most difficult and demanding job because its wings push the air to the sides so those behind have a somewhat easier flight. When the lead bird gets tired, the next stork moves into this critical spot. You will find in your life that it is frequently more difficult to be the first to run before anyone else."

"It is a long and difficult flight to Africa," explained Didoon. "They have to fly above the high, windy, and cold Alps. They have to fly across the Strait of Gibraltar and over the coast of the Holy Land to reach their home down south. It is a treacherous journey, and they will lose some members of their flock. Yet they will return next spring to enjoy the happy life in Ukraine!"

CHAPTER FOUR

A View from the Carpathians

In the autumn of 1930, as I was sitting one afternoon in our one-room schoolhouse being tutored in Polish by our teacher, Miss Vojtkiv, I saw out the window my Uncle Sidorko sprinting for the teacher's woodshed. To her consternation, I watched him lock himself inside. A few minutes later we saw why: Fifty Polish soldiers were galloping into town, their guns and swords flashing in the sun. They dismounted in front of Chitalnya and the adjacent school. The entire village, we soon discovered, was encircled by mounted troopers. No one could enter or exit without special permission.

These soldiers knew exactly where to go and whom to apprehend: Anybody who had anything to do with promoting Ukrainian history and heritage. They were above all looking for Sidorko because he was the de facto head of Chitalnya. But he couldn't be found.

The troopers did manage to round up about a dozen others on their list. They did not bother with the school or the schoolmistress because the school was run by the Polish government. Nor did they mess with our Greek Catholic church, because that might land all of Poland in the dock facing the ire of the Pope, for this was a Polish government-sanctioned raid directed at some 450 villages in Halichina and called the "Pacification." It was an attempt to stamp out nascent nationalism among the Ukrainians living in what we called "Occupied Ukraine."

The soldiers broke down the door to Chitalnya, destroyed the pictures of Ukrainian heroes, and with a sword slashed the picture of the cannon commemorating those who had died in the fight for Ukrainian freedom. The soldiers also broke down the door to the small library and threw out all the Ukrainian books, tossing them through shattered windows into the dirt outside. There the horses' hooves finished the job, tearing the pages to shreds in the dust.

Finally, the imprisoned men were taken inside and tied face-down on the benches. The horsewhips then came out. When it was all finally over, many of the prisoners could not walk and had to be carried out on blankets by the women of the village. The floors were covered with human blood and excrement.

Several soldiers even visited Didoon Semen's farm looking for Sidorko. Naturally, they did not find him in the stables or barns since he was hiding elsewhere. They did, however, steal several hundred pounds of grain from our granary to feed their mounts.

The Polish troopers terrorized our village for two full days. On the morning of the third, they trotted off to pacify other villages, leaving behind traumatized and embittered people with hearts brimful of hate.

Historians might point out that Ukrainians actually began this latest round of tit-for-tat savagery. In July 1930, our more extremist nationalists began a campaign of sabotage, launching hundreds of small attacks on Polish property and interests in Halichina. Only in September did the Polish government retaliate, ordering the Pacification. But as I was soon to learn, our extremists represented only a portion, and not necessarily a large portion, of the Ukrainian population. As we would see, all too clearly, a decade and a half later, reprisals directed against innocent people only leads to an escalation of violence and terror.

That commemorative picture slashed by the sword would never be repaired. It remained as a permanent reminder of Polish terrorism.

Thus did my education begin, in a schoolroom—even though that was not the lesson Miss Vojtkiv had planned.

Education in Poland, as in most of Europe, had two paths. After a few years of the children being taught together the most common outcome was to go straight to work on the farms or enter a vocational program to be clerks, carpenters, bricklayers, and so on.

The other path was academic and might lead to a university education and a professional degree. That involved attending a gymnasium, or secondary school, for six years and passing another and more formidable general examination called a Matura, from the Latin for "mature," after which young people had the right to seek higher education at a university.

This second path was the one my parents hoped I would follow. My initial experiences in elementary school, however, may have shaken their confidence in me.

I started school in September 1930. I was already a year late, having inadvertently been knocked unconscious by Uncle Petro when he was fixing the iron turnstile on the well. The injury was so severe that Babunya Marina had held me back. So, I was a tad older when I joined the line of kids standing in the school yard. The doors opened at 8:00 a.m., and after we wiped our shoes or bare feet, we took our places on the rows of benches. None of us pupils understood Polish, and we were apprehensive about our new Polish teacher.

She was a small lady, and she was hardly visible when she sat at her desk. Behind her hung the emblem of the Polish state, a white eagle on a red background, and on either side of it were pictures of Marshal Pilsudski, the de facto dictator, and Ignacy Moscicki, the official president of Poland. There were twenty-five pupils in my class, all Ukrainian. But on this first and every subsequent school day, the teacher started our education with a Polish prayer we did not understand. For the failure to speak Polish, she punished pupils in front of the class. We had to extend our hands with the palms up and she would strike them with a stick several times. It was fun, however, to watch when the hands of some pupils were quicker than the teacher's stick and she swatted empty air.

From the very beginning my teacher and I did not like each other. She knew my father was a representative to the Polish Parliament, and it irritated her that even the child of the Posol did not know the Polish language. She was reluctant to punish me, but she made unpleasant jokes about my linguistic clumsiness. One day, however, she could not resist temptation and I finally had my hand swatted. After several such hand spankings, I decided to find a way to get away from this teacher. In addition to my difficulties with the language, I did not like her because she spoke and behaved as if she were superior to us—not to mention that she was not as pretty as I thought my teacher should be.

So, I played truant for a few days. But that backfired when I took my little cousin, also named Ivan, out into an early snowfall and he almost suffered frostbite. It was back to the classroom for me. Fortunately, the Polish teacher was transferred to another school, and we received a Ukrainian teacher by the name of Evhenia Vojtkiv.

Now we started and ended our school day with a Ukrainian prayer. We also sang Ukrainian songs while walking in The Forest or fields during our class excursions. We learned quickly how to read and write in our native language. The only time the nice Miss Vojtkiv punished me was for my stubborn mispronunciation of a word. She later found out I was not at fault; the pronunciation was printed incorrectly in my old textbook. The next day, she apologized to me in front of the class.

Miss Vojtkiv was so nice, in fact, that the reason why Uncle Sidorko was hiding in her woodshed during the Polish raid was because they were already lovers and would soon be married. And the reason she was tutoring me in Polish was because Volodimir Kochan had asked her to do so. My father was coming back into my life. And coming with him was a long baggage train of Ukrainian history, heritage, and politics.

No one railed more effectively against "polonization" than did my father. As a Ukrainian delegate to the Sejm in Warsaw, he had stood up and denounced the militantly Roman Catholic Jesuits who were clandestinely bombing Ukrainian Orthodox churches. After he explained to his constituents that the "invading pagan Tatars in the Middle Ages did not destroy our churches, but now the Catholic Poles do so because they happen to belong to a different Christian sect"—he was finally arrested.

Born in 1898 in the village of Nismichy, near the old Russian border some four miles south of Tudorkovychi, Volodimir Kochan had graduated from the Academic Gymnasium in Lviv just after the beginning of the First World War. He had then served in the Austro-Hungarian Army on the Italian Front. After the Austro-Hungarian Empire collapsed in 1918, he supported the "West Ukrainian People's Republic's" proclamation of independence in November of that year.

Widespread civil wars were already burning through Eastern Europe, ranging from the Baltic to the Black Seas. My father joined the Ukrainian

People's Army in defending our new republic against the onslaughts of both Russian Bolsheviks and Poles hoping to reinstate a Second Polish Republic after a century of having no national existence whatsoever. The Polish state had been partitioned by the Germans, Austrians, and Russians at the end of the eighteenth century.

After seven months of vicious fighting, in which my uncle and name-sake Ivan was killed, the Poles won, in large part because they were aided by the French, who even lent them tanks, much to the furor of other Western powers. France was committed to rebuilding a strong new Poland as a buffer against the new Soviet Union and a backdoor check on any renascent Germany. So Paris did not favor an independent Ukraine because that would weaken an otherwise strong new Poland.

France won. By the terms of the 1921 Treaty of Riga, which settled these civil wars, predominantly Ukrainian Halichina was indeed given to Warsaw—with the stipulation that all national minorities, including Ukrainians, be permitted "free intellectual development, the use of their national language, and the exercise of their religion."

The Poles paid no heed to that stipulation. On the contrary, they promptly set out to "polonize" our culture in the same way the hated Russians had tried to "russify" the vast majority of our brother and sister Ukrainians long subjected to the ruthless rule of that harsh empire. This was so alarming that my father was galvanized into action. He ran for the position of Posol in the Polish Sejm, representing the Sokal district, embracing most of our neighborhood, and won.

And promptly landed in prison, or so it seemed. He was so often under arrest for defending Ukrainian rights that he met many other like-minded prisoners. From them he learned the nuances of politics and the nature and goals of the various Ukrainian political parties. So he was well-prepared when in 1930 the people of the Sokal district re-elected him to the Sejm, despite his being behind bars. Eventually, even a Polish court could not find him guilty of any crime, and he was finally freed, to be re-elected again in 1932.

Now Volodimir Kochan wanted to take me out of the village school and put me into a better one in Sokal. There I would live with him in his apartment.

Didoon Semen gathered up my meager belongings and together we climbed not into his sleigh but into the horse-drawn wagon. Once again, we clomped through eighteenth-century Sokal, across the railroad tracks, and over the wooden bridge into the old city.

My father's apartment looked the same: one large room furnished with two double beds, a desk, and two tables. There was also a smaller room that we would use for washing and cleaning our shoes and clothes. An outhouse was hidden among the trees in the back yard. At night, I was afraid to use that dark and isolated place and preferred to hide myself behind some bushes.

Didoon Semen replaced the old straw in the mattresses with fresh wheat blades. This apartment, he said, was rented from a Polish lady who lived with her daughter in another part of the house. Our window looked out upon the front garden with its low fence. Across the dirt street stood an empty lot that belonged to the Ukrainian Cooperative Store.

I barely knew the man who then came up the stairs. Tall and handsome, with the light blondish-red coloring of the Kochans, my father was thirty-five years old and outwardly very likable and friendly. He was attentive to the needs of his constituents, argued forcefully for their rights, and was a careful listener. He was truthful and never forgot to fulfill a promise. As a capable politician, he also had the ability to choose the right people to help him achieve his goals.

Not long after Didoon Semen left for home even I as a child began seeing my father's other side. Yes, he was usually level-headed, but he had a hot temper that quickly shifted into unreasonable anger and sheer stubbornness. I was soon uncomfortable whenever he was around. He had little time to speak to me—or to any other family member, for that matter.

He disliked physical labor. He always found excuses when it was time to do housework. He had little interest in the farm back in Tudorkovychi. And money? As a member of the Sejm, he received 1,000 zlotys per month plus free railroad transportation within Poland. Yet he never seemed to have enough cash on hand. I later learned he supported a gifted Ukrainian student at Lviv University and was also sending Uncle Miron, his brother, to that commercial school in Lviv. Unfortunately, money never stayed in his pockets for long.

Although I lived with him in Sokal, he was never involved in my activities. He didn't know how I spent my time after school or whether I even did my homework. He spent most of his time at his office in the Ukrainian Cooperative Bank a few blocks away, where he served as a director. There he held meetings with many people, the discussions always returning to the plight of the Ukrainian people living under "Polish Occupation."

I would often sneak over there and listen to the political talk. Ukrainians were clearly a divided lot. The younger ones favored violence against the Poles. The older ones did not. The latter hoped to *persuade* the Poles to remove all discriminatory sanctions. The others favored armed revolution to "build a free Ukraine." One slogan was, "You will liberate Ukraine or die fighting for her!" They even favored dictatorship to achieve that goal.

It must have been around this time, with all this swirling about my young ears, that I first heard of two organizations that would later come to haunt me. One was called the Ukrainian Military Organization, founded in the early 1920s as an armed underground movement aimed at liberating Ukrainians by means of terrorizing primarily Poles via bombings and assassinations. The second organization, which would come to absorb most of the Ukrainian Military Organization, had just been established in 1929. It called itself the Organization of Ukrainian Nationalists, or OUN for short. It embraced the same violent means and ends, but gave them an even more extreme twist, one based on Mussolini-style fascism.

And there sat my father, amid all this seething ferment, trying to reason with the fundamentally unreasonable.

Meanwhile, throughout the two years we lived in that apartment, we had our everyday routines. I always fixed our breakfast, boiling eggs that we ate with buttered bread and hot tea. I ate my midday dinners at the home of Pani Zerebecka, who lived across the street from my school and prepared excellent dishes. We ate our evening supper in our one-room apartment, where a young woman named Lydia Knish made a dish of eggs mixed with chopped onions and fried to a golden color that, served with mashed potatoes, became our standard dish. Pani Lyda, as I always called her, dropping the "I" in her Christian name, was my minder when my father was in Lviv or Warsaw. It turned out she was more than my minder, but I was still young and innocent.

Sokal mirrored most old Ukrainian towns. Most of the citizens were Poles or Jews, who tended to align with Poles. There were a few Ukrainian stores, but Ukrainians dominated the countryside and not the towns. Here lived and worked lawyers, dentists, priests, and physicians serving a fifty-bed hospital. Not a single house or office boasted indoor plumbing, though. Water had to be carried in buckets from water pumps and each building had an outhouse that was built as far as possible from the main structure. Several streets were paved with bricks, but the majority were little more than rutted dirt lanes, muddy and pockmarked by rain-filled potholes. Both sides of an unpaved street were lined with twelve-inch-wide boards laid flat on the ground to serve as sidewalks for those who wanted to keep their boots clean. To walk on them, one had to possess good sight and balance; when two people going in opposite directions met on such a board, they tried desperately to find a place where they could pass each other without soiling their shoes.

There was also a teachers' seminary, several elementary schools, and a good Gymnasium. The name of my school was "Shkoolka," and it prepared pupils to pass the entrance examination to that Gymnasium. In my class were twenty-eight boys of whom only two were Ukrainians, six were Jews and the rest were Poles. The Polish boys called me names, but the Jewish boys were friendly, even if their parents did not welcome me into their homes.

One Jew, in particular, became my friend. His name was Jankel, and his delicatessen sold the most delicious moskaliki in the whole world! Moskaliki were small fish steeped with onion in a heavenly-tasting marinade. Jankel would scoop the fish from a big barrel, fill my jar with them, and ask how much marinade he should add? I suspect he enjoyed bartering with me because I spoke a funny Polish and, at the same time, tried to imitate his Jewish way of speaking. I started all my sentences with "Oy vey" and we both had a good laugh. I always received as much marinade as I wanted and Jankel always invited me to come again soon.

Otherwise, my two years in Sokal were difficult and even, at times, traumatic. I stumbled through Polish lessons and was frequently prey to the bullyings or cheats of the Polish boys. This was a far different world than that of a Ukrainian country village.

Back in Tudorkovychi for one summer break, both Didoon Semen and Didoon Kindrat were each assembling some 200 kilograms—about 450 pounds—of wheat apiece to help alleviate a famine said to be killing our brother Ukrainians in the Soviet Union.

The few emaciated skeletons who managed to stagger past the Soviet border guards and into Halichina had told appalling tales of starvation wiping out entire villages over there. Mass cannibalism was said to be setting in, people digging up cadavers for food or mothers eating their children and vice versa, one horror piling on another. This was far worse than the Great Hunger in Ireland a century earlier or to those colossal famines one heard about in faraway places like Bengal or China. That's why our good Christian farmers were assembling these massive relief packages—only to be blandly assured by Soviet authorities that nothing was needed, there was no famine here.

It didn't take long for realization to set in. This was *deliberate* mass murder. Uncle Joe Stalin not only had tried to eliminate an entire class of prosperous yeoman farmers called Kulaks; he was now revenging himself on the stout-hearted Ukrainians who refused to collectivize their inherited family farms! This would come to be known as Holodomor, "The Starvation Killing" of millions of people, and its memory would haunt every subsequent generation of Ukrainians as the later Holocaust would that of Jews. In 1933, everyone in Halichina was staring eastwards in frank horror, for hanging over Russia now was an enormous dark cloud of unimaginable evil.

The ethnic hostility so apparent during the day in Sokal was missing on Sunday evenings when the people came out for a stroll on the wide sidewalk, called the "Corso," the main street of the town. Men doffed their hats and kissed the hands of ladies. They exchanged small talk about the weather or the performance of the local soccer team. Recently engaged couples would show their intentions by holding hands. Teenagers walked in groups and teased one another.

But on Monday mornings our problems returned. The year 1933 was proving a hard one for Volodimir Kochan. His centrist political party, the Ukrainian National Democratic Organization (UNDO), had reached an accommodation with the Polish government in which it surrendered all claims to any independent status whatsoever in return for a dubious full equality of citizenship for Ukrainians. My father quit the party over this "normalization" and resigned his position as Posol, an honorable decision to many because the parliament had been largely co-opted by the Pilsudski regime but a disastrous one for us. Suddenly we had no money! Didoon Semen brought us food from the farm and the bank board finally agreed to pay my father a hundred zlotys a month, a poor wage even for unskilled workers.

We were also forced to find less expensive accommodations, renting a one-room apartment in the middle of a lumberyard. The outhouse here was so far away I made my own private one in the midst of a stack of wood. The saving grace in this new apartment was its proximity to a friend of my father's whose own father, Andrej Chaikivskij, had been a noted writer. So I could curl up with his books about Cossacks, imagining myself a participant in the heroic deeds of those wild warriors.

Otherwise, my schooling was falling apart. My classmates were now calling me *Rusyn*, a derogatory name meaning a boorish savage from Kievan Rus. Things had deteriorated to the point where it seemed impossible that I would be accepted to the Gymnasium. So, my father decided to send me to a private school instead. That might help me develop more of the self-discipline he did not have the time nor inclination to teach me. By going to a private school, I might have a better opportunity of entering a gymnasium and hence a university. His choice was a school in Lviv maintained by the Belgian Monks of the Order Redemptorist.

In the meantime, however, my father dispatched me to a former Boy Scout camp in a village high in the Carpathian Mountains. This camp, named "Sokil," was built on ground donated by Metropolitan Andrey Sheptytsky, a former nobleman who had been Archbishop of Ukraine's Greek Catholic Church since 1901. That's why its gates were still open, for in 1930 the Polish government had outlawed the Boy Scout movement in Halichina, probably because they feared it was a training ground for separatist terrorists. Sokil, meaning "falcon," was now staffed by monks.

My father bought me a rucksack and a pair of heavy shoes. He took me to Lviv and left me with the family of Dmitro Paliiv, a well-known figure in Ukrainian life and politics. He was a tall, handsome man with deep-set blue eyes and a soft voice. Even then I held him in awe because, as organizational officer of the Ukrainian Military Committee, he had been largely responsible for the November 1918 proclamation of Ukrainian independence. After we lost the ensuing war with Poland, he became one of the founders of the underground Ukrainian Military Organization; but by this time, he had become disenchanted with that extremist group, preferring my father's centrism and advocating forcefully for it in the papers he edited.

I spent the evening with him and his family, and I'll never forget the kindly look in those blue eyes. The following morning, after Pani Paliiv made me breakfast, he took me on the streetcar to the railroad station. I was placed in a group of ten boys being supervised by a young monk we called Brother Taras.

We took a train to Stanyslaviv, a large city located at the foot of the Carpathians. Then we transferred to an open-car train, sitting on wooden floors and enjoying the cold mountain wind blowing into our faces. After a winding, two-hour journey through rocky slopes and along white-water streams, we reached the small village of Pidlute, located close to the River Lymnytsia.

The camp was outside the village, situated in a heavily wooded forest. Upon reaching it, we were each given a large bag of straw to make our beds on wooden platforms in the dormitory. In front of each bed was a bench for our personal belongings.

My group was located in a room on the first floor, near an outside assembly where the Ukrainian flag, not the Polish one, still brazenly flew from a flagpole. Not far away stood the dining hall where a hundred hungry boys were fed every day. Between these two buildings was a paved walkway behind which was a closed gate always patrolled by one person. There were no fences anywhere around, so the function of this guard seemed only ceremonial. Or maybe he was just a lookout, keeping a watchful eye peeled for the approach of Polish authorities.

Our day started at 6:00 a.m., when, wrested from sleep, we quickly made our beds and washed our faces sparingly in that ice-cold stream. We stood in the assembly area in straight lines, starting with the tallest and ending with the shortest boy. We sang the outlawed Boy Scout anthem and were told the itinerary for the week.

When the time for breakfast finally arrived, we marched with as much discipline as we could muster to the dining hall for eggs and freshly baked bread. We were given our eating utensils and had to clean them in a nearby stream— or by licking them, which we did quite effectively. After breakfast, we had an hour to ourselves—mostly standing in line for our turn in the outhouse.

My group was under the supervision of Brother Taras. He spoke to us about his education at the University of Lviv and began instructing us in Ukrainian history. It was history scaled down to boyish ears; but it was history, nonetheless. We learned about our origins more than a thousand years earlier when a polity called Kievan Rus was established on the Dnieper River. There, Norsemen from the Baltic, called Varangians, or *Rus*, intermingled with the local Slavic tribes in an area tailor made for trade: The place where the forests of the north and west met the grassy steppes of the south and east. Here they established the trading post that would later become Kiev.

It was already a prosperous place when in the year 988, the ruler of Kievan Rus, Vladimir the Great, brought Christianity up from Byzantium to our people, inaugurating a Golden Age of high culture lasting for centuries. That explained why Kiev became our Holy City; it held the rock-cut catacombs of our ancient kings, and its Cave Monastery once drew hundreds of thousands of pilgrims annually. Even its poets became famous for ballads and love songs.

Sadly, though, it was a city many if not most of us sitting around Brother Taras would never see. Although less than four hundred miles to the east of "Sokil," it might as well have been on the moon. Kiev might still crown the bluffs above the Dnieper, but we were separated from it by what was now an alien border, the one separating the Soviet Union from the Second Republic of Poland. A great gulf fixed—or, during these years of the Holodomor, so we hoped.

Although most of my fellow campers squirmed with boredom during these morning history lectures, I sat enthralled. The next day we learned nothing lasts forever. Oh, there were times, centuries after the Golden Age of Kievan Rus, when successor states flourished, some of them boasting as many as eighty major cities. But in the Middle Ages the Black Death and Mongol invasions from the eastern steppes ravaged most of

Eastern Europe, perhaps halving its population and leaving it prey to even more predatory invaders from the steppes. This was the era of foreign domination, when we Rus—or Ruthenians, as most of the world called us—turned to the famous Cossacks for protection.

Brother Taras was a spellbinding speaker. He brought the beauty and melancholy of the steppes alive for us campers: How high the grass grew in places, higher than a horse and rider combined, allowing raiders to creep up unseen; how clean and fresh it smelled in summer, when it was spangled with flowers; how grim and desolate it appeared beneath the lowering gray skies of winter. Above all, he brought out the character of the Cossack himself: Whether "outlaw" or "freebooter," whether a Ruthenian or escaped slave or even a Turk or Tatar, he was as brave as a lion, as boisterous as a stallion, and possessed fighting skills second to none.

The Cossacks, we learned, patrolled the border marches of southeast Europe, setting up unruly quasi-republics of their own, calling their general assembly a *Rada* and their commander a *hetman*, words that would be brought into Ukrainian life and lore. For in the makeup of the average Ukrainian, the legacy of the Cossack, despite his Orthodox rather than Catholic religion, is second only to that of Kievan Rus. After all, for over a century the hetman of the Zaporizhian Host ruled much of the territory of Ukraine.

At this I piped up, telling Brother Taras of a play I had just seen in Sokal. It was about Hetman Ivan Mazepa, I said excitedly, head of the Zaporizhian Host. He had angered Tsar Peter the Great of Russia and as a result, a scoundrel of a Russian general named Menshikov had burned his capital city to the ground and then tortured and murdered all its citizens!

I must have been wearing a stern scowl on my features because Brother Taras turned to me with a smile. "Yes, Ivan," he said. "Mazepa was a dashing figure. He was well-educated and spoke numerous languages. He was so dashing and romantic that a great English poet named Lord Byron would write a famous epic about him. Other people you might learn about in school, like Victor Hugo or Franz Liszt or even Russians like Pushkin and Tchaikovsky, would find inspiration in his story, too. But remember, Ivan, there is nothing simple in this part of the world."

"You see, where we live there was once something called the Polish-Lithuanian Commonwealth, and it stretched from the Baltic to the Black Seas. We Ukrainians were a part of that; but we were always fighting wars with the Poles, who dominated it." There was some stirring among the campers at that remark. "So, in the year 1654 or thereabouts, Mazepa's predecessor, Hetman Bohdan Khmelnitsky, made a devil's bargain with Peter the Great's father, Tsar Alexis. In return for Russian help against the Poles, he let Russia take over much of Ukraine."

"Before that, Russia had been a Slavic nation that worshiped a gang of Asian cutthroats called the Golden Horde, learning nothing from them but cruelty. They then tried commandeering out heritage, calling themselves Rus, or Great Russians--as opposed to us, whom they demeaned as Little Russians. So, when Peter the Great came to the throne, Mazepa served him loyally until he felt betrayed—and only then did he turn and fight against Russia to free himself and his fellow Ukrainians. The tsars of the Romanov dynasty never forgave this 'treason' and finally Catherine the Great, in the 1770s, dissolved the hetmanship and began the long and brutal campaign to exterminate every vestige of Ukrainian culture."

We were all facing east, scowls on every young face.

"Nothing simple, Ivan," Brother Taras was saying. "Catherine the Great was born a German in Prussia. But she had Varangian ancestors."

We were running out of time. So he quickly reminded us that after Russia, Prussia, and Austria-Hungary had divided the remains of the old Polish Commonwealth, we were lucky that Austria scooped us up. We might be poor, but we have been, until recently, free to keep the Ukrainian flame burning brightly. That chimed with what my father had been saying.

Our group fell quiet for a moment. Then one boy spoke up: "So it's either the Poles or the Russians, eh?" To which Brother Taras shrugged slightly and responded, a little hopelessly, "I suppose so."

This awakening interest in my heritage received a further boost the following Sunday. Metropolitan Andrey Sheptytsky was visiting the church in Pidlute and we went to see him at his mountain retreat. Born in a village near Lviv in 1865, Count Roman Aleksander Maria Sheptytsky came from old Ruthenian nobility and inherited a vast fortune. He chose not the path of worldly success, however, becoming a monk instead; and although born and baptized a Roman Catholic—his mother's family being partially Polish—he chose to become Greek Catholic and share the spiritual lives of his Ukrainian neighbors. He even took the name Andrey (Andrew), after the Apostle considered to be the founder of our Ukrainian Church. He received a doctorate in theology from the Jesuit Seminary in Krakow and, only a few years after being ordained a priest, he was enthroned in 1901 as Metropolitan Archbishop of Lviv, the titular head of the Ukrainian Greek Catholic Church. He was only thirty-six years old.

Over the years, he had donated most of his considerable landholdings to charities and other civic causes. Yet fate was not always kind in return. When the Tsar's armies occupied Halichina in 1914, this physical giant of a man was arrested and subsequently imprisoned in numerous places in Russia, a grueling experience that ultimately broke his health. Because he supported the 1918 establishment of the Western Ukrainian Republic he was also, at a later point, arrested by Polish officials, even though his brother was a general in the Polish Army.

By 1933, Metropolitan Sheptytsky was the most revered figure in Halichina. That's why I felt almost overwhelmed when told that of the hundred boys at camp I had been chosen to present him flowers and thank him for giving us such a beautiful place for the training of body and soul.

When we arrived, this literally larger-than-life figure was confined to an old-fashioned wheelchair. Nevertheless, he remained an impressive man, his pleasant face and bright blue eyes framed by a long white beard and an unruly shock of white hair. Even his head seemed abnormally gigantic, despite his entire countenance radiating peace and goodwill. Upon hearing my name, he turned those expressive eyes on me with genuine interest. He knew of my father, he told me, and hoped I would grow up to be like him.

I kissed his ring and thanked him for his kind words. I turned from his presence with tears in my eyes and walked back to my place, a boy now immensely proud of his father.

Although "Sokil" was no longer officially a Boy Scout camp, in practice it amounted to one. We marched and hiked and learned wood-lore and engaged in all the other activities typically associated with a Boy Scout summer camp. We had a weekly bonfire, for instance, for which each group of campers had to collect dry wood and at which each group was in turn responsible for giving a short performance. Twice each week we sunned ourselves on the huge boulders on the banks of the cold, swift-flowing River Lymnytsia. There we enjoyed the warmth of the stones and the view of the surrounding peaks. We also studied the Ukrainian people of the Carpathians. They were called Hutsuls and dressed in colorful costumes, the older women smoking pipes while riding comfortably on tiny horses. These people spoke a Ukrainian dialect we could not understand.

Once a week, we all went on a daylong outing into the mountains. While hiking, we sang many songs and I gazed at all the rocks and boulders. That summer I realized that rocks are commonplace and not exceptional. It is only the chernozem underlying our Ukrainian farms that was devoid of rocks. On one hike, we climbed a peak higher than the tree line and explored old dugouts made during the First World War. This was Makivka Mountain, Brother Taras said, a very important site to Ukrainians.

That day the history lesson was focused on that shattering 1914-18 conflict. In August 1914, when Europe blew apart, the green fields of Austrian Galicia, now spread out before us or glimpsed between distant peaks, became one of the principal battlefields. Here the main Austro-Hungarian formations met the Russians pouring south in a series of titanic engagements, most of them fought less than fifty miles west of Tudorkovychi. The Austrians appeared to have the upper hand; but Russian counterattacks from south of my village ended up routing them and winning all of Galicia for the Tsar.

The scale of devastation, we were told, cannot be imagined. Cities like Lviv were badly damaged but not destroyed. Villages, hamlets, farms—all and anything else in the way were pulverized, burned to the ground, utterly eradicated. Attack after attack was hurled into a maelstrom of artillery and machine gun fire. Men and standing grain were cut down and winnowed without distinction, the tallies of humans and horses quickly reaching into the millions.

What was left of the Imperial armies retreated here, into the

Carpathians. But there was no safety in these hills, Brother Taras said, gesturing toward a four-hundred-mile line of peak after dimly seen peak. The Russians followed them up the mountain passes; but once the winter snow and ice fell few provisions, ammunition, artillery, or even overcoats could be delivered. The worst possible warfare ensued, endlessly violent with as many men freezing to death or dying of starvation as being killed in battle. Beneath the somber evergreens clothing every slope, he said, lie a million skeletons amid an endless shamble of discarded equipment.

If this was intended to make us fear and loathe war, it was working. Then we examined the eroded dugouts around us. Spring comes late to the mountains, Brother Taras was telling us, and there may have been snow still here when for five days in late April and early May 1915 in these very trenches, around eight hundred heroic Ukrainian soldiers held off one major Russian assault after another. They were the elite Sich Riflemen, the only purely Ukrainian unit in the Austro-Hungarian Army (a *sich* being a fortified Cossack camp). Eight companies of them had been recruited in Lviv in August 1914 and they would go on to distinguish themselves in a number of Eastern Front engagements. But this victory was an emblem of our pride and resilience.

That made us all stand the straighter. We were nearly on our tiptoes when Brother Taras reminded us about our forbidden Boy Scout organizational name, "Plast." It came from *plastun,* he said, the name for a Cossack Scout.

I craned my neck, hopping on boulders for any possibility of seeing my home village from these heights. But I couldn't even find Lviv. I had to imagine it out there, somewhere, wondering what had happened there during the last war?

Today I can tell that lad what happened. In 1915 the Germans and Austrians won Galicia back in an equally bloody and violent campaign, one that also drove at least a million people out of their burned-down houses with barely the clothes on their backs, nearly half of whom would die within weeks, mainly of starvation, their bones to be picked by crows and later gathered to fertilize fields. I can tell him that, fortunately, our village escaped serious damage. In July 1915, Russian armies did retreat to the line of the River Buh at Sokal. That meant their outposts would have been in our woods and fields. They would have ransacked our barns for food and fodder, and we would have hidden our animals, if possible. But the Russian soldiers were probably too weakened by fatigue and hunger to offer much resistance to the First Austro-Hungarian Army, which soon thundered upon the scene and pushed them beyond the Buh and out of Sokal.

One Russian artilleryman, however, sick of looking at the golden dome of our hated Greek Catholic Church, let fly a round at it in a parting gesture, destroying our church out of spite because it was not a Russian Orthodox one.

I would also tell him, as I watch him scrambling about those trenches, looking for souvenirs in pieces of shrapnel or rusted bullet casings, that he would grow up despising war and the man he would become would thank him for it. I would also remind him that one thing about Makivka Mountain might have escaped everybody there that afternoon celebrating the glory of the victory. There was tragedy here, as well because many of the Russians attacking our Riflemen were ethnic Ukrainians from beyond that border. It was brother against brother, the tragedy of a people who didn't have a strong and independent national existence.

The Metropolitan had hoped I would grow up to be like my father. In that I was only partially successful. I was never adept at politics, but I did espouse his moderate, non-violent path. Like him, I am a loyal Ukrainian from Halichina. I believe Ukraine deserves an independent status among nations. I do not believe in unwarranted violence to achieve that goal. I do believe in living to fight another day—fight when only absolutely necessary, but then fight like the Sich Riflemen. Because I'm also quite sure that subjugated nations pay a heavy price in blood for failing to achieve independence.

CHAPTER FIVE

Blitzkrieg!

In August of 1933, I turned ten years old, an unpleasant birthday for me because nobody remembered it. My family was all focused on my imminent departure to the Redemptorist Gymnasium in Lviv.

I traveled to my new school in the back of a horse-drawn wagon with a friend named Ihor. We slept on straw mattresses while his father drove us the seventy miles. The night was moonless and the sky full of bright stars, so many of them I could just gaze and gaze in wonder. Eventually I fell asleep to the swaying rhythms of the road.

We awoke upon approaching Lviv and ran alongside the wagon to stretch our legs. We had some breakfast and gave hay to the horses in a small park before arriving in the village of Zboiska, just over the Poltva River from the city. On a hill overlooking us were the grounds of the Redemptorist Gymnasium.

Metropolitan Andrej Sheptytsky had donated this property for use as Redemptorist monastery, a Belgian-based order he had brought to Ukraine. The school, originally intended to prepare students for the priesthood, stood next to the monastery and was encircled by an eight-foot wall with glass shards embedded in its top. It was unclear if that was to keep intruders out or to keep in the students. The doors were always locked, and visitors and family had to meet in special reception rooms.

The main building housed classrooms and a lecture hall. Each student had an assigned seat and in class he was never allowed to speak to one of his fellows, all questions being directed to the master. On the second story was a chapel with a polished wooden floor where students prayed on their knees three times a day. My dormitory room, with its iron bedstead and straw mattress, was on the third floor. From its window I could see the rooftops of Lviv.

Our day started at the dark and painful hour of 5:00 a.m. We had a half-hour to wash, dress, and leave the bed wrinkle-free. Then we were on our knees in the chapel, convinced the morning mass was devised to test our endurance and strengthen our spirits. After a few months, however, the skin on our patellas thickened.

Breakfast in the dining room was at 8:00 and that's when announcements were made. Classes began promptly an hour later. Each lecture lasted exactly forty-five minutes, giving us fifteen minutes to prepare for the next one. There were four sets of lectures, all delivered by Ukrainian or Belgian priests, then prayers again, then dinner. In the afternoon there was one hour for recreation. Lectures resumed until supper. Then prayers in the chapel at 7:00 p.m. with some singing of hymns. At 8:00 we went back to our rooms to prepare for bed.

At 9:00 p.m., the priest serving as hall monitor wished the students good night and turned off the lights. He then enforced silence and made sure no secret visitations were made. Some students tried reading adventure books by flashlight beneath the covers, even though discovery and punishment were swift and painful. If you were lucky, the director paddled you. If unlucky, more kneeling in the chapel.

It was, let us say, a disciplined and tedious routine.

I lived several years beneath this spartan regime, relieved by only occasional outlets. On Sunday afternoons we were allowed to play on the hills behind the school. We could organize soccer games, enjoy the freedom of unsupervised walks, and engage in conversations, quarrels, and fights. We could help the monks next door collect fruit from their orchard, a welcome treat because they allowed us to eat some of it. And whenever we were allowed into Lviv we wore caps called Mazepinki, after the Ukrainian hero Hetman Ivan Mazepa, who frequently wore one. They were blue with yellow trim and a V-shaped design on the front—and they annoyed the Poles because they were reminders they were living on Ukrainian soil.

For holidays I took a train to Sokal, spent a few days with my father before Uncle Petro picked me up in the horse-drawn wagon for the ride through the fields to Tudorkovychi. My village friends were happy to see me, and I got to visit Chitalnya, the village store, and the blacksmith shop. I spent time with Didoon Semen and Babunya Marina and sometimes moved across the creek to stay with my mother, Alexandra, at the Dula family farm.

During these years my father remained active in Ukrainian politics. Alongside his friends Dmitro Paliiv, now a Posol in the Polish Parliament and editor of a popular Ukrainian newspaper, and the philosopher Mikola Shlemkevich, Volodimir Kochan had organized yet another political party, the Front for National Unity, or FNU.

Besides being another in the bewildering sea of acronyms, the new party essentially boiled down to a repudiation of both the old moderate party's "normalization" program with the Poles and a continuing strong rejection of the extremist nationalists. What new ground it now opened I never could discover, but the FNU grew very quickly and at its First Congress in Lviv in 1936 Volodimir was elected its director of membership. After proving quite adept at this new job, the extremists decided to assassinate him.

One night as he and Yarko were walking home down a dark street in Sokal, two masked men leaped out of the shadows and would have killed my father had the knife cut his spinal cord. As it was, the blade struck the cervical vertebra and pierced his lung but did not cut vital nerves or blood vessels. My father fell to the ground unconscious and my nine-year-old brother ran to a nearby house and asked for help.

My father was taken to the hospital but was released ten days later. The two men who attacked him were apprehended, but he never pressed any charges. Any trial would have revealed the deep cleavages within the Ukrainian movement, and he wanted to present a united face to the outside world.

My father's prominence in the Front for National Unity was well-known in the Redemptorist Gymnasium. Many students therefore considered me a traitor—an important index of how deeply extremist ideas were penetrating our society, for these students were barely teenagers! Father Kochut, who taught physics, learned about my difficulties and notified the school's director. They suspected someone from outside the school was spreading destructive and hateful ideas among the students—but they had no idea who it might be.

Father Kochut happened to be a very good portraitist, and in the year 1936, he painted my portrait, the only thing I still have from my home in Ukraine. It depicts a thirteen-year-old boy with wavy, blond hair and a self-conscious smile, dressed in an embroidered shirt tied with a red ribbon, a gift made by my mother.

My years in the Redemptorist Gymnasium were good for me. I developed self-discipline and emotional stability. Living among priests gave me new respect for living a spiritual life. But in February 1937, when I was still thirteen, my father decided it was time to attend the most noted of all Halichina's gymnasia, his own alma mater; therefore, I took my entrance exam at the Academichna Gymnasium in Lviv in August of 1937, the month I turned fourteen, and I was admitted for the upcoming school year.

Because of its famous architecture, beautiful churches, and lovely parks, Lviv (or Lw'ow in Polish or Lemburg in German) was often called "Little Vienna." Although the city was founded in the thirteenth century by Prince Danilo Romanovich and named after his son, Lev, the site had been settled at least four centuries earlier. After the Holy City of Kiev, Lviv is the most important cultural, religious, and political center in Ukraine.

The oldest part lies in the depression of the Poltva River, which in my experience was a small and smelly creek. By contrast, its most glorious monument, in my view, was its four-storied marble Opera House, built during the reign of Empress Maria Theresa on the most prominent hill in the city.

During the early twentieth century, it might have passed as a Polish city. Lviv in the 1930s still did not have a single Ukrainian restaurant or hotel and very few stores that sold Ukrainian books or newspapers. Most of the businesses were owned by Jews and this led to widespread dislike and envy of them. There were several Ukrainian factories, though, the most famous of them being "Maslo Soyous," Butter Enterprise, which made delicious butter and other milk products. And our farmers might sell their produce in vegetable markets scattered all over the city.

Academichna Gymnasia was located on a lovely street lined with chestnut trees, next to the famous Lviv Polytechnic University. The school's chief feature was a grand, imposing three-story building adorned with flower-filled window boxes. The Gymnasia was established in 1784, the oldest secondary school in Halichina and a continuation of a Jesuit Gymnasium founded over two centuries earlier. Until 1849, Latin was used as the language of instruction and German as its auxiliary, as the German phrases painted on the walls—"MorgenStunde hat Gold im Munde"(morning hour has gold in its mouth), "Morgen, Morgen nur nicht Heute sagen alle faule Leute" (tomorrow, tomorrow, but not today say all lazy people), or "Ubung macht den Meister" (the practice shapes an expert)—amply testified.

The school was considered one of the best in the Austro-Hungarian Empire and many of our teachers were authors, scholars, and public figures, known and respected in the community. It was also expensive, and the limited number of places made it competitive, too.

Fortunately, there were reasonably priced boarding houses on the edge of the city. I lived in one about a half-mile away on Khshanowska Street. It bordered a prison—the infamous Loncky Prison—in which many Ukrainians, including my father, spent time for political trespasses against the Polish Government.

This boarding house accepted only Ukrainian students, and each of us had a narrow bed and a desk with a compartment for books. There was a common dining hall where we ate our meals; but unfortunately, the boarding house had no recreation room and only occasionally were we permitted to play table tennis in the dining hall. When not engaged in any other way on Saturday and Sunday afternoons, we played soccer on the fields outside of the city.

The man who ran the boarding house was Mr. Zoobricki, a heavily built, middle-aged fellow who tried to maintain discipline by hitting us with his large set of keys. He forced us to accompany him to national festivities, where we listened to speeches on our weary legs. These speeches were boring; standing in one place was like kneeling on the hard floors of the Redemptorist chapel.

Lucky for me, my friend Bohdan Yourchuk from Sokal not only followed me to the Gymnasium but also ended up in the same boarding house, sharing a room with four other boys—some of whom were already infected with the Organization of Ukrainian Nationalists' extremism. They set out to make life difficult for me, knowing about my father's role in the formation of FNU. Since I resisted the pressure to join their ranks, they declared a friendship boycott on me. It would have been easier to give in and pretend to share their beliefs, but I could not.

My class of twenty-eight students was composed of approximately an equal number of boys and girls, the girls sitting up front, the boys in the back. We all wore blue uniforms embroidered in gold braid with matching caps. We started each school day with a prayer. We stood up whenever a teacher entered or exited and whenever we spoke or asked a question. Each day we had an hour of physical education and every Sunday we assembled in the corridors and walked to the baroque St. George's Cathedral to pray and listen to the High Mass. As it happened, Metropolitan Sheptytsky lived nearby.

For entertainment, the occasional string quartet or violinist would play for us; and in 1938 we all went to see a newsreel of the recent Olympic Games in a nearby movie theater. Those were the Berlin Olympics, and we enjoyed the ceremony and sporting events onscreen, especially the hundred-meter dash of Jesse Owens.

Sometimes we saw, while dressed in street clothes, other films at movie theaters. Not just "cowboy movies," but also vaudeville, because dance revues showed attractive young girls with high-stepping bare legs and musicals, where I learned many American showtunes that I found exciting and romantic. Naturally, my friends and I had to take special precautions not to be caught in such morally questionable places.

My vacations from school I generally spent in Tudorkovychi, staying either with my father's parents or with my mother in Kindrat Dula's house. I would ride a bike that my mother had bought for me to see places and to visit friends.

One Sunday, during my 1937 vacation, Didoon Kindrat allowed my cousin Mitonko and me to take two horses to the River Variazanka, where he had some pastures and a hay meadow. We were familiar with horses but we were still too small to mount them without the help of a stool; but once we were on them, we rode well, without saddles, firmly pressing our knees to the horses' sides.

We began our trip to the Variazanka about an hour before sunrise. Along the way, we picked up our cousin Vlodko with his two horses. The morning was rather cold and we enjoyed the warmth radiating from the bodies of our mounts.

Outside the village, we passed the thirty-foot cross erected in commemoration of the Black Death victims. Beyond that landmark was a vast open space where villagers mined for sand and clay. Then we hit the open road where we urged our horses to a gallop as we held on tightly.

Upon reaching The Forest near the river, we slowed our pace. The air was fresh and fog was close to the ground. The horses were nervous and blew steam and moisture from their noses, raising their heads high. They probably smelled animals that had crossed the road during the night.

After passing through the oaks and hornbeams, we reached pastures with fresh and plentiful grass. There we hobbled the horses and, to warm ourselves, climbed high into the trees, where the upper branches were already touched by the rising sun. There we sang songs and told funny stories. Around mid-morning we bathed in the deep pools of the river, then rode the horses into the water and gave them baths, too. After more swimming, we let the horses dry in the sun as we grazed on wild strawberries and blackberries growing in dappled groves in The Forest. The ride home was slow, our bellies being full and the horses too lazy to run.

That same summer of 1937, I met a girl a year older than me and we became friends. Her name was Slava Shchoocka, but everybody called her Slavka. We met in Chitalnya and I fell for her beauty and friendly smile. Slavka was tall and had a well-proportioned body with shapely legs. She also had a sharp mind and an even sharper tongue, one that scared off most of the village boys. At our first encounter we both felt an attraction for the other, and soon I was often in Chitalnya, regaling Slavka and her friends with tales of my life in Sokal and Lviv.

Eventually she and I started meeting in Didoon Semen's orchard at twilight. There we'd kiss to the accompaniment of singing nightingales and croaking frogs. Mitonko knew of our trysting place and frequently had to drag me home, almost ripping me away from Slavka and her sweet kisses. Her family was rather poor because her father was not interested in farming and rarely participated in any local activities. Some people thought he might even be a Communist. Slavka's mother was also a very pretty woman and the envious village matrons claimed that in her younger years she had many lovers.

When I wasn't fishing for Slavka I was fishing with a long bamboo rod I found in the attic. I used the black tail hairs of a horse for line and the quill of a goose feather tied to a cork for the bobber. I fished in the early mornings on the banks of the Variazanka using grasshoppers for bait. On a good day, after several hours, I usually caught several sunfish and some pike-like fish we called *plotichi*. My mother prepared the fish for our dinner, dipping them in a beaten egg mixture, coating them with flour, and frying them in salted butter.

One day while fishing on the river I noticed some fish floating close to the surface with their bellies turned up. It seemed like I might be able to catch them with my hands. Curious, I walked up the river a distance and encountered some people who were taking wet and rotting plants out of the water to dry on the banks. I learned this was hemp that had been buried in mud for a few weeks. This incubation in an anaerobic environment induced the growth of bacteria, which then digested the organic matter, leaving the fibers intact. The hemp bundles were then spread on the banks to dry in the hot sun before being spun into threads from which rope and rough linen were made.

I also learned some of these people felt funny, sort of drunk. I was told that hemp releases something toxic that disturbs not only the human mind but also the behavior of fish. This was my first encounter with the psychoactive properties of *Cannabis sativa*, the common hemp, which as marijuana and hashish would become such a popular recreational drug.

Usually I fished alone since farmers had no time to cast a line. But there was an older man, also an angler, even if dressed in white linen and wearing a straw hat. I saw him frequently but never could engage him in conversation. It was the straw hat that brought us together. One day, I arrived on the riverbank wearing the straw hat Didoon Kindrat had made for me. Upon seeing my hat, the old fisherman stopped and asked to examine it, holding it carefully in his curly, arthritic fingers. After studying it with much interest, he said Kindrat was still doing good work. He explained that in our region only he and my grandfather could make straw hats that were symmetrical and pleasing to the eye. "Since I did not make your hat, then it was made by Kindrat," he pronounced.

In later conversations I learned that both these mad hatters believed that straw hats prevented headaches and that trousers made of dog skin protected the wearer from rheumatism and colds. At that point, I realized why my grandfather's trousers looked familiar to me. My mother confirmed the origin of Kindrat's trousers and said probably the smell of the leather scared the diseases away. I also noticed the pouch in which Kindrat kept his tobacco was made out of a pig bladder, no doubt secured during hog-killing time.

In the autumn of 1938, when I was fifteen and had returned to school from summer break, the atmosphere in Lviv had changed. The Spanish Civil War had divided public opinion everywhere. Because the Republicans, although supported by writers and artists, were widely thought to be infiltrated by Communists and controlled by the Soviet Union, Ukrainian Nationalists tended to support Franco, many young men enlisting in the Nationalist Army. In Italy, Mussolini's wars of aggression against Abyssinia and Ethiopia looked like an attempt to re-establish a Roman Empire in Africa. But the greatest threat lurked right next door to Poland, where in only five years Adolf Hitler had built in Germany an aggressive and militaristic regime that was already de-stabilizing the continent of Europe.

In September, the very month of my return to school, a major war was only narrowly averted over Germany's proposed annexation of the German-speaking Sudeten borderlands of Czechoslovakia. Poland and Hungary had even partially mobilized their armed forces; but then Great Britain, France, Italy, and Germany agreed to the "Munich Betrayal" that began the dismemberment of the two-decades old nation. The next step came in November, when the First Vienna Award continued that process, stripping Czechoslovakia of one of its four original provinces, Subcarpathian Rus. A month later that little slice of Carpathia formalized its independence as Zakarpatska Ukraine, commonly called Carpathian Ukraine, with its capital in Chust.

Many of my classmates were jubilant. This small mountainous enclave promised to be the nucleus of an independent Ukrainian Republic!

Hitler, however, had other ideas. After marching into the remainder of Czechoslovakia in March 1939 and dividing it into the Protectorate of Bohemia and Moravia on the one hand, and a Slovak Republic on the other, he gave Hungary the nod. Budapest then seized the territory of Carpathian Ukraine. Tens of thousands of Ukrainians were summarily executed, including many who had crossed over from Halichina hoping to fight for freedom. Once more the flame had leapt up, only to be ruthlessly quenched. Again.

I thought this development would have my Organization of Ukrainian Nationalist friends thinking twice about Herr Hitler's plans for Ukraine, should he ever be allowed to turn it into lebensraum. Perhaps this should moderate their views.

On the contrary, the dormitory room I shared with four other boys was an OUN haven. My brother, Yarko, was now also enrolled in a branch of the Academichna Gymnasia and living with us. But our roommates kept nightly contact with members of OUN by letting them climb into our room through open windows. Their political discussions kept Yarko and me awake until the late hours and finally I asked them to stop these nocturnal powwows. They outright refused my request, and in retaliation for my even lodging a complaint they proclaimed me an enemy and submitted me to a general boycott. Most boys in the dormitory had already stopped speaking to me because they said my father was a traitor for criticizing the activity of OUN.

The nightly visitors were urging teenagers to slip out and fight Poles in the streets. The relationship between our two ethnic groups in Halichina had now deteriorated to that point. After the destruction of several Ukrainian businesses and offices in Lviv by Polish thugs, we suspected there would be an attempt made by Polish students on our dormitory. The director asked us to keep the doors locked and to avoid standing at windows. Expecting an imminent attack, we started to collect and store brick bats on the second and third floors of the building. We planned to hurl them at the Poles if they were rash enough to try to break through the front door.

We didn't have long to wait. One Saturday afternoon about fifty Polish students assembled in front of our dormitory yelling, "Beat the Ukrainians!" They threw bricks at the windows and tried to break down the door. We retaliated with a few bricks fired from the upper-story windows but suddenly, as if on command, all the attackers ran away.

A few minutes later, about twenty Polish policemen arrived and asked the director to open the door. They charged us with throwing bricks and shooting a revolver at peaceful Polish citizens! The policemen ignored our complaint about the broken windows and remained deaf to our assurances that we did not have a gun. They searched every room and naturally, the police used the imaginary gun as a pretext to destroy our beds, books, and furniture while doing so. The search of our dormitory and the destruction of our belongings continued for several hours. But of course, no gun was ever found.

Before leaving, the policemen took all our names and told us to come to the Loncky Prison on Monday for an interrogation. It was surprising, at a time of such turmoil in Europe, that the Polish government was terrorizing teenage Ukrainian boys. Instead of befriending the Ukrainian minority in Lviv, they once again alienated them. The police imprisoned Ukrainian politicians for any hint of anti-Polish activity and the censors frequently confiscated Ukrainian newspapers. Polish jails were filled to overflowing with Ukrainians; and to keep more "dangerous" prisoners in seclusion, the Polish government had built the first concentration camp in their supposedly democratic state, a hellhole called Bereza Kartuska, where prisoners were kept in filthy conditions and regularly beaten by brutal camp guards.

Somehow, the high academic standards at Academichna Gymnasia were maintained despite this increasing violence. The latest worry, in the spring and early summer of 1939, was Herr Hitler's renewed demands concerning the "Polish Corridor," the twenty-mile-wide slice of Polish territory, vouchsafed by the Versailles Treaty, dividing East Prussia from the rest of the German Reich and containing the busy port of Danzig. Even the recent Anglo-Polish Alliance, alongside a similar French guarantee for military assistance should the Germans invade, did not dispel the prevailing gloom. The removal of this corridor from Poland would isolate it from the Baltic Sea and would constitute a major impediment to the growth of its economy.

Yet the Poles were a very proud people and believed that they had an army capable of stopping a German invasion. They did not ask but demanded Ukrainian help if this came to pass—the help of Ukrainians who, only a few years earlier, had been beaten senseless during the Pacification! Defiance is what we were thinking if it should ever come to that.

After finishing my second year at the Lviv Gymnasium, I spent most of my summer break in Tudorkovychi. As the weather in July and August 1939 was hot and dry, Bohdan Yourchuk and I frequently rode our bicycles to the river where we cooled ourselves in its refreshing water. On our way, we usually visited Petro Voroby, our friend from Starhorod, only two miles from Tudorkovychi. Petro was four years older than us and he had already attended the University of Berlin. Lying on the hot sand on the bank of the Buh, Petro told us tales of life in Germany and the fun you could have as an undergraduate. That's what we wanted to do, Bohdan and I—go see foreign lands and attend a famous university.

Even when he was still at the Sokal Gymnasium, Petro was tutoring his fellow students and earning enough money to pay for his education. We teased him by saying he was lucky God had given him such a big head to fill up with useless knowledge! And he did have a big head on a rather small body. Unlike us, he wasn't interested in sports and disliked swimming in the river. He preferred to read or to discuss intellectual topics with knowledgeable people. We forgave him. He was always such a smart, interesting, and reliable friend.

When I wasn't with Bohdan and Petro I was with my cousins, Vlodko and Mitonko. We resumed our horseback excursions to the rivers nearly every sunny weekend. Vlodko was a moody boy; he did not like participating in anything, whether play or conversation or simply messing about. And he was as secretive as an owl. His meager verbosity was partly due to a slight stutter and his lack of enthusiasm the expression of his strange nature. Mitonko and I never knew what he was thinking.

Mitonko, on the contrary, was very outgoing and talkative. His ears always stood straight out from the side of his head but he was always ready to play any game you wanted and always tried to do his best whatever the activity.

For one thing, we enjoyed hiking into The Forest to harvest spicy-scented wild strawberries that were sweet to the tongue. One sunny day Bohdan Yourchuk joined us for our hike and brought with him a package of cigarettes called "Plaski." They were packed in a very elegant silvery box and Bohdan assured us they were the best cigarettes one could buy in Sokal. We were not permitted to smoke at home but here in the woods the temptation was too much and so we hid ourselves behind some thick bushes and lit the best cigarettes money could buy.

Hmm, I did not like either the smell or the taste of my cigarette. But like the others I pretended that I did. We lit a second cigarette. That made us light-headed and almost nauseous; but at the same time I began feeling tranquil, too. After this, we began to frequent The Forest more often; not that we enjoyed smoking all that much but simply because it was a new experience in our young lives and seemed to be another step to adulthood.

I lived with my mother that summer of 1939, but I often crossed the creek to visit my father's parents, too. Sometimes it was easier to spend the night there as well. Semen and Marina were quite happy to have me because now their house was nearly empty. All my uncles were gone, pursuing lives in different directions—all, that is, but Petro. The farm had become progressively smaller, as we liked to put it. The tool shed and one barn had been taken apart. They were no longer needed to serve a smaller number of farm animals and a decreased area of seeded fields. I was sad to see the house that was once so full of life and joy look so empty and desolate.

Here as in Lviv everyone was talking about the approaching war. Many villagers hoped the Germans would eventually defeat both Poland and the Soviet Union. Then they might create an independent Ukraine for the benefit of both our people and the Germans. My family, however, had no such expectation.

Earlier that summer Uncle Miron had bought in Sokal a copy of Hitler's book, *Mein Kampf.* He was pointing out to all who asked and any who didn't that Hitler's doctrine of lebensraum—"living space"—included a vision of Germany extending east as far as the Ural Mountains. Miron couldn't find any mention of this "Grossdeutschland" dwelling peaceably side-by-side with an independent Ukraine. On the contrary, we would apparently supply the slave labor force for the Master Race.

Yet war was clearly coming. In August, the delivery of newspapers to

Tudorkovychi was stopped. So Miron decided to buy a radio, one that would give us not only Polish stations but also foreign ones. We all wanted to know when the fighting would begin, who would start it, and how would Britain and France respond. Since we had no electricity in the village, Miron bought two large batteries and an antenna that we attached to the roof of Chitalnya.

The radio set was placed on the table where many people could see it and listen to the news from around the world. When we first turned it on, Chitalnya was jammed full of people and those who could not get into the hall stood listening at the open windows. After we made several adjustments, many villagers for the first time in their lives heard voices and music being broadcast from a wooden case. Their faces radiated satisfaction and joy.

On the evening of August 23, 1939, the radio informed us that the German foreign minister, Joachim Ribbentrop, and his Soviet counterpart, Vyacheslav Molotov, had signed a nonaggression treaty. Although details of that agreement were not announced, it was clearly ominous when two inveterate enemies make common cause like this. A few days later, Great Britain signed a mutual defense pact with Poland, and the Polish government announced the mobilization of all citizens from twenty-one to forty years of age.

Despite all the warning signs, Poland was not prepared for war. Such government-sponsored slogans as "Seelnee, Zvarcy, Gotove"—"We are Strong, United, and Ready"—were always being supplemented by a joke: In this case, ready "for flight."

The German Wehrmacht's lead elements were motorized to a much greater extent than were the Polish units, which were much more reliant upon horsepower. The Poles had been especially impressed by the pivotal role cavalry had played in the Russian Civil War and so they had fostered that arm of their service. They were also impressing horses at a furious pace—including animals from Tudorkovychi.

Mikhalko, Aunt Stefonka's husband, had heard that if horses are not given water for a few days, they might not be able to walk—and then the military commission might reject them. He tried this strenuous treatment on our animals. On the second day the thirsty horses started to cry and lament with heart-piercing whinnies and screams. We could not sleep, but fortunately the commission came around on the third day of treatment and that ended the experiment. The Poles impressed three of our horses and left us but one that was unable to do all the work necessary for running the farm, for we still had crops in the fields.

On the morning of September 1, 1939, as every schoolboy now knows, Germany invaded Poland, touching off the Second World War.

The long spell of dry weather helped the German armored spearheads drive deep into the countryside, encircling vast numbers of Polish soldiers. Attacking from three directions, within just over a week they were at the gates of Warsaw, which their Stukas were dive-bombing ruthlessly; and just under two weeks they had arrived before Lviv! One night, about that same time, several convoys of cars—loaded with Polish government officials, other dignitaries, and probably gold and secret documents—drove right through Tudorkovychi. They were on the way southeast to a safe haven in Romania, and the drivers had chosen dirt roads to avoid discovery by the Germans then patrolling the paved thoroughfares.

We villagers did not disturb these refugees or try to take their possessions. The compassionate treatment of Polish refugees by Ukrainians is often forgotten. Polish politicians frequently accused Ukrainians of not helping the Poles in the defense of their nation against the Germans. But the fact is that the Polish Government did not adequately prepare the country for war; and with its unfair policies towards seven million Ukrainians, they had failed to make us loyal citizens.

Soon afterwards, we discovered what was left of the Polish Army had also been ordered to withdraw to the southeast, where the countryside east of Lviv still offered good defensive positions as well as an escape route to Romania and ultimately to Great Britain. But a day or two later, on September 17, the Soviet armies poured across Poland's eastern border and raced to close that escape route. Stalin had broken a non-aggression pact with Poland, preferring a secret codicil to the recent Nazi-Soviet Non-Aggression Pact, a codicil that split Polish territory between Germany and Russia.

Trapped, a major part of the Polish Army was encircled outside of Rawa Russka, a road and rail juncture not that far northwest of Lviv that had seen at least two major battles during the Galician campaign of the First World War. Now another tremendous engagement was fought there, the Polish remnants staging a fighting retreat north to more fields west of a town called Zamosc, about fifteen or twenty miles from Tudorkovychi. And there they were forced to surrender.

The Germans, however, had captured Polish soldiers; but they had no means of corralling all of the Polish horses that had escaped the slaughter. They simply shooed the mounts off. The woods and fields between our village and Zamosc were rumored to be full of horses wandering dazedly about.

So Mikhalko and I went out to look for some of them. Although I was now sixteen years old and well-muscled, he took me along primarily because I knew some German and could assure any soldiers we might encounter that we were neither partisans nor spies. Or so I hoped.

We left at dawn, dressed like farmers and carrying nothing threatening. We struck west, heading for the dirt highway linking Sokal with Hrubieszow, paralleling that for a while but keeping well to the bordering hedges and woods. We spent most of the day proceeding in that furtive manner; and when we judged we were about ten miles south of Hrubieszow, we ate a cold supper out of the rucksack and lay down to rest for a few hours.

We rose with dawn and, very carefully looking up and down the road and seeing nothing, hopped across it; then did the same thing with the railroad tracks running from Sokal to Hrubieszow. Then we struck dead west. We had hardly seen anybody on the journey so far, and no sign of horses. But the closer we crept to the neighborhood around Zamosc, the more cast-off debris, wrecked fences and hedges, and abandoned wagons we encountered. While sitting on a hill somewhere close to that town and eating our lunch of bread, we concluded the surrender must have been further to the west of town than we had hoped.

Then we saw an unforgettable sight. From the forest opposite our hill, a squadron of Polish cavalry emerged from the trees and picked its way carefully towards us over the grass of an intervening valley. Then we heard the piercing roar of German tanks! They crawled slowly across the valley and stopped the cavalrymen. A German officer climbed out of the forward tank and ordered the troopers to dismount, discard their weapons, take off their boots, and walk home.

The Polish cavalrymen did all he asked of them and quit the field, leaving behind horses, boots, and shiny swords and guns. The German tanks rode back and forth over the pile of weapons and scattered the horses with several shots. We moved in the direction of the horses, keeping to the cover of woods until we found a few frightened mounts dashing about among the trees. We selected two of them, quieted them down, discarded their saddles, and rode them bareback through the fields, avoiding all roads. Any German who may have seen us would surely take us for farmers—or so we hoped. Again.

Late in the evening of the second day we arrived back at Didoon Kindrat's, tired but happy with our war booty: Not plough horses but two handsome cavalry mounts to help us with the farm work.

Within four weeks, Poland had ceased to exist. Although war was declared on September 3 by France and Britain there was no fighting with them yet because these two countries, like Poland, were not prepared for war. Now we Ukrainians had to face the consequences. The Red Army was poised on the right bank of the Buh—less than three miles from Tudorkovychi.

What had been the Second Republic of Poland was now divided between Nazi Germany and the Soviet Union. By their Secret Protocol, Germany took the western two-thirds of Poland and Lithuania. Moscow was given a free hand in Latvia and Estonia and also annexed eastern Poland. They adopted as their new boundary the Curzon Line, first drawn up in 1919 by a British Foreign Minister as a proposed border but now resuscitated because it gave them half of Halichina, including all the southeastern parts, especially Lviv. That meant no more school for me. The Communists would close the Gymnasium.

Our village had been lucky the new border ran along the Buh in our sector. Sokal, however, was split. The old city was now in Soviet hands, but the western suburbs with its train station was now part of the Generalgouvernement, as Germany called its new eastern portion of Poland. So was Tudorkovychi.

Before the closure of the border, most of the Ukrainian intelligentsia had fled west because they did not want to live under Communism or expected the Communists to all-too-willingly comply with that wish.

The Reds would persecute and kill as many Ukrainians as they could. Many of these refugees, like my father and Pani Lyda, settled in the medieval town of Krakow where, among other political and social organizations, the Germans permitted the establishment of a Ukrainian Relief Organization.

There was certainly nothing inviting upon looking across the Buh. The Soviet soldiers patrolled the river day and night with trained dogs and anyone who tried crossing the border was shot on sight. These unsmiling, gray faced soldiers were dirty, dressed in poorly fitted uniforms and stole whatever they could. Occasional conversations with these guards convinced most farmers and villagers who encountered them that Communism was a big lie.

The Germans wanted nothing to do with them, either. In Starhorod, where my friend Petro Voroby lived, was a German outpost that overlooked that new border. He got to know them and that's what he told us. In Uhryniv, the village two or three miles west of Tudorkovychi, was stationed another detachment of German soldiers. To show good faith towards them, the citizens of Uhryniv and its surroundings invited them to a celebration of their victory. Soon the soldiers were visiting a different village every Sunday, eating good home-cooked meals and being entertained by local musicians and singers.

Eventually it was time for Tudorkovychi to play host. The women organized everything, despite strong opposition from my Uncle Miron and my family.

First, they had some men build a welcome gate near Chitalnya. On one corner of the gate, they hung a Ukrainian flag and on the other corner they wanted to place the German flag—but the villagers didn't know the colors in the German flag. So Miron made a deal with the women. If they would accept a second Ukrainian priest with his family to our parish, then he would show them the German flag.

A year earlier, in 1938, the village had undertaken to build a new gold-domed church to replace the one lost to the Russian shell. But our old married priest had died, and he was replaced by new, unmarried Father Hardibala. He was, let's say, flirtatious; and the village women were soon responding in kind. Yet there were so many married priests who had just escaped from the newly occupied Soviet zone and did not have a parish so their families were starving. Being in a difficult situation, the women finally agreed to accept the second priest and Miron told them the colors of the German flag.

All day Saturday the housewives of Tudorkovychi cleaned Chitalnya and arranged tables and chairs to accommodate the German soldiers. On Sunday morning the girls decorated the hall with embroidered table-cloths and placed freshly cut flowers on every surface. After the Sunday mass, the housewives produced enough cooked dishes to have fed not twenty but fifty soldiers. The tables literally groaned beneath the heavy weight of the food. Meanwhile, Father Hardibala, dressed in festive church robes, and his parishioners stood at the welcome gate awaiting the arrival of the Germans.

Exactly at 1:00 p.m., we heard the singing and soon a company of twenty-five soldiers marched down the burok toward Chitalnya. Leading them and riding a frisky brown horse was their officer. Before reaching the gate, he dismounted and led his soldiers through it on foot. It was a real pleasure to see these troops in their clean, well-cut uniforms and shining boots, despite their having marched on dirt roads. There was something precise and military about them, and I was impressed.

Father Hardibala formally welcomed them and in turn the German officer thanked everyone for the invitation. Then, according to an old Ukrainian custom, two girls offered the officer a *Korovai*, celebratory bread and salt placed on a beautifully embroidered towel, as a token of friendship. The officer accepted it and shook hands with the girls—one of whom was Slavka, who looked beautiful and graceful.

Then the soldiers stacked arms on the lawn and took their places at the tables. The village headman, Korolchuk by name, stood up and of-fered the first toast. Miron had prepared the text and translated it for him. It was a speech of welcome and a hope that the war would soon be finished, and Europe restored to peace and freedom. The German offi-cer thanked him in turn, professing his hope that Ukrainian wishes for freedom would soon become a reality. Those remarks occasioned much applause. After all, they were exactly what the villagers wanted to hear.

I sat on stage behind the curtain and listened to all this because none of my family would attend the celebration. The village choir sang a few Ukrainian songs during the dinner and afterwards the soldiers responded with German songs which the people seemed to enjoy. The musicians played their instruments and the soldiers and villagers all danced waltzes and polkas. At seven o'clock the Germans left and returned to their station in Uhryniv.

When I returned home, I described the look and behavior of the soldiers, but Miron was not in the mood for praise. He still believed Hitler would enslave the Slavic people exactly as he had stated in *Mein Kampf.*

Miron notified the Ukrainian Relief Organization in Krakow that Tudorkovychi would accept one married priest, a refugee from the newly occupied zone. In a few days, we learned the Organization was sending us a former chaplain of the Ukrainian Army by the name of Hoora who was married with three children. When Miron told the villagers about the new priest, the men were happy to accept the deserving priest, but the women objected. They completely ignored their promise to Miron, claiming it was made under duress and thus was not binding. In spite of this revolt, the men decided to bring Father Hoora to Tudorkovychi and asked my uncles to arrange his transfer.

Miron and Petro drove a wagon to the small town Variazh, loaded Father Hoora and his family onto the wagon, and brought them to our village.

Expecting some unpleasant demonstration from the enraged housewives, Miron stopped the wagon before entering the village proper and asked Father Hoora and his family to go to the parish using the back streets. Five village boys, dressed in large overcoats, took the places of the priest's family on the wagon. On both sides of the burok the women were waiting impatiently for the arrival of the new priest. When the wagon came into sight the women began their protest. At first very softly they repeated, "Father, we don't want you." But getting no response, they became quite angry. At that point they turned their backs on the wagon, raised their skirts, and mooned the passengers!

The boys on the wagon removed their coats, laughing and ridiculing the protestors. Later these women were quite ashamed, and they never forgave Miron for this deception.

During and after the war, all the village schools were closed. There were no police, but neither was there much crime in our villages. The

Germans did impose orders, though. They were issued from Khorobriv, the new headquarters for the several villages of the former Sokal district. It was announced to the villagers in the age-old fashion: A village elder would beat a drum while marching through the streets. Stopping at pre-scribed places, he would shout loudly the text of the order.

This first *diktat* called for all weapons and radios be handed over to the German Military Government. Failure to comply would be pun-ished very severely. Miron angrily parted with his radio, and it was the only such item the Germans received from our village.

Shortly afterwards, a second order called for the collection of an agri-cultural quota to be submitted to the German Army and Administration. Each farmer had to donate an established amount of farm products per cultivable acre to the Occupation. In return, the farmer received stamps that entitled him to buy certain manufactured goods, such as materials for clothes and leather for boots.

The quota, however, was very high and the amounts of available man-ufactured goods were correspondingly low—and moreover expensive. Eventually, the farmers started complaining that whatever grain was left them, after the quota was met, barely sufficed to feed their families, much less provide seed corn for the following year. Many began drink-ing heavily, alcohol being the only commodity the Germans happily supplied in bulk. Village morality declined steeply, as often happens in times of war.

City dwellers, however, had only food stamps to survive on and they often were not enough. This drove them to the villages to exchange their possessions for food. Polish money was now worthless, and this led to the development of a black market that grew in dimension throughout the duration of the war. Many people were making a comfortable living acquiring food from farmers and reselling it in towns for much more money. The penalty for such activity was severe, of course, black marke-teers commonly being sentenced to death by hanging or imprisonment in one of the numerous concentration camps.

In attempts to eliminate the black market, the Germans performed unexpected searches of people's possessions in the streets or on public transportation. Frequently they stopped a train and would order people to leave the cars, then subject their belongings to a search. The Germans were specifically searching for guns, illegal literature, food, tobacco, soap, and larger amounts of manufactured goods. At such an "oblava," as they were called, the black marketeers would simply discard the illegal items and walk to the examination places without them.

Since the schools were closed, I lived in Tudorkovychi and helped both my grandfathers with their farm work, especially with the harvesting of beets and potatoes. In my free time I fished in the river and, as autumn deepened, collected hazelnuts and wild berries in The Forest or raided Uncle Sidorko's orchard for autumn apples and pears. In the evenings I always found time to make love with Slavka, listening to the singing of village boys but missing the nightingales, long since flown, and the songs of the frogs now buried in mud beneath the creek.

Life in our isolated village was peaceful, even tranquil; but occasionally we heard something about what was happening under the Soviet regime a few miles away. Someone was always illegally crossing the Buh and visiting their families on the sly; and they told us life under Soviet domination was very difficult. The Bolsheviks eradicated everything with a hint of Ukrainian about it, banishing most of the educated people to faraway Siberia. The Soviet government nationalized factories, businesses, stores, land, houses, and all private possessions. Farms were organized into collectives called "colhosps" in which farmers worked as laborers and were paid very little. The Soviet government became the owner of all material goods and controlled the lives and activities of all the people.

That was so discouraging and distressing it seemed to bring the snows earlier that year. It also inspired me, once the winterizing chores were finished, to help in Chitalnya to prepare a festival commemorating the anniversary of the Proclamation of Ukrainian Independence in January 1918. I was fast inheriting the educational job in Chitalnya that had once been Sidorko's and later Miron's. I threw myself into the preparation of various festivals and patriotic plays, especially those about the fight for Ukrainian independence at the end of the First World War.

It was the winter of 1939-40, the winter of the "Phony War," of stasis, of snow. I started reading Jack London's adventure stories set in Alaska. But one day, in our small library, I found a copy of Shevchenko's poems and soon I was reading his verse all day, every day. More and more

I understood his love of the uneducated, suppressed, and poor village people and why he hated those of the intelligentsia that had left them to die not just physically but spiritually as well. That small volume of Shevchenko's poems, much of which I memorized by heart, awoke a deeply Ukrainian spirit in me that I was determined would become my guiding star—especially knowing what lay just across the River Buh.

CHAPTER SIX

Strewn Roses

During the winter of 1940, while I was immersed in Shevchenko, my father and Pani Lyda finalized their move to Krakow. He had been appointed the director of a Ukrainian bank there, supervised by German overseers. In Krakow he finally married Pani Lyda and they leased a nice apartment on Zylona Street, in the center of this ancient and beautiful Polish capital.

In the early spring they invited me to visit. I was happy to oblige because I had not seen my father since the war began and was anxious to get out of Tudorkovychi for a change of scenery. Didoon Semen took me in the wagon to the railroad station at Sokal, now so perilously close to the Soviet border. While buying a ticket I was warned that now the trains rarely kept a regular schedule. After the German invasion most public transportation in the Generalgouvernement was spotty and unreliable. In fact, it took two days to travel from Sokal to Krakow, approximately 200 miles.

First, I was routed northwest to the city of Lublin, about halfway to Warsaw, and then I had to wait there overnight for the connection to Krakow. I didn't see any nearby hotels, which was strange. Then two small boys came up and asked me if I would like to spend the night at their house?

I thanked them and said I would await my train at the station. They then informed me the station would close, and the nights were very cold.

Acknowledging I needed shelter, I accompanied them to their small apartment that was indeed close to the station. Their mother fed me potatoes with sour milk and a piece of bread. I slept in one of their unused beds and in the morning, I thanked these good people for their hospitality. I gave the lady a piece of soap—an item practically unobtainable even on the black market—that Miron had secretly made. The two boys accompanied me back to the station and I was on my way to Krakow. I arrived in the city that evening and took a taxi to my father's apartment.

Volodimir and Pani Lyda were pleased to see me. They fed me well and I told them news about our family and all the new rules in the village. The next morning was clear and sunny and while exploring Krakow I could see in the distance the bluish silhouettes of the Carpathian Mountains.

The city was certainly picturesque. Steeples pointed skyward everywhere. Monasteries and convents, churches and basilicas all seemingly clustered around the large medieval market square with its large Renaissance-styled cloth hall. There you could buy, legally or illegally, foods, fabrics, and manufactured goods. Looming above everything was the castle complex, a city within the city, where the prominent Nazi, Hans Frank, ruled like a medieval landlord over the Generalgouvernement— and over several generations of Polish kings buried in the crypts beneath.

The Old Town was encircled by a belt of trees, walkways, and benches where once the city walls had stood. This was Planty Park, and on its western side was the very old and famous Jagiellonian University. Adjacent to that was a small Ukrainian Catholic Church that I attended.

One day when I was strolling about, I was picked up by the German Military Police and taken to their headquarters. Fortunately, I knew some German and asked them to telephone my father. He would confirm that I was both a citizen and a student too young for military service. Nothing came of this encounter, except a potentially useful facet of my blond hair; I could pass for German.

Before returning home my father and I discussed my education, which had been suspended now for nine months. He had heard from a friend that permission had been obtained to open a new Gymnasium in Belz, a town located about eighteen miles south of Tudorkovychi. His friend was planning to send his own son to this new school and was organizing a dormitory to house four boys. The families of these four would share the expense of feeding their sons. I agreed to be one of them. Another would be my friend from Sokal, Bohdan Yourchuk.

A few days later I took the train back to Sokal. It was packed with people. They filled not only all the cars, but also all corridors, platforms between cars, steps leading into cars, and even the bathrooms. Fortunately, the train started its run in Krakow and I was able to get a seat. At each station, though, more and more people boarded and finally there was no more room whatsoever—except perhaps on the roof. But with night coming no one wanted to ride there.

Of course, the first three cars were nearly empty. Each of them had a big sign, "Nur für Deutsche," attached to its side. Only for Germans. The supermen could relax and enjoy their journey in comfort.

After a few days in Tudorkovychi, I packed my things to go to the school in Belz. Didoon Semen prepared our weekly contribution of food products for the new dormitory kitchen. I finished my job of helping the village boys and girls prepare a concert in Chitalnya to commemorate Taras Shevchenko. It was well received, and I was proud to have been a part of it. Toward the end of March 1940, over muddy lanes and potholed roads, Didoon Semen took me by horse-drawn wagon to the dormitory in Belz.

Belz was yet another picturesque small town about a thousand years old. Standing on the banks of the slow flowing Solokiya River, it was encircled by a belt of forested low hills. It, too, had seen its share of wars and sieges over the centuries. Its Ukrainian church once boasted a revered icon of St. Mary, but a Polish magnate stole it and now it is world-famous as the miracle-working Black Madonna of Czestochowa.

The town also had a miracle-working rabbi and a large synagogue noted for its beauty. Yet when I arrived in Belz in the early spring of 1940, everything looked desolate and lifeless. The war destroyed business, and both the synagogue and the residence of the miracle-making Rabbi had been burned. The synagogue's walls were still standing, but there were no Jewish people left to rebuild it. They had all been transferred to ghettos in larger towns and their houses were now occupied by the German Special Forces.

The town was under military rule and even for minor infractions the punishment was severe. The curfew from 8:00 p.m. to 5:00 a.m. was strictly enforced. No civilians were allowed on the streets of Belz and if you were caught being out during curfew you could be shot. All the shops were closed and there was no place to buy even a piece of bread. All meetings and assemblies were forbidden and during the day people could not walk on the street in groups larger than three. You could, however, attend both church and school.

The house rented for our dormitory was located in the outskirts of town, close to a railroad track with only a few other houses nearby. There were three rooms, one for cooking and eating, one for sleeping, and one small room became the bedroom for our cook, Mrs. Mikhalchuk, who was the mother of one of the students living in the dormitory. All four beds were placed on one side of the room and a large table filled the center. The only way you could sit near the table was by perching on the end of your bed. All your belongings stayed in your suitcase under the bed. There was an iron-plate in the kitchen that was to heat *both* rooms. There was no running water. Water had to be carried in via pails from the water-pump across the street.

Looking at this pitiful arrangement, Didoon Semen asked me whether I wanted to stay. I replied I could not do otherwise because I promised my father I would go to school and it was too late to find another place to live. Later I regretted that decision and felt my father had been misled. The worst feature of the dormitory—which I didn't know before Didoon Semen's departure—was the lack of an outhouse. With no outhouse and the inevitable delays in the delivery of food, our lives were made miserable. Cold and hunger interfered with our studies. Not until the sun began to warm the earth and dried up the roads could we leave our cramped room and enjoy the natural world just waking up from its long wintry sleep.

Several weeks after my arrival, the town began piling up soil and making a high mound. It was soon topped by a large wooden cross—a cross dedicated, per the plaque, to those who died while fighting for Ukrainian independence.

One Sunday in early spring, a local priest said mass for the souls of the fallen fighters and officially sanctified the mound. The choir sang nationalistic songs and several young men delivered long and extremely patriotic speeches. After this dedication all the neighboring villages were soon putting up mounds and crosses. It seemed to me this was excessive nationalism and I decided such celebrations could take place without me. My roommates did attend because most of them were members of the Organization of Ukrainian Nationalists and followed their party without question. From the war's outset, it was clear to me the Nazis did not and would not recognize Ukrainians as partners in the building of the "New Europe."

Though I was only sixteen years old in early 1940 I thought I could foresee the day when this OUN movement would fracture and fall into mutually hostile camps. This flash of foresight would prove all too true. Years later, the warring factions would tear each other to shreds over such picayune matters as the color arrangement of the proposed Ukrainian flag. At meetings, they would destroy each other's flag designs, arguing about the exact placing of the blue and yellow stripes. To me, this was reminiscent of the Kingdom of Lilliput as described in *Gulliver's Travels*. The Lilliputians fought among themselves about the best method for cracking a boiled egg, whether from its wide or from its narrow end.

The school in Belz was located close to the city square, the heart of town through which all motorized and pedestrian traffic had to pass. In the center of the square was the kiosk where the German Military Administration posted its edicts and announcements.

I had been accepted to the highest class in the new school. There were twenty-two of us in a student body of about a hundred. There were no textbooks and all we had to study were the notes we took during lectures. There were only around eight teachers whom we called professors, and they emphasized the study of mathematics and the German language.

Mr. Demchuk, a former Ukrainian officer in the last war, was behind the establishment of the school, a considerable achievement considering the hoops he had to jump through. The building needed considerable renovation to turn it into classrooms, and then there were always the Germans to placate. We learned that last bit fast.

While walking home from school one afternoon with my friend Bohdan Myhal, we passed the ruins of the burned synagogue. Because the debris had spilled over the sidewalk we had to walk in the street.

As we were doing so we saw three German officers on beautiful horses riding toward us. Both the riders and mounts were an impressive sight. The Germans sat erect in their saddles and inspected, with a sweep of their superior gaze, all the buildings and people huddled in doorways. Because it was a wide street, we passed them with room to spare.

Suddenly we heard a shouted "Halt!" We stopped and turned around. One of the officers had reined in and was trotting back towards us. He ordered us to take off our caps. We must have been paralyzed with fear. Seeing no reaction to his order, he struck me across the face with his riding crop and knocked off my cap. His horse was startled by this sudden motion and began to buck. Thanks to that unruly horse we avoided severe punishment. If we had shown any defiance whatsoever, he might have shot us. He shouted that we should remember to stand aside whenever a German officer approached us on the street and always to take off our caps! There was no anger in his eyes; he was only behaving in the manner he had been taught—the manner for dealing with slaves.

That crop had sliced into my left cheek and blood was seeping out of the swelling tissue. Bohdan helped me stanch the flow with my handkerchief before it permanently stained the only jacket I owned. Greater than any pain I felt from the swelling, however, was the rage and humiliation I felt at such treatment. That recovery took much longer.

Living in that dormitory on the edge of town, it wasn't long before I found a little path leading off the hill and down to a creek that eventually fed into the slow-flowing river. One Sunday, when my friends were away attending yet another celebration on a mound, I walked down the path. Before I reached my favored spot by the creek, however, I encountered a girl.

She was riding her bicycle and as she passed me, she lost her balance and fell on the soft grass. The potatoes she carried scattered from an open bag and rolled all over the place. I helped her up and set to collecting the spilled tubers. I thought I recognized her from the school.

She told me she was bringing the potatoes from her grandfather's farm to her parents' townhouse just off the square in Belz. Yes, she was a student at my school but she was two years behind me. That made her about fifteen years old, but she seemed quite poised. Conversation came naturally to her and soon I was inviting her down to my favored spot by the creek. She walked her bike down first and I followed with the potatoes.

She had a nice figure, with long and shapely legs and black, shiny hair neatly braided on both sides of her head. From time to time, she looked back at me, as if checking whether I was still following her, and each time she gave me a warm smile.

While we sat on the bank of the creek, she told me she had wanted to meet me but had not yet had an opportunity to do so. She had heard I had been in Krakow and she wanted to know what I had seen in the old Polish capital. I described to her the ornamental facades of the old buildings, the castle on the hill, the majestic buildings of Jagiellonian University, and the beautiful Planty Park. In return, she invited me to visit her family in the house across the street from the school.

After she departed, I wondered about this unusual meeting with Darka Tkachuk, for that was her name. She was an interesting and certainly a different girl from any I had met previously. I liked her openness, that absence of shyness that was otherwise so prevalent in Ukrainian girls. Then again, I wondered whether she was a Ukrainian girl at all? Her skin was olive while her eyes were black and framed with black, long lashes. She also had a thin straight nose and a delicate face.

There was no question she was a beautiful girl and I wondered why I had not noticed her earlier. Asking around, I learned that she was indeed Ukrainian and the daughter of elementary school teachers. I was also told her grandparents lived on a large farm on the outskirts of Belz, a farm with a church on it that her ancestors had built long ago.

I let several days pass, and then approached her and asked whether I might not come for a visit that weekend? The next day she told me her mother had invited me for Sunday dinner. I should be there at 1:00 p.m.

My roommates did not approve of these arrangements. "You are do-ing this all in the wrong way," they said. "If you like the girl then take her for a date, but do not get involved with her parents!"

I disagreed. I thought this girl was different and, after all, her mother *did* invite me. But there was no convincing them, so I turned my atten-tion to making myself presentable. I had only one decent suit, so before going to bed Saturday night I cleaned the pants and placed them under my mattress to flatten them and give them creases. I wore my embroidered shirt and tied it beneath my chin with a red ribbon. When I put on my blue jacket, I thought I looked respectable enough and certainly colorful.

At Darka's house I met her father, mother, and younger sister, Natalia. We then sat down and spoke about the life of my family in Krakow. I think they cocked an eyebrow or two when I spoke of my father's living with Pani Lyda for so long before they married. I hastened to explain I also spent time with my mother, who lived very comfortably in Tudorkovychi. But most of my vacations I lived with my paternal grandparents.

We ate a nice dinner and finally Darka and I could sit alone on the balcony, watching people walk by on the street below. I then thanked Mrs. Tkachuk for dinner, kissed her hand, and shook the hand of Darka's father before wishing the house a heartfelt goodnight.

I met Darka the following Sunday at our trysting place, my former perch above the creek. She invited me to go to her grandparents' farm. We strolled through flowery meadows and jumped over small streams before we reached it. On our way, we sang songs and enjoyed the sweet smell of fresh grass and blooming trees. Darka's grandparents welcomed us warmly and fed us sorrel borscht with fresh buttered bread. This borscht was enriched with sour cream and with crumbled hard-boiled eggs.

I asked them for permission to see the church that was on their property, and they gave us the key to unlock the door. It was an old structure with one cupola and I wondered how it had survived the terrible First World War, not to mention the recent German invasion. Covering the inside walls were depictions of saints; but wherever they were exposed to the weather the colors had faded. Screening the sanctuary was a beautifully carved and painted iconostasis. A silver-framed door beckoned and, stepping through it, we entered into the presence of the high and hallowed altar itself. Darka and I then crept up narrow stairs and sat in the choir stall, looking at the still and solemn beauty below and above us. I was enraptured—so enraptured that, on impulse, I leaned over and kissed her cheek.

To my surprise, she seemed shocked. And then upset. Tears brimmed in her eyes as I hurriedly whispered apologies and explanations. I couldn't understand her reaction. The kiss had been an innocent one, after all. Nevertheless, she fled to her grandparents' farmhouse and I went disconsolately home.

My roommates merely laughed at my misadventure. When I proposed that maybe I should send her some flowers, they guffawed. This was wartime and there were no cut flowers for sale. Then the eyes of Bohdan slowly lit up. He knew where to get flowers. Frequently we passed a convent's gardens on our back trail to school. Surely they wouldn't miss a few flowers! We decided to invade that night.

Before we left, our lady-cook reminded us it was close to curfew and dangerous to leave the house at night even for a short walk. We decided to chance it. The Germans were unlikely to patrol this far from the center of town in the dark. As we slipped out we felt fairly confident we wouldn't get caught. As we walked my friends asked how I planned to deliver these flowers to Darka? They joked that I would be carrying flowers to the school, kneeling in front of her, and asking for forgiveness. They imagined the expressions on the faces of our professors and friends when witnessing such a performance. They were having fun and could not control their laughter. Fearing they might change their minds about our plan, I did not reveal to them how I planned to deliver the flowers.

Upon reaching the garden we climbed the wire fence and began to look for the red roses. We knew approximately where they were; but at night, we could not see their color and had to identify them by touch. It was painful to cut and gather them and our hands were very sore. We left the garden with about thirty full-blown roses emitting a strong, almost dizzying fragrance.

Now I told my friends I intended to throw these roses onto Darka's balcony. They thought I had lost my mind! It was now one hour after curfew and her house was in the center of town. I told them that strewn roses were better than no roses, especially in a time of darkness and war.

Well, once they glimpsed the romantic angle, they decided to take the chance and help. Using only back streets, we reached Darka's house. I took off my shoes, climbed onto the shoulders of Bohdan, and was just able to reach the bottom of the balcony with my hands. Another friend handed me the prickly roses, a few stems at a time, and I threw them over the railing. After a several minutes the job was done.

We reached our dormitory without encountering any Germans. Our hands were scratched and bloody, but we washed them in cold buckets of water, disinfected them with iodine, and disregarded the pain.

At school the next morning the students were all abuzz about the roses on Darka's balcony. Although she claimed she didn't know who covered her balcony with flowers, many of the students did not believe her. Most of the girls considered the nocturnal gift, delivered at the risk of losing one's life, to be a very romantic undertaking.

At recess, Darka came to me and thanked me for the beautiful roses. We met after school that day in an empty classroom and fell into each other's arms, kissing passionately. Afterwards, she told me her mother wanted her to marry our teacher, Mr. Kozak, who was twelve years older than her. Not only that, but he was also boring and dislikable. She had cried when I had kissed her in the church because she didn't know what to do!

She was clearly too young to be married and I consoled her by suspecting her mother would surely change her mind with time. I told her I loved her, adding, however, that we were too young to marry in these dangerous times—for I secretly knew I could not marry this early in my life.

For Easter 1940, I decided to walk home for the holiday. The weather was warm and sunny and the roads were dry. Leaving early in the morning, I enjoyed striding down the road, seeing the beauty of the countryside unfold, listening to the singing of birds and the buzzing of insects, and just being solitary.

I covered nine miles by noon, about half of the distance to Tudorkovychi. I waved to people working in the fields and was invited to eat lunch with one family as I walked past the back of their wagon. They shared their freshly baked bread, garnished with salted pig fat and garlic, and we drank sour milk. It was a pleasure to speak with the farmer. He was intelligent and skeptical of the nationalists' hope of achieving independence with the help of Nazi Germany.

I reached my mother's house just as the sun was setting. I was pleasantly tired and hungry. My mother fed me buckwheat kasha steamed to perfection, enriched with freshly prepared skvarky, and sour milk. The next day was Good Friday and many people were preparing to celebrate by spending most of their day on their knees in church.

It was good to see the rest of my family. Mitonko had decided to work in an administrative office in Chorobriv, a village about four miles south of ours, and was preparing to move. I visited Didoon Semen, Babunya Marina, and Uncle Petro. They were happy to see me. I told Didoon that my school was good but the dormitory was lousy and without a proper outhouse it was barely tolerable. They again tried to convince me to move but with only two months of the school year left I felt it wasn't necessary.

There were, however, disturbing changes in the village. The boys and girls who worked with me in Chitalnya seemed to avoid eye contact when speaking. Then I saw the earthen mound close to the church with a tall cross on top and learned that everyone was forced to work at least one day to construct this memorial. The villagers no longer seemed relaxed or eager to hear about Ukrainian politics and the progress of the war. Before 1939, nearly all of them subscribed to newspapers published by the Front of National Unity or other organizations. Now they weren't reading so much but were drinking more horilka.

I should have known. The OUN adherents had decided to promote patriotism by building these mounds and holding rallies. I was not surprised that my friend, Bohdan Yourchuk from Sokal, was the local promoter of this program. He now paraded around town in a semi-military outfit and was preparing the boys and girls to march to the village of Starhorod to dedicate a new mound. He greeted them by extending his right arm in a fascist manner and saying, "Glory to Ukraine!" and they answered, "Glory to our leader!" Even my mother had heard about my disappointment with such developments and now called me a Communist.

That was it. I took my bicycle and headed back to Belz.

I was so agitated I pedaled fast. Everyone should know by now how dangerous extremist ideologies are. Communism and Fascism have been causing untold suffering and death for millions of people. This Ukrainian Nationalism will end up the same way. And now they are imitating the Nazis!

Back in Belz I was hungry but there was no food in the larder of the dormitory. Everyone had gone home. The next day I went to church but inside I was still unhappy and still hungry. After Mass, Darka was surprised to see me, and we went to say hello to her parents. I avoided telling Darka about my quarrel with my own mother and my leaving home angry.

The weather was warm, and I went to our creekside trysting place to contemplate what I should do. Except for a few candies, I had not eaten anything for twenty-four hours. I was sad about missing Easter dinner, but I knew one other person who did not eat it, either, and probably cried as well. That was my mother. I resolved never to tell her about the hardships that ensued after she called me a Communist.

I couldn't give her flowers, either. She grew her own roses.

CHAPTER SEVEN

Barbarossa

The week after Easter, after everyone had returned to the Belz Gymnasium, I noticed my roommates, after eating their evening meal, were going back to school—a most unusual change of habit. When I asked them what that was all about, they gave evasive answers. Finally, I learned they were training to cross the Soviet border as Organization of Ukrainian Nationalist spies. From what I had heard, that usually ensured young recruits met an early and violent death. I told them that.

A few days later a classmate of mine named Ilnytski informed me at recess that he had been appointed to be my defender at my trial. Trial? I did not understand. He then said he could not tell me who had made this decision or what crime I was accused of having committed. I laughed and told him that as my defender he had already failed if he didn't know these things.

I told him I was unlikely to attend such a trial unless I knew what my crime was supposed to be. Ilnytski replied the trial would take place irrespective of my presence. In that case, I replied, I had no need to inform him whether I would be there or not. I knew such show trials were common in places like the Soviet Union and people could be sentenced to death by secretive courts. After all, the director of Academichna Gymnasia in Lviv had been murdered for opposing the spread of nationalistic literature in his school. I am sure the attempt on my father's life was decided at a secret trial by an OUN court.

I decided to attend this kangaroo court anyway and learn more about these accusations. At 6:00, in the designated classroom, the members of the tribunal entered one by one. They identified themselves as Bohdan Mihal, the judge; Bohdan Yourchuk, the prosecutor; Serhij Ilnytski, the defender; and Cerhij Olijnyk, the recorder.

After they sat down, I asked, "Who gave you the authority to perform this trial?" They seemed confused and finally Mihal replied they acted under the authority of OUN. I replied I was not a member of OUN and therefore they had no right to judge me, whatever the nature of the charges. Mihal asserted OUN Courts could judge anyone.

Then Yourchuk accused Uncle Miron of opposing the welcoming of the German soldiers in Tudorkovychi and, furthermore, accused my father of belonging to FNU and hence opposing Ukrainian independence. Whatever the merits of these charges they did not pertain to me. And anyway, "Judge" Bohdan Mihal's own father had also belonged to FNU! Why didn't they put him on trial? Finally, since not one accusation had been leveled against me personally, I was not going to participate in this farce any longer. I left the room and went back to the dormitory.

I never heard anything further about these proceedings. Bohdan Mihal and Bohdan Yourchuk both behaved as if nothing had happened. Much later, however, I found out the leader of OUN in the Sokal district, Petro Bashuk, had indeed ordered my trial—and he was the same man who had ordered the unsuccessful assassination of my father several years earlier.

The school year ended in July 1940, when we took our final exams and received our grades. Mine were good, except for arithmetic, a subject with which I was having problems. In the wider world the pivotal Battle of Britain was underway, and if the Nazis triumphed Hitler might turn the full might of German arms against the Soviet Union. Yet we weren't celebrating anything. We just shook hands and wished each other success in our lives.

Darka and I went to her grandfather's farm. We ate currants from the blackcurrant bushes and visited the old church once more. It was a melancholy setting in which to say a final goodbye. She knew I dreamed of higher education and, not yet being seventeen, I had already told her I was too young to marry her. I knew her mother was determined to wed her soon to the older Mr. Kozak. We kissed and held that embrace for a long time. She said she would always remember me and the huge collection of roses on her balcony. And thus, I left this girl that I loved and would always fondly remember.

The next day, Didoon Semen arrived by horse-drawn wagon to take me home. We loaded my belongings; and since it was late afternoon and both he and the horses disliked traveling at night, we turned the team northward and left Belz far behind.

When I arrived home, there was a letter from my father notifying me his friend Volodimir Kubiovich had received permission from the Generalgouvernement to establish a gymnasium in Cholm, an old and beautiful town twenty-five miles to the north in Kholmshchina Province.

Volodimir Kubiovich was a well-known Ukrainian scientist who had been asked by the Germans to head the Ukrainian Relief Organization in Krakow, with which my father was now associated. Although its principal duty was to help people in need and encourage young men and women to volunteer for work in German factories and farms, the URO also organized elementary schools. According to the Germans, Ukrainians should know how to read and write—but they didn't need any further education to work in fields or factories, our presumed destiny in a Nazified Europe. Permission to establish a gymnasium in Cholm was therefore a significant achievement.

My father also informed me that he spoke to Dr. Oles Babij, who used to work as a writer for Front for National Unity-affiliated newspapers and had asked him to enroll me into the gymnasium since he was to be a professor of Ukrainian literature there. Dr. Babij agreed to enroll me—warning, however, that I would have to pass an entrance examination in the Ukrainian and German languages, biology, and mathematics. Therefore, my father advised me to review these subjects because he had heard there were many applicants to the new school.

During one of my visits to the German-controlled part of Sokal I had met Mr. Mihal, whose son was Bohdan Mihal, my "judge" in the farcical trial at Belz. While visiting him I told this friend of my own father's how excited I was to be given the chance to attend the new school in Cholm. He warned me, in turn, about the splintering of the

Organization of Ukrainian Nationalists into two factions. One faction was called "Melnikites" after Andrij Melnik, a former officer in the Ukrainian Army during the First World War and a moderate nationalist. The other, much more violent, faction was called "Banderites," after its uncompromising leader, Stepan Bandera, an unscrupulous hothead who condoned any act to win independence. These two factions would never see eye-to-eye and that would lead to much killing and suffering over the next few years. Furthermore, they would probably be infiltrating the new school. I thanked him and took my leave, deciding not to mention anything about his own son's affiliations.

I left for Cholm at the end of August 1940, boarding a train one morning in Sokal and arriving later that same day. It was a difficult trip, however, because I carried a heavy suitcase and two large bags packed with winter clothing, sheets, bedcovers, and some books. I had to change trains in Hrubieszow and boarding the Cholm-bound one was almost impossible. It was packed so full I had to throw my baggage on the platform between two cars and squeeze myself behind a door. I watched my bags by leaning out of the car to make sure they did not fall off.

In the old Ukrainian language, a "kholm" meant a hill and the name couldn't have been more appropriate for this picturesque place perched atop a small plateau and overlooking an undulating agricultural plain. At the center of the old town stood an ancient Sobor, or Greek-Orthodox cathedral, complete with bell tower, hoary cemetery, and quarters for priests and bishops. Spacious parks adorned with old trees and flower gardens were ideal places for friends and lovers to meet. The cobbled main street, lined with stores and offices, was called Hrubieszowska Way, and the new Gymnasium, with spacious grounds for games and sports, was located nearby.

As soon as I walked through its doors a secretary suggested I seek lodgings with a Mr. Kovaluk, who had a six-room apartment not far away in a large building originally constructed to house railroad workers. Mr. Kovaluk used four of his rooms for his large family and rented the two others to prospective students, one room for girls and the other for boys. In the former room I glimpsed a pretty face framed by golden curls. It belonged to a girl named Halya Pona and she was there with two of her young cousins. And in the latter room—well, the first two boys I saw were Bohdan Yourchuk and Bohdan Mihal. All of us were applying for admission to the new Gymnasium.

I did not want to live in the same room with the two Bohdans and their crazy politics. And seeing such a large number of applicants for the same limited places, I decided the next day to try and find another room where I could study. Sure enough, that night various young people kept dropping in to learn techniques for illegally crossing the border into the Soviet Union. The Bohdans were not interested in passing the upcoming Gymnasium examinations. They probably hoped to recruit students into OUN.

Thus I began my search for another place to live.

It was an ancient city I set out to explore. Cholm was established when in 1237 Prince Danylo Romanovich of Volhynia, the wooded province northeast of my home village, built a castle on this hill, reinforced with a stone wall and defense towers. It was so strongly built it withstood the Mongol invasions of 1240 and 1261. In 1387, it was annexed by Poland and shortly thereafter received Magdeburg law, the legal framework adopted by most towns in medieval Central Europe. In the fifteenth century, Cholm was an important trade center and remained so throughout the heyday of the Polish-Lithuanian Commonwealth. After the Third Partition of Poland in 1795, however, the town was subjected to the untender mercies of Imperial Russia, and during those bleak centuries, only ending with the First World War, it became predominately a Jewish city.

When I arrived, it contained about 21,000 inhabitants, equally divided between Poles, Ukrainians, and Jews. The houses of Poles and Ukrainians were scattered all over town, but the Jews had already been confined to the ghetto. There were no restrictions upon entering or leaving this ghetto, however, so I promptly went in there to buy bread and Hungarian cigarettes, the latter sold only on the Jewish black market. In the ghetto one could buy most items needed for daily life.

Except lodgings, of course. Then a kindly fate stepped in.

Stopping for dinner in a restaurant and unable to find an empty table, I asked a man of about my age whether I might share his table. He invited me to sit down and, to my great surprise, I discovered he was from Sokal. To my even greater surprise, he was the son of the same Mrs.

Zerebecka who had fed me all those tasty dinners when I first lived in Sokal with my father and Pani Lyda! His name was Mykola Zerebecka and he was starting his education at the Technical Institute in Cholm. Like me, he was looking for a place to rent. So, upon leaving the restaurant we decided to go door-to-door and see what we could find.

Wherever we knocked, we asked the same question: Would you rent a room to a pair of good-looking and pleasant-mannered students? We were, In truth, tall and reasonably handsome young men. Mykola had dark hair, light-brown skin, and perpetually smiling blue eyes while I was blond with golden twists in my curly hair. Nevertheless, we met disappointment after disappointment.

Then, at one house that was separated from the street by a neglected flower garden, a very pretty woman opened the door. We repeated our line about the handsome students looking for a place to live and she replied that indeed she did have one room to rent—but only for good and polite boys. When we assured her that her requirement described us exactly, she laughed good-naturedly. This nice lady's name was Mrs. Romanovska, a Polish woman who lived there with her daughter and her father, who was sick and rarely left his room.

We rented the room immediately and saw it had a bed, a couch, a table with four chairs, and a wood stove. According to an agreement between us Mykola would sleep on the bed, and I would sleep on the couch. Then, after six months, we would switch. We established a common food supply in one of our suitcases and decided to share anything further we received from home. According to our budgets, we could afford to eat dinner in a restaurant, but we would make breakfasts and suppers with the food from home.

We could have lived in a dormitory that offered three cooked meals a day for nearly the same money, but we did not want the noise and pressures of life with so many people. After living in dormitories for two years I just wanted to get away from other students and their social and political prejudices. Mykola disliked crowds and fortunately we agreed on political issues. We both thought OUN members were puffed-up mannequins, with no thoughts of their own, who did whatever their leaders ordered.

During the evenings we often visited with the daughter of Mrs.

Romanovska, named Noosia. She was a pretty girl with long blonde hair and a nice figure. She said we were lucky to be able to go to school because the Germans did not allow Poles to establish schools, so she studied on her own. Noosia was close to our age and though she said she desired an opportunity for education, I never saw her with a book in her hand. Her mother worked at the post office and supported both her and her sick father.

Noosia was very nationalistic and frequently told us the Poles would liberate their country at the first opportune moment. I suspected she was a member of the Polish underground organization, which attracted many young Poles. She liked Ukrainian boys, though, and during cold winter days she sometimes invited us to study in her room because it was heated by a wood-burning stove. We weren't using ours because we couldn't afford the firewood. Noosia's mother liked Mykola because he reminded her of a Russian officer whom she had loved during the First World War. From the way she spoke about her lover, and never mentioned her husband, Mykola and I suspected Noosia had some Russian blood in her veins.

We enjoyed our room and liked the Romanovskas. Since we our room was cold, we spent most of our time studying at our respective schools. We lived in our winter coats. We wore them in class to stay warm and used them as blankets at night. Our room was so cold that water froze in our glasses and our blankets became stiff with frost. Occasionally, Mrs. Romanovska or Noosia invited us into their warmer rooms, but most of the time we simply endured. When our bones became very cold, we visited friends whose families lived in Cholm and enjoyed the warmth in their houses.

I passed the required entrance examinations and embarked on the seventh year of the eight required before taking the Matura. Dr. Oles Babij, the noted poet, friend of my father's, and editor, had indeed administered the exam and as one of about twenty teachers at the new school would be the one to introduce us to Ukrainian literature. He was a short man with a large head who couldn't take his eyes off a certain blonde. Nor could I.

Halya Pona, whom I had met in Mr. Kovaluk's apartment, was proving to be an interesting and spirited girl whose smile lit up every face she encountered. She was also a very good student and soon I found I needed help preparing essays in Latin. She was more than willing to assist me, and because Kovaluk's was within walking distance of the room Mykola and I were renting, we met as frequently as possible. We also spent time in the beautiful park near the Sobor. On one side of this park was a fenced cemetery so isolated it eventually turned out to be a good place to prepare for the upcoming Matura.

Between Halya and me a little romance was always brimming, but it never quite spilled over into an out-and-out love affair. Nevertheless, we remained close friends for the two wartime years we were at school together.

Anyway, the program of education in the Gymnasium was rigorous and demanding. Our teachers disregarded the cold and hunger to which their students were exposed and expected us to work as hard as we did before the war. We did not have uniforms, but our clothing was neat and clean. We drank alcoholic beverages on occasion but always moderately. Many of us also smoked cigarettes—but never at school, where they were forbidden.

There were some politics in our class. One girl was an OUN leader, but she never recruited her classmates and most of us didn't take her seriously anyway. Bohdan Myhal and Bohdan Yourchuk were still preparing themselves for the war they believed to be coming between Germany and the Soviet Union. Yet only a few weeks after the academic term began both were back in Sokal, where another, and far easier, school had opened.

Nevertheless, it was annoying to see on the streets OUN members saluting each other with their right arms extended in the Nazi fashion. They also looked silly in their semi-military, Hitler-style overcoats with raised collars—especially in hot weather. Some students even started greeting their professors in this Fascist fashion, forcing the teachers to respond in like manner, however half-heartedly. For if you didn't respond that way, you were labeled a Communist and an enemy of an independent Ukraine.

Fortunately, this behavior was uncommon in our class, and we enjoyed being students rather than playing politics. I also knew Mykola's friends at the Technical Institute and none of us took any of this seriously.

As the days grew longer with the approach of spring, Mykola and I enjoyed the increasing warmth of the sun as it chased our chilly winter blues away. Although we knew smoking cigarettes was unhealthy, we did so anyway, smoking so many good but expensive Hungarian cigarettes that it seriously impacted our food budgets.

Thus, every month either Mykola or I went home to collect whatever provisions were available: solonina, kovbasa, smoked ham, apples, cookies, and horilka. Such hunting-and-gathering expeditions could be dangerous because carrying too much food was the sign of a black marketeer in German eyes. They requisitioned the same products to feed workers in Germany. Whether Wehrmacht, SS, or Gestapo, they arrested all the black marketeers they could catch.

You could still get practically anything you needed in the Cholm ghetto, which was not yet closed. At least some Jewish people could move back and forth—if the Germans found it convenient for their own purposes. I knew one of them.

Moshko was a barber, a happy and friendly man around thirty years old. He would cut my hair and if I had extra money, I got a shave as well—not that I needed it, but it was something a fully mature man might do. After a few visits, however, Moshko gave me a shave whether I could pay for it or not.

One day, when no one else was around, I brazenly told him he should flee to the forests before the Germans closed the ghetto. They had already directed several unimaginably bloody spasms of violence against the Cholm ghetto and it was now or never. He could join the partisans already infesting the Volhynian woods and swamps.

He listened to me with a face that masked all emotion. Either he outright disagreed with me, or he was indulging in what all of us did at some point during the war years: Simple denial.

A few days later I found him very happy. He had just returned from barbering some German soldiers, all of whom had been friendly and given him generous tips. He also said his friends who remembered the First World War had told him German soldiers could be very nice to Jews. From what he had just experienced, they hadn't changed. He scoffed at Hitler's rants against the Jewish people.

The next time I passed his shop, however, the front window had been shattered. I found Moshko inside, very upset because there was no place to buy a large enough pane of glass to repair it. I helped him board up the window as best we could. I agreed with him it wasn't the German soldiers who vandalized his shop. But it served as a warning of what was probably coming. Go to the forest! I again urged. He just insisted on taking his complaint to his new German friends. The next time I passed his shop it was locked and I never saw Moshko again.

March turned to April 1941, the mud hardened and dried and it was fighting season again. One balmy April night Mykola and I heard vague rumblings coming from the street. The sound was so muted by the large trees in the front garden, though, that we decided it wasn't worth getting up to investigate. Another night in early May, however, it was so loud and persistent that we could not sleep. We had to get up and identify it. We were surprised to see the street filled with German soldiers on the march. They were followed by trucks loaded with military equipment. All were heading East. Toward the River Buh.

We realized a showdown with the Soviet Union was imminent.

By the end of May, the Wehrmacht columns, with tanks and self-propelled guns and artillery pieces, were not even using the cover of darkness to move forward. Night and day they were pouring toward the border. The German Military Police even requisitioned our school building for the use of the army. We were temporarily transferred to a smaller building on Hrubieszowska Street. The soldiers we saw were well fed and were marching enthusiastically, weapons slung jauntily on shoulders, followed by an endless convoy of vehicles.

More than three million men were moving into position along a thousand miles of front for what might prove one of the largest and most pivotal assaults in history. Most of them were Germans, but some were Romanians and there was even a "Ukrainian Legion," divided into two battalions, the "Nachtigall" and the "Roland." Stepan Bandera had recruited his soldiers from his OUN fighters, sponsored by no less a figure than Admiral Canaris, the head of the Reich's spy service.

Of course, we didn't know about those units at this time. We were busy preparing for our annual examinations, scheduled for the middle of June and lasting several days. Afterwards, we had to wait to receive the certificates listing our marks in each subject, including religion and behavior. It was June 20 before they were handed out. My grades were good and so I passed to the eighth and final level of secondary school. The next day, Mykola and I said goodbye to our friends and packed our things, most of which we left with Mrs. Romanovska because all the trains were being used exclusively for military transport. We could only carry what we could load onto our bicycles. Since Tudorkovychi was only two miles from the border, we wondered whether the Germans would even allow us to ride into the war zone.

We awoke early on Sunday and got underway. The roads were empty because the Army was already at the Soviet border. Or rather, over it, for at 4:00 a.m. that very morning—Sunday, June 22, 1941—the Germans launched their massive attack—codenamed Operation Barbarossa— with heavy bombardments and air strikes. They met little resistance in our section of the continent-wide line, probably because it was fronted by the vast forests and swamps of Volhynia—surely the primary reason we never heard anything.

We stopped in one village to eat our dinner. A farmer was standing by the road and asked us if we had any information about the attack. He spoke a surprisingly good literary Ukrainian, and when he heard we were students from Cholm, he invited us into his house. His wife served us *vareniki*—for Ukrainians the best of dishes, filled with potato and cheese or sauerkraut, sprinkled with skvarky and covered in fresh sour cream. We had not had vareniki in a very long time and this was a most memorable treat.

The farmer told us how glad he was to hear that in Poland a young Ukrainian could attend a Ukrainian school and speak the Ukrainian language. He even hoped for a free Ukraine one day. When I told him that, before the war, my father had been elected by Ukrainians to be a Posol in the Polish Sejm and that he had been imprisoned for defending the Greek-Orthodox churches from destruction by Polish Jesuits—well, there was no end to his joy in meeting us.

We gave the farmer a few Hungarian cigarettes—a treat in an era when country people only smoked homegrown tobacco—and thanked his wife for such a good dinner. Then we climbed back aboard our bicycles. It was about sixty miles from Cholm to Tudorkovychi, through Hrubieszow and Uhryniv, and we made good time all the way. We were surprised to see no soldiers whatsoever along the way. The only indication of something different were the green nets on the roadsides under which the Germans had concealed their trucks and tanks.

We arrived in Tudorkovychi in early afternoon and even there we saw very few signs of a German presence. My mother and the rest of the family were thrilled to see us and were bubbling over with the excitement of the past few days. We learned the Germans had taken one large room in our house for an office and living quarters for one of their generals! The regulars occupied all the available space in the barns, stables, and other buildings of the village. They did not take anything from the farmers and paid for anything they wanted. They were polite, did not attack any women, and tried not to interfere in the activities or lives of the villagers.

Few people today would understand our excitement on behalf of the Nazis. But to us the greatest evil imaginable was bolshevism, and Russian bolshevism at that. We were for anything and everything that might destroy that or at least remove it to the far side of the continent. So yes, when I went to sleep the night of that most momentous day it was the soundest slumber of my life.

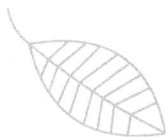

CHAPTER EIGHT

Nur Für Deutsche

As the tide of war rolled inexorably east, the Wehrmacht's panzer wings making sweeping encirclements of vast numbers of Russians, life resumed its immemorial pattern in Tudorkovychi. The fighting was now far away, and the wheat harvest was already upon us. Farmers were hard at work in the fields, diligently collecting the crops, not only to feed their own families but also to fulfill the hated grain quota imposed by the Germans. The punishment was severe for failure to meet it, including the loss of those all-important coupons for buying soap, leather, and fabrics.

My mother told me that Mot, now the only Jew living in Tudorkovychi, had been severely beaten by the Germans because he did not have enough grain to fulfill his quota. I couldn't believe nobody in the village was willing to help him out with a little surplus grain. Mot and his sister, Yidka, had inherited their small farm from their late father. But they weren't born farmers and never could fulfill their quota.

Knowing only what the Germans told them about the war and sus-pecting most of that was propaganda, the villagers summoned up their age-old ability to make do in times of shortage and scarcity. Salt, sugar, soap, matches, and leather were all in short supply. It was too difficult to find a replacement for salt, so food was less flavorful. For sugar, however, they substituted molasses prepared from the sugar beets. It was sweet-er than cane sugar and I liked the taste of it when used in jam on my bread for breakfast. Miron and Sidorko learned how to make soap, but it was difficult to find the fat that was needed for its production. Wooden matches were rarely available and when obtained, they were split with a sharp knife into four pieces. Since every household needed a fire to cook meals, the housewives were responsible for maintaining glowing embers all day long.

Lack of leather for shoes and boots was keenly felt on cold days when farmers had to work in their fields. Didoon Kindrat overcame it by making shoes out of straw, but they didn't look very good. And coffee? A pipe dream—we used toasted oat grains mixed with chicory gathered from the meadows. People also learned to make alcohol from potatoes and soon forgot about the work ethic maintained before the war. Young people broke the accepted social rules that had kept our village spiritually healthy. A few youths even volunteered for work in Germany, hoping to make some money and to see life in a foreign country. There was a palpable feeling of unrest I had never noticed before.

One piece of apparent good news arrived within days of my return for summer break. On June 26, the Nachtigall Battalion of the Ukrainian Legion, to a rapturous welcome from its citizens, helped free Lviv from the Soviets. These heroes were, of course, accompanied by their shadowy twins, the "Banderites" of the Organization of Ukrainian Nationalists. Having won control of the city's hilltop radio station, these OUN revolutionaries announced on June 30 the "Proclamation of Ukrainian Independence" for all the world to hear—an Independent Ukraine, even if allied to Nazi Germany.

A few weeks earlier, at a meeting of prominent Ukrainians in Krakow, this Banderite faction had sought advance approval of such a proposed declaration. Most attendees approved—but not my father. Volodimir Kochan stated he would not affix his signature to a proclamation glorifying the German Army and Hitler. He also asserted that one faction of the Ukrainian movement should not act by itself in matters of independence. And with that, he turned on his heel and left.

Proponents of the Proclamation triumphed anyway, many believing its propaganda value outweighed other factors. The Soviet Army, after all, was full of Ukrainian conscripts. After hearing about a German-sponsored independent Ukraine, how likely were they to fight hard on behalf of continued Soviet oppression of their countrymen?

As the Ukrainians began to organize their new state, I was on my way to Lviv, too.

Hardly had the city been liberated when my father was called to be a director of the Central Bank for the Province of Halichina and moved from Krakow to Lviv. He received an apartment on Tarnawsky Street and a nice office in the Centrobank building. I arrived there three weeks later to visit him, Pani Lyda, and their newborn son Vsevolod, or "Roman" Kochan. I had decided to accept the fact of their marriage and try to be happy for them. Here they could start over in a new place without the gossip that had dogged their every step in Sokal.

Soviet occupation had lent to Lviv a tainted and dingy feel. That was in large part due to the sickening discovery, after their forces abandoned the city, that the prisons had become charnel houses. In those cells and basements, the true nature of Communism was revealed: Thousands of political prisoners, both men and women, had been murdered in the most savage and brutal manner imaginable. Many had been subjected to cruel tortures. Facing this, the Germans seized Jews off the street and forced them to bring out the corpses and wash them—the Nazis, of course, believing Communism to be a diabolical Jewish creation. Corpses, quickly decomposing in the summer heat, then had to be identified by relatives. This was happening in every Polish city the Soviets had occupied. Historians have asserted these crimes were followed by waves of murderous anti-Semitic pogroms, but I never saw this during my brief stay in Lviv.

Indeed, I remember, as I strolled those streets, seeing no animosity between the different nationalities residing in the city. The Jews had been ordered into the ghetto, located behind the famous old Theater. They were free to work in other parts of the city but most of them attended to their stores in the ghetto. Several days after the German re-occupation the German Military Government formed Ukrainian, Polish, and Jewish Committees to deal with the affairs of the town and its varied people. The Jewish police were an executive arm of the Judenrat, or Jewish Committee, and they enforced order in the ghetto, while the Ukrainian and Polish police were to maintain order in the rest of the city, helping the Germans to curtail the black market.

Many civilians from Germany came to live in Lviv to help administer the Occupation. They lived in nice houses that were confiscated from the owners. They used the street cars or trains labeled "Nur für Deutsche," but since most Germans traveled by automobile these reserved cars were nearly empty while the ones for common people were jammed to over-flowing. This German "superiority complex" was so infuriating one wag took a fearful chance when he posted a "Nur für Deutsche" sign on the gate of Lichakivskyj Cemetery.

When I returned to Tudorkovychi after visiting my father I found two young men waiting for me at my mother's house. I recognized them immediately: They were schoolmates of mine from the Cholm Gymnasium—both of them living in the apartment next to Halya Pona and her cousins. They were reluctant to tell me what they were doing in Tudorkovychi, but eventually I learned they were coming back from Volhynia Province. Both were members of OUN and had received an or-der to follow the German Army into the liberated Ukrainian territories and spread OUN's extremist dogmas. There they experienced the mur-derous infighting between the Melnikites and Banderites—and decided to return home to Hrubieszow, where it was safer.

A day or two later I had a more welcome guest. Mykola biked into the village for a visit. My mother instantly liked him and tried to make his stay a pleasant one. We slept on hay in the barn, where we could talk late into the night until sleep finally overcame us. In the morning, we washed our bodies, above the belt, with ice-cold water and rubbed our-selves with homemade towels. Mykola initially recoiled at this spartan regimen, but later he felt its invigorating effect.

For breakfast we ate soft-boiled eggs with buttered bread and hot milk. We then spent most of our day fishing in the spot where the Variazanka River joins the Buh. Mikola liked the sound of the name "Variazanka," claiming it originated with the Varangians, the Norsemen widely re-garded as the "Founding Family of Kievan Rus." As we lolled about in the fine weather, we imagined the Varangians actually rowing their long-boats up the Vistula and Buh to this very spot. Perhaps they had camped here. Perhaps they had built a temple here or even buried a hoard of gold and treasure somewhere in The Forest. While war was raging hundreds of miles to the east of us, we were having fun speculating about history and heritage. We concluded this was, after all, enchanted ground.

Our fishing hole was next to a ruined bridge that still had a few boards nailed across the horizontal beams. There we sat above the water with our feet dangling in the cool flow. The water was crystal clear, about ten feet deep and we practiced jumping in when we got too hot. We caught several sunfish and then just enjoyed lying on the boards in the hot sun. Mykola was a strong swimmer who tried to teach me how to jump and flip before hitting the water, but I could not overcome my fear and failed to perform the trick, which he called "salto mortale," a somersault. All our jumping loosened the string holding our catch, the sunfish sinking to the bottom of the river. Mykola recovered them on his first dive and I was impressed by his ease in the water. It was a peaceful place we were reluctant to leave when it was time to ride home for supper.

My mother cleaned the fish and we had them as a crispy appetizer before digging into wiener schnitzels with svarky-sprinkled mashed potatoes, the whole washed down with cold sour milk from the hillside cellar outside the house.

On our last day together, Mykola and I drove a horse-drawn wagon almost to Sokal to meet my Grandmother Maria, who was returning on foot from her annual pilgrimage to the monastery at nearby Krystynopol, where she spent three days in prayers, thanking God's Mother for her healthy family and listening to preaching about the life she would have after her death. It was a fifteen-mile walk and Didoon Kindrat always offered to take her, but she always declined. However, I thought that if we waylaid her on the road with a wagon, she would gladly accept a ride. Her legs would be weak and tired after three days of kneeling in church.

She was happy to see us and told us how much she enjoyed her pilgrimage, meeting friends from previous gatherings and listening to those uplifting sermons.

The next day Mykola and I rode our bicycles back to Krystynopol so he could return to his mother, who had a farm on its outskirts. Mrs. Zerebecka was also glad to see us and since the day was quite hot, she offered us cold apple soup, which was as good as I remember it being when I dined in her restaurant in Sokal. Before June 22, she had employed two German soldiers to help run the farm. They had been farmers in Germany and, instead of watching the border with the Soviet Ukraine, had preferred working the soil and eating her delicious home-cooked meals.

While visiting with her, Mykola and I rode our bikes across the Buh to Old Sokal to see what shape the town was in after two years of Soviet occupation. The streets were ruined, and all the buildings looked gray with peeling paint. The Jewish synagogue had been burned but the marketplace was still open. The most beautiful church, the Church of Peter and Paul, where I used to pray when I attended school there, had been used to store grain. The Communists had also used the Polish church and Bernardine monastery-- an old complex with many gold-framed pictures ornamented with precious stones--as asylums. It was encircled by defensive military constructions that were built in the seventeenth century, when Sokal and its surroundings were occupied by Cossacks serving in the army of the Ukrainian Hetman, Bohdan Khmelnytsky.

I wondered if Mykola had a father. He never spoke about him, so I assumed he was dead. He had an older brother who was married and was a fabric merchant, but he had been killed by Soviet soldiers when he tried crossing the German-Soviet border along the Buh River. Or so it was said—there was some suspicion, however, that he was instead murdered by Ukrainian partisans because he had refused to join them. He had been an officer in the Polish Army before the war and the partisans wanted him to train them in the military arts. He did not join them because he had children at home and the Germans would have retaliated against his family.

Another victory for OUN, I thought grimly.

In August of 1941, I returned to Cholm to finish my schooling at the Gymnasium. Mykola and I would room again, as he was finishing up at the Technical Institute. But this term we decided to find a new and warmer place to rent. The room we found was closer to school and behind it stood a bakery. We hoped to persuade the baker to sell us some bread without coupons. He refused but the smells were still heavenly! Our new room also featured two single-pane windows overlooking a field on the edge of town.

This was the year for Matura, and so I settled down to concentrate on my studies. I hoped to play more soccer and occasionally escort a girl to the movie theater, but now I didn't want a serious relationship. A few kisses but no deeper feelings.

At the movie theater we did see the newsreels. It had been a summer of victories for the German armies in Russia. The vast encirclements were netting millions of Russian prisoners. Army Group North was approaching Leningrad. Army Group Center had taken Minsk and was now targeting Moscow. And Army Group South, after a titanic encirclement that killed nearly a million Russians, had finally, on September 19, 1941, captured Kiev, our Holy City. What we didn't know until much later was the story of the clandestine but thoroughgoing mining of the city. A few days later the mines and booby-traps were remotely detonated, destroying much of central Kiev and killing a thousand German soldiers. In retaliation, the SS Einsatzgruppen—Heinrich Himmler's execution squads—murdered nearly 34,000 Kievan Jews in the infamous warren of eroded gullies outside of town called Babi Yar. As if they needed an excuse! Tens of thousands of Ukrainian civilians would also be killed there by the Germans.

At the same time, the Germans finally abrogated the 30 June 1941 "Proclamation of Ukrainian Statehood" issued by Stepan Bandera in Lviv. The Nazis had finally shown their hand: They were no friends of an independent Ukraine, after all. Nur für Deutschen.

While this was happening in the wider world, a new student from Warsaw arrived in Cholm to join our class. Her name was Tatiana Sawycka, and she was a tall, slim brunette with beautiful blue eyes. She was a year younger than me, and since she came from a Polish school, the administration had difficulty evaluating her academic standing. The director decided to place her in my class on a probationary basis. The most difficulty she had was with mathematics and I tried to help her with that subject. Although she was as Ukrainian as me, she had mostly attended Polish schools and so was also weak in Ukrainian literature. Despite a few weeks of hard work, she was transferred to the Seventh Grade. But I continued to check in on her and eventually introduced her to Mykola and my company of friends.

One day Mykola and I looked out of our two windows toward the empty field and saw German soldiers building a fifteen-foot-high barbed wire fence with several towers around its expanse. It certainly appeared they were building a concentration camp, but there were no buildings inside the perimeter. The fence enclosed a huge vacant piece of ground with no accommodations or even trees for shelter from the coming winter.

Nevertheless, a few days after the completion of their work, the Germans started to fill the camp with Soviet prisoners of war. Once shoved inside the enclosure, these guys did not know what to do or how to behave. When it rained, they just stood there in large groups like caged animals. They also spent their nights in a standing position and hoped for sunny days so they could warm up. Each week, even more POWs arrived at the camp until it finally contained thousands of prisoners. But I never saw anything approaching a mess tent, nor even the appearance of an open-air latrine.

This was the notorious Stalag 319, which eventually held hundreds of thousands of POWs, many if not most of whom would starve to death as a result of deliberate policy. Another Nazi version of the Holodomor.

Fortunately for these first prisoners, the fall of 1941 was long and dry. Maybe because the weather was fine and the trees were on the turn, Mykola and I decided to arrange a dance. After the Germans had occupied our large school building, all such entertainments had to be held in private houses. We asked our former landlady, Mrs. Romanovska, and she gladly gave us two rooms for the party. One was our previous bedroom, which we designated for food and drinks; and the other room would be turned into a ballroom, its central feature a borrowed gramophone.

We invited friends from the Gymnasium and from the Technical School and everyone could bring a guest. I made sure the two most beautiful girls at my school, Halya Pona and Tatiana Sawycka—a study in opposites—were there. They busied themselves making sandwiches of kovbasa or smoked solonina topped by slices of dill pickles. Another pretty girl, Noosia Romanovska, made horilka diluted with tea for the ladies. I brought two liters of good undiluted horilka for the men, and Mykola supplied homebrew for when the good stuff was gone. Our friend Oles Dekhnich surprised us with several salted herrings that we cleaned, cut into small pieces, covered with thin slices of onion, and sprinkled with vinegar and pepper. They tasted heavenly!

A grand time was had by all. Even Mrs. Romanovska joined us. She waltzed around with both Mykola and me and after a drink or two performed a Russian "Knife Dance." She threw a knife into the wooden floor and twirled about it in a manner that she learned in Russia, and she did it beautifully. She was a most unusual and interesting woman.

The party lasted until 2:00 a.m. and such was its success our teachers were soon asking for invitations to the next one—also reminding us to study for our Matura, that final oral and written examination not only testing us on what we had learned during our school years but also determining where our future paths might lead.

From employees of the Ukrainian Relief Organization in Cholm, I learned there were many Ukrainians who served as Soviet conscripts in Stalag 319. But these employees also said they had attempted to send food to them, but the Germans did not permit giving prisoners any food or help. We later learned that the only way for Ukrainians to get out of this hell was to volunteer to serve as guards at other camps.

Those POWs who still had their wits about them began thinking about the freezing winds of the coming winter. They made dugouts in the soil and covered them with sticks held together in large clusters with grass roots. The snows began flying in December, and soon such improvised dugouts were covered by the deep white drifts. Yet there was only enough room in them for a small percentage of the prisoners. So enormous numbers of thinly clad skeletons milled about waiting their turn to go inside and warm themselves. As the winter deepened, the mortality rate of these unprotected and starving men increased dramatically. Every morning we watched from our window the dead bodies being collected on a wide two-wheeled cart that prisoners pulled to the gate of the camp. Rumors about cannibalism were rife.

Small groups of POWs were occasionally led by German soldiers through the streets of town to shore up German military buildings or unload coal and wood at the railroad station. Two German soldiers usually walked behind them with guns at port arms, ready to shoot. Civilians were not allowed to feed the POWs, but many still threw bread, cookies, or fruit in their direction. Since the prisoners were not allowed to bend down, their rotting boots often trampled the food.

Mykola and I tried to throw bread over the barbed-wire fence but eventually the guards chased us away. I've often wondered whether one of those we were trying to help was a fellow Ukrainian, but one doomed to serve in the Soviet Army. Ivan Demianiuk was a poor peasant boy who was indeed standing somewhere across that fence. But to save his own life he "volunteered" to help the Germans guard camps holding mainly Jewish prisoners. Forty years later, John Demianiuk, as he then was called, would be accused of being the infamous "Ivan the Terrible" at Treblinka. The U.S. government would strip him of his citizenship and send him to Israel for a show trial. He would be sentenced to death, but after the disintegration of the Soviet Union secret documents appeared which showed Demianiuk was not guilty of any war crimes, after all. The American government reinstated his citizenship but awarded no compensation for the time he unjustly spent in prison.

It was too easy to blame Ukrainians. They of all the subject peoples of the USSR had no love for Stalin. Given half a chance in a hellhole such as Stalag 319 it was all too easy to volunteer to wear the black uniform of the Special Police and become a camp guard. Passing them by, I'd speak a few words of Ukrainian. By their uneasy reaction I knew that's who they were. They had chosen to postpone their own deaths while watching from the towers as their brothers starved.

It grew so cold that our upcoming Christmas vacations were extended to two weeks. Mykola and I decided to go home to warm our bones before the family hearths. Just before departure, he brought out two half-kilograms of finely cut tobacco. He had decided to smuggle it to Krystynopol and sell it there for more money than he had paid in Cholm. I tried convincing him that this was a stupid idea. If he were caught, the Germans would place him in a concentration camp. Or, should he be lucky, he'd end up working in a German factory or farm.

But Mykola entered what I called the "stage of a donkey." He was usually so agreeable but sometimes he became "stubborn as a mule," a weaker English equivalent—and then he would not listen to anyone. He insisted on placing one half-kilo on my bed and the other in his rucksack. After all, he said, we needed to find a warmer apartment and by selling the tobacco we could afford one. He only smiled when I told him it would be better for him to carry all the tobacco himself because if caught by the Germans, I would then be free to send him packages at the concentration camp. But if we both were caught—well, we'd both be hungry and would freeze to death, pointing to those two windows and the camp of human misery beyond them.

It was no use. I gave up. I wrapped my half-kilo in white paper and put it between the covers of a book in which, admittedly, I had carved a hole in the text. I then placed it alongside several other books I was taking home to read.

The next day, we boarded the train that was rolling in the direction of Sokal. It was packed with people and with Christmas coming, most of them were carrying something that could be construed as smuggling. Sure enough, when we reached a small station that evening, our train was stopped.

The railroad police boarded and ordered everyone to leave the cars. Since it was hard to find baggage in the dark, there was much jostling and pushing. Some people thought they were being transferred to another train—which frequently happened during the war whenever overworked locomotives broke down—and they would rush the door to find better places on the next train. When Mykola and I climbed down, however, we realized it was an "oblava," a German Police hunt for smugglers and black marketeers.

Already the tight crowd was getting restless and people were pushing each other, making room to surreptitiously discard illegal items from their bags. Mykola and I were quickly separated, and I was so hemmed in I could not open my suitcase to get rid of my own stash. Slipping and stumbling over a litter of butter, kovbasa, pig fat, tobacco, bottles of horilka, dead chickens, hams, and other abandoned goodies I realized I could not even rid myself of the suitcase because I would lose my notebooks! My heart hammering, I was pushed helplessly along toward the table where German policemen were examining belongings.

Suddenly I was there. Put your suitcase on the table and open it! I tried countering with my student identification card, hoping that they would let me pass. The policeman barely glanced at it and asked me again to open my suitcase. When I did, all my dirty linens tumbled out onto the table. The policeman was so reluctant to touch them that he missed the one book caught up among them. Close up and move on.

Heart still hammering I re-boarded the train but never saw Mykola. Only in the Sokal station did I finally find him. Crestfallen, he told me he had discarded his half-kilo of tobacco. But did he ever perk up when I told him I still had mine! He said he at least would not lose any money because selling this half alone would return the funds he had paid for the entire kilogram. So, he took my part of the tobacco and even forgot to thank me for saving it for him. Our unsuccessful smuggling caper ensured we had to face our cold room for the rest of the winter.

The films at the movie theater had not improved much once we returned to Cholm in January 1942. The newsreels before the main feature were still boasting about German victories on both the Eastern and Western Fronts. We did not know much about the Western Front, except that America had just entered the war on the side of Britain and, theoretically, the Soviet Union. That was…troubling, if the struggle were really one to destroy Bolshevism.

But we did know something about the war in Russia. Although reports showed the German Army advancing farther and farther into the USSR, we had also heard the Wehrmacht was mired in mud on Russian roads barely worthy of the name. The winter of 1942 was very cold and German tanks were frozen in place. Most infamously, the troops had little in the way of winter clothing. Most ominously, what was not shown on the newsreels was the retreat of German armor before Moscow itself.

The German Administration in occupied eastern Ukraine forced young people to "volunteer" for work in Germany on farms and in factories. Unsurprisingly, such volunteers were treated very badly, being severely punished for minor mistakes or shot for having illicit romantic affairs with native Germans. They had to wear armbands emblazoned with the word "OST" (East) and could not leave or change their place of employment under any circumstance. They were slaves who had to work for the German masters.

You could slave or you could fight: Nearly every country in German-occupied Eastern Europe had many young men and women serving the German war machine—such was the fear and loathing of Communism in our lands. Yet in the end it would still amount to "Nur für Deutsche."

The Italians, though, acted their part with style. They were present on the Eastern Front in large numbers. They were not very enthusiastic soldiers, however, and as individuals they often disliked Germans and German policy in the occupied lands. They were also dressed in Italian uniforms while soldiers of other nationalities usually wore some variant of Wehrmacht gray. Frequently one saw Italian officers choosing to ride with us commoners in streetcars, disdaining those other cars with their obnoxious labels.

That awful winter finally turned into spring, and still there were living skeletons standing huddled in Stalag 319. Human endurance can stagger the imagination.

I meanwhile began my intensive preparation for the Matura. Eight years in a Gymnasium were coming down to this two-day multi-subject examination. For breaks I played a little soccer, went occasionally to the cinema, and had quite a few walks with Halya or Tatiana. My relationship with Halya remained very friendly but noncommittal. I think she sensed how unsteady in relationships I could be and might even have cast a jealous eye at Tatiana. For her part, Tatiana did appear to my friends as rather cool and aloof in demeanor. She was smart but very strong-minded, and because she often wore a fur jacket some of the boys nicknamed her fox. But I was intrigued by this pretty girl with the large blue eyes, curly brown hair, and dimpled smile. She was not only tall and slender but also—whenever I could steal a glimpse of them—had very shapely legs.

She was also very guarded. About what, I couldn't guess. But we seemed to share some hidden bond. Perhaps it was only that we both grew up in broken families—her father had left when she was very young.

But these were dalliances. Mostly I studied.

In May, the Germans began liquidating the nearby ghetto. One morning about twenty German Special Policemen invaded it and with the help of the Jewish Police marshaled about 2,000 people, mostly older adults, then marched them peacefully down to the train station, loaded them onto cattle cars, and transported them to a concentration camp, I assumed. Only it was not your ordinary concentration camp, I found out much later. They were taken to a place I would never hear of until after the war, a place called Sobibor, where they were exterminated by poison gas—a place not that far north of Cholm.

Were there no attempts to escape or resist? I have a vivid memory of killings occurring in the street in front of our school that was so close to the ghetto: Germans with pistols shooting young Jews who must have been resisting their fate in some way. Nevertheless, by November 1942, the human element of the ghetto was finally eradicated.

Life during wartime is full of moral incongruities. Not long after that horrible day for the ghetto, I was playing in a soccer match. A team from Hrubieszow had challenged us students in Cholm. The time—three weeks before the Matura—couldn't be more inconvenient, but we accepted the challenge. We did not have uniforms but managed to assemble enough white shorts and white jerseys for every player.

In Cholm, we boarded the train early in the morning and were in Hrubieszow well before when the soccer match started at one o'clock. Our opponents were older than us, and they appeared strong and well-fed. They played a physical game and pushed us around. We were faster, however, and our ball-handling skills were better. At one point during the first half, we were even leading the game by a goal.

Close to the end of the second half, the score was two to three in their favor. Five minutes before the end of the match, I was in a perfect position to score and tie the game. Their goalie was down but just as I was about to nail it an opponent snuck up from behind and pulled my shorts down. I wore no underpants and suddenly I was standing naked in front of all the spectators—including beautiful girls that came to see us play soccer!

So I promptly sat down—to a roar of laughter coming from the spectators. The referee was not sure whether there was a foul or not and let the game continue. I pulled my shorts up but when I got to my feet, I had to hold them in place because the supporting elastic had snapped. A pretty girl came out of the stands to the edge of the field and offered me her belt, much to the applause of the spectators.

After the game my friends couldn't stop kidding me. "We could have tied our opponents with a 3:3 score but we lost because Ivan lost his pants!" was all I heard. I found the girl, Martha, who gave me her belt and together we spent a pleasant afternoon.

That evening our team took the train back to Cholm. During the war, of course, train cars were blacked out at night. As all Ukrainians love to sing to pass the time in the dark, we sang popular Ukrainian songs. That annoyed one of the Polish guards, who, passing down the aisle, ordered us to shut up. I asked, "Why?"

There was no light to see by, but he found me—smacking me with the butt end of his rifle: "That's why!"

The next day, I had a few bruises but no major injury. When the director of our school heard about our soccer game, he was upset we had chanced injury instead of studying for the Matura. He warned he would be paying special attention to the soccer players during the examinations. It was pure show: I learned from Professor Babij that the director laughed when he heard we lost the game because I had my shorts yanked down just as I was in position to score.

During the second half of June 1942, we were tested on our "knowledge and maturity"—the Matura. I had no difficulty with mathematics, and I received a geometry assignment to perform on the blackboard. In the middle of my demonstration, I was stopped because the committee decided I clearly knew the subject well enough. Latin was tested with a written exam, and I received a Latin text I successfully translated into Ukrainian. I passed oral examinations in Biology and Chemistry as well.

Surprisingly, I had some difficulty with Ukrainian literature because the absent-minded Dr. Babij asked me about a literary era he had never discussed in class! I stumbled through some generalities while slowly directing the discussion to Polish literature of that same period, which I knew better.

I still vividly remember my examination in German literature. It was conducted by our teacher in the presence of Professor Stavnichij and Dr. Stechman, a German representative. Dr. Stechman asked me what I knew about the poet Goethe. I told them Goethe described his early life in a short poem:

> Vom Vater hab ich die Statur, Des Lebens ernstes Führen,
> Vom Mütterchen die Frohnatur Und Lust zu fabulieren.

> From father I get my physique, Also my earnest nature; My story-telling bent, glad heart I have from my dear mother.

I explained what that meant for Goethe and how I felt it applied to me as well. From my father I had inherited my height and sense of high purpose; from my mother, I hoped, an outgoing nature and a poetic soul. Dr. Stechman was very pleased with my answers and tried to convince the other members that I deserved a grade of "Sehr Gut." I thought maybe I'd secured a place on those restricted tram cars. But I received a mere

"Gut" because my earlier grades in this subject did not justify the highest accolade.

We all passed the Matura, except for two girls who now had to repeat the final year. I'll admit they probably had not ripened enough; yet I still would have passed them, considering all the turmoil of the times. It's hard enough to study when you're hungry and cold, and harder still when thousands of men outside the town are being deliberately starved to death and thousands of other men and women living just next door are being led off to summary execution.

It was time to say farewell—to friends, teachers, and the beautiful, haunted old town of Cholm. Farewell to the teachers was the easy parting. The town, we felt, would endure, could withstand another layer of accumulating sorrows. Friends? Well, we needed a party for that.

Mykola and I organized it, inviting only our closest friends, the ones with whom we had shared joys, sorrows, food, lack of food, the warm days of summer and the long, cold days of winter. We had a wonderful celebration together. Yet it was a difficult party, too. It wasn't just that this might be our last time together. It also had to do with the recognition that we, too, had not yet ripened enough; and that millions of Europeans in our generation would never approach ripeness at all.

"If God wants to punish someone, he doesn't need a reason" is an old and tough-skinned Ukrainian proverb. We knew Germany might lose this war and we felt a gathering storm was approaching, the sky just perceptibly darkening, and the wind already stirring the tops of the trees. We were just another generation of leaves doomed to be torn off our branches and scattered haphazardly over the face of the globe.

CHAPTER NINE

In the Shadow of Death

When I returned home from passing the Matura in late June 1942, I put my two bags down in my mother's house and, outside of accepting congratulations from half the village for an achievement all too rare in Tudorkovychi, I spent several days just eating and sleeping. My mother was happy to have me back home and enjoyed seeing me devour all she prepared for me in the kitchen.

But as my two suitcases were being cleaned out, Mot was packing his bags. He had just received a letter from the Generalgouvernement to appear with his sister, Yidka, at the train station in Sokal with no more than four suitcases.

This was alarming news. On the day before they were supposed to leave, I went down to their small house to see if there was anything I could do. These were the last two Jews in the village, and I had nothing but the fondest recollections of them. Mot was as stone-faced and silent as ever; but Yidka used to feed me matzah when I was a child, and the memory of those delicious unleavened flatbreads remains with me today. I took her gnarled hands in mine and thanked her for her love and affection. She stared straight through me.

The following day the entire village turned out to see, rather awkwardly, their departure. I remembered that no one had helped Mot meet his grain quota. Did that have anything to do with this? Didoon Kindrat was bent double by now and clearly dying. Didoon Semen was still losing acreage on an annual basis. Everyone else just stood in silence and watched as this tragedy unfolded before their eyes. They watched as Mot piled the four cases onto a wagon pulled by his last horse. They watched as he closed the door to the house in which they both were born. They watched sullenly, as they were not always on the best of terms with these our neighbors. And they watched in bewilderment, as so many could not register what was happening, hoping that what they were witnessing was not true.

As Mot took the rope, pulling the wagon while he walked beside his horse, his sister stood up and turned to everyone. "The Germans will bake bread from us all," she cried. "They will use us as the yeast. And they will use you as the flour!"

That summer of 1942, Bohdan Yourchuk shifted from foe back to friend. He had finished Gymnasium in Sokal, his hometown, and passed his Matura. Together we realized it might be our last summer to enjoy complete freedom and have a good time in the waters of the River Buh. Under my tempering influence, and perhaps more that of Petro Voroby of Starhorod, Bohdan eased back from some of his more extreme attitudes and curtailed his childish preoccupation with the marital and political activities of my father and uncles. This was a welcome change because Bohdan proved himself an interesting and friendly young man.

The other Bohdan—Bohdan Myhal—chose a different path. He told me he planned to go to Eastern Ukraine to spread Bandera's nationalistic ideas. He was at odds with his father and wanted to get away from him. And that is just what he did. We never heard what became of him. He just vanished, as many did during those years.

One day Bohdan Yourchuk and I heard from some teachers in Sokal that the German Government had given permission for Ukrainians to organize a Medical and Pharmacological Institute in Lviv. The teachers said if we were interested, we should apply by assembling the usual reams of paperwork and submit our applications. We spent nearly the whole night at this most unwelcome labor; but the next morning we sent the documents in and, to our great delight—we both were accepted.

I spent the few precious summer weeks before moving to Lviv visiting family and friends. Uncle Miron was at his leather store in Sokal. Uncle Sidorko was at his home. His daughter, Lesia, was about five years old and, like all Kochans, was blonde and tall, quite pretty but rather reserved with people.

Mitonko, who had two years of business school under his belt, was working in a government office in Chorobriv. There he made me some very important documents, especially the "Kennkarte Generalgouvernement" with which I could identify myself before the German police. It was written in German, Ukrainian, and Polish. I visited my other cousin, Vlodko, and we got drunk with the alcohol that farmers received as a part of their payment for the German quota. It tasted like rotgut, but it did the trick. Even when drunk Vlodko was not completely relaxed. But he did lose his stutter. After four years of education in our village school, he had attended two years of business school in Sokal alongside Mitonko.

Several times I met Slavka. She told me about changes that were taking place in our village. It seemed the ties to Chitalnya, and even to the church, had become very strained. The war seemed to cause people to drink more alcohol and neglect their responsibilities both to their families and to the village. The new church was nearly finished, and Sunday services were already being conducted there. The villagers liked Father Hoora, but the women of the village were still angry with Miron for provoking their foolish behavior when the new cleric arrived in Tudorkovychi.

Slavka had also heard rumors that in the forests of Volhynia a new leader, Taras Bulba by pseudonym, was organizing a partisan movement to protect Ukrainians against German, Polish, and Soviet excesses. The anti-German activities of partisans were being severely punished, of course, by the Nazis. Support for the partisans ensured the murder of innocent Ukrainians and the burning of their villages.

Although the Germans were in the heart of Russia itself, close to Moscow and approaching Stalingrad on the distant Volga, we weren't sure they were really going to win the war. The Russians can always trade space for time, sucking an enemy ever farther, ever deeper. Slavka might never have heard of Napoleon. But I had.

Now it was time to go to Lviv and enroll in the Medical Institute.

My father was still a director of the Centrobank and was still renting the apartment at 36 Tarnawsky Street, only a block away from the street-car station that connected us with the rest of the redeemed city. I was going to live with them and share a room with Yarko.

Because the weather was warm and pleasant, I sat on the passenger car steps and enjoyed the cool breeze as we rolled down the tracks toward Lviv. Looking ahead, as we rounded a curve, I could see the locomotive pushing an empty platform car before it, a dubious means of protecting the engine against any bomb a partisan may have attached to the rail. There would soon come a time when such trains would be preceded by two and sometimes three platform cars. But on this August day in 1942 it sufficed to just sit on the steps of a passenger car and drink in the passing panorama of rural Ukraine at harvest-time.

It never failed to astonish me that these rolling hills, often stretching out as far as the eye could see, could be infamous fields of battle. Yet not thirty years earlier hundreds of thousands of men were killed here during the Galician campaigns of the First World War. Doubtless many a skeleton in many a forgotten mass grave still fertilizes what I perceived as a smiling landscape.

It was a patchwork countryside, one strip of grain alternating with another of root crops or fallow ground in a rotation changing every season. Small villages nestled beneath shade trees and bountiful orchards cropped up here and there. I studied the waving grain with particular care, a loving family taunt still precious in memory: "Ivan, you are like a blind man who can't distinguish wheat from barley!"

Most of the wheat had been harvested by now, but I always found it difficult distinguishing ripening barley from rye, especially from a moving train. Soon waves of high grass covered the meadows and glistened like silver in the sun. Come autumn, the farmers would cut the grass, dry it in the sparkling air, and use it to feed their animals throughout the winter.

To me, though, the fields of buckwheat were always the prettiest. Their golden color was unmatched by other grains and their aroma saturated the air with delicious hints of honey. Besides providing men and bees with food, buckwheat carried a concealed meaning for Ukrainians. Whenever a man is discovered having an illicit affair with a woman the whispered gossip always contains a telltale clue: "He has jumped into the buckwheat!" In other words, he has lost his head amid the dizzying fumes of buckwheat and committed a sin as sweet as honey but as sticky as flypaper.

I was smiling at this when the train passed the first barbed wire entanglement and entered the fortified outskirts of Lviv during wartime.

My father's apartment was large, and the room I shared with Yarko was furnished with two beds, a large desk, some shelves for books and linens, and two chairs. Through our window we saw a large orchard which belonged to the officers of the Italian Army, whose headquarters were in the neighboring building. It was good to see Pani Lyda with her one-year-old son, Roman. He had a nickname already and members of the family called him Dada. I was happy to be visiting, sharing stories, and enjoying tasty meals with them.

One day I went to visit my father in his office in the Centrobank building, which was located one short block from the Lviv Opera House on the street now called Prospect Shevchenka. In the middle of this wide avenue was a long narrow park with two rows of trees lined with planters filled with various flowers. Between the rows of trees was a sidewalk also lined with benches on which people relaxed or played chess. The street ended at a large square in front of the Opera House and behind it was the Jewish section designated by the Germans as the ghetto.

On the opposite end of the long park was a statue of King John III Sobieski, the Polish king who, in 1683, with the help of Ukrainian Cossacks, had liberated Vienna from a Turkish siege.

From my father's office on the second floor, I could see both the Opera House and the statue of Sobieski. It was an impressive place, the chairs covered with blue leather and the furniture being made of rosewood. A map of Halichina Province covered one wall of the room and on it the bank's branches were marked with colored beads. It was quite a change from the tiny office he had in Sokal.

My father introduced me to his fellow directors and to a German supervisor who liked my Germanic "look" and asked me whether I would like to join the German Army. I thanked him for his kind words and told him I planned to become a physician and only afterwards would I consider joining the Army. He laughed and said by that time the war would be over, and it was—but not with the results the German supervisor had in mind.

Back in the apartment, Yarko told me to look out the window. Several Italian officers with slingshots were in the orchard, hunting for sparrows. They had already killed several of them and were pleased with their prowess. Father said they made a tasty soup from these small birds and that he had tried it while a soldier fighting in the Italian Alps during the First World War. I had my doubts about those small birds, but the hunt did lend a human face to these allies of the stern Germans.

I went to the Medical Institute to ensure Bohdan and I were still enrolled. On the board in front of the building was posted a list with names of students admitted to the first year and there I found both my name and that of Bohdan Yourchuk.

Lviv University is one of the oldest universities in Ukraine. It was established in 1784 by Emperor Joseph II of Austria and its medical school was one of its four traditional divisions, alongside theology, philosophy, and law. I was proud to be enrolled here, even if that coincided with the city's occupation by the German Army. Fortunately, enrollment protected me against impressment as labor in German factories or in the building of roads and bridges. I could also register as a permanent resident of Lviv and that enabled Pani Lyda to obtain my ration of food stamps.

It was August 1942. Bohdan and I were duly enrolled in the first year of Medical School. I was living with my family and he was renting an apartment. We set out to see the town.

After a year of German occupation Lviv resembled the thriving city it had been before the war. The street fighting of 1939 and 1941 had left few noticeable scars. Many longstanding businesses were open, and the electric streetcars were apparently still running on time. On closer examination, however, there were some crucial changes.

While walking home I read several announcements from the city government and orders from the Military Government that were posted on prominent boards. One reminded citizens about blackout restrictions: Cover Your Windows at Night! Another threatened the severest punishment for hiding fugitive Jews, Gypsies, and black marketeers. Yet a third stipulated that for the killing of a German soldier or German citizen, 20 citizens would be hanged on the city square. A fourth and final announcement listed the actual names of people that were recently executed by hanging for the killing of a German policeman. I later heard that on the day of that execution, the Germans forced passersby to observe the hideous proceedings.

The people of Lviv tried to live a semi-normal life in the shadow of death the Germans imposed on them. Yet it was understandable why many people of Lviv were reluctant to leave the safety of their homes.

People were not allowed to walk on the sidewalks in front of government buildings or to eat in German restaurants or ride in streetcars marked "Nur für Deutsche." German restaurants had better food than restaurants for common people, their movie theaters had more recent films, and their stores had an inventory of products that were not available to ordinary civilians.

Our stores were open, but merchants had little to sell. Frequently storekeepers hid some merchandise and later sold it to those who were willing to pay higher prices. Restaurants served various dishes but only to those people who had the required food stamps and money. Everyone received monthly food stamps allowed them to buy a certain amount of food. However, to live only with food stamps was impossible. It was a slow starvation diet. Without additional food, older people died rapidly.

The lucky people had relatives with farms where they could get vegetables, fruits, bread, some meat, oil, or butter. To transport these precious items from the farms to Lviv was very dangerous, though. The Germans examined the contents of packages in every train station. If forbidden items were found that person was arrested, his goods were confiscated, and he was sent to a concentration camp or to forced labor in Germany. Nevertheless, people took chances and risked their freedom or life for food.

The electricity was frequently shut off to save energy. That meant the streetcars really didn't run on time but stopped dead on the track. The result was a walk home in complete darkness. There were no longer streetlamps: That and the curfew limited most activities after dark.

The Medical Institute was located in the eastern part of Lviv. It contained not only the various departments of medicine but also hospitals where advanced students acquired practical knowledge about the art and science of healing. The first two years of our study program were called "pre-medical," the last three years "clinical learning." To go from one stage to another in any such academic environment, of course, involved passing extensive examinations.

There were about three hundred students in my class, by no means all of them as interested in medicine as in obtaining an identification card with his or her picture on it that served as protection from arrest. Students carried identification cards because it helped them to avoid the "oblavas" and dragnets for forced labor. About half of the class were young women.

The lectures were given in big auditoriums dating from Austro-Hungarian days. Our professors could deliver them in Ukrainian, Polish, or German. Bohdan and I started our study of Anatomy, for instance, by learning the names of bones and muscles, their places of attachment, and the location of various blood vessels and nerves. There were no plastic models; we had to learn by using the real thing from cadavers whose mortal end we didn't want to imagine. Going through the basement one day, we saw hundreds of human skulls stored in glass cabinets. Since Bohdan and I badly needed some skulls for our studies, we slipped two of them into our bags. Unfortunately, they had no lower jaws—but you can't have everything!

Bohdan kept them in his apartment, where we'd relax with horilka and toast our unknown guests. Friends like my old Cholm roommate, Mikola Zerebecky, now attending the Polytechnic Institute in Lviv, found it a bit macabre; but *memento mori* lay all around us during the war years. I eventually carried my jawless skull back to Tudorkovychi—but when I left it there, my mother promptly gave the ghastly thing a proper Christian burial.

Next Bohdan and I received a human leg to dissect. The smell of the formalin preserving it permeated our clothes. Working on "our" leg kept us busy for an entire semester. We were clumsy with the use of the scalpel and frequently cut some nerves or blood vessels. A young Polish woman who was an assistant in the Anatomy department supervised our work and always made cute remarks about our sewing abilities. But she passed us at the end of the semester.

While practicing dissection, we also attended Anatomy lectures given by old, semi-paralyzed Dr. Markowski. He'd sit in his wheelchair and deliver humorous remarks about the organs under discussion—including the male sex organ. That had some of the women students squirming. Once he mentioned that in Japan there was a man with a penis measuring twenty-five centimeters. Some women began leaving the auditorium. Markowski smiled and said, "Ladies, please don't leave right now! The train to Japan leaves late at night so you still have plenty of time to catch it after my lecture!" That brought a roar of laughter from the male students.

Mostly, however, it was grim studying while a grim autumn and winter started falling on Lviv. In faraway southern Russia Generals Ewald Von Kleist and Friedrich Von Paulus had respectively reached the all-important oil fields around Grozny in the Caucasus Mountains and the sprawling new industrial city and model worker's paradise obsequiously named Stalingrad. But they were very deep into Russia—too deep, many people feared.

Those worries appeared justified when in November the Soviets sprang a trap on Von Paulus's Sixth Army, trapping it in Stalingrad, while Von Kleist barely extricated his forces from the Caucasus. Riding among them were many of the fiercely anti-Communist Kuban Cossacks—descendants of the Zaporizhian Host—on their way, often in family groups, to a new home eventually promised them in the Italian Alps.

When we weren't studying, Bohdan and I were usually making merry with Mikola and his friends. I even found time to go to the theater and opera, the latter still featuring excellent actors and singers. Many of them were newcomers from occupied former Soviet Ukraine who grabbed at the chance to move further west, away from Stalin's commissars. They helped make the Lviv Opera, during these few months, probably one of the best in Europe. There I heard Verdi's "Aida," "La Traviata," and "Il Trovatore"; Bizet's "Carmen," and Puccini's "Madame Butterfly" and "Tosca." Frequently I attended the vaudeville "Veselij Lviv," which means Joyful Lviv, where I learned by heart some very romantic love songs.

And to think the ghetto was right behind the Opera House.

Around 65,000 Jews remained in the ghetto as 1942 began winding down. That's about half of the number living there when I arrived in Lviv in August. What had happened, while I was busy getting established at the Medical Institute, was called the "Great Aktion." Upwards of 50,000 people were carted out of the ghetto and eventually sent to Belzec, one of the death camps we never heard of until later, located north of Lviv. There, about the time I received my skull for anatomy studies, they were gassed and buried in mass graves, there being no furnaces at Belzec. Many others in the ghetto were reportedly shot on site. Add to that toll the usual hangings of prominent Jews—and the assault on the ghetto was well under way.

How many noticed the Great Aktion? How many noticed Mot and Yidka's departure from Tudorkovychi? Probably not that many. Life was rough enough during the Occupation. At all times people were being checked for their identification documents and persons caught without "Ausweis Karte" might be imprisoned and perhaps sent to forced labor in Germany. All visitors to Lviv were required to register at the district police station within twenty-four hours. It was a police state, almost as bad as Stalin's.

The Germans had lots of lackeys they could summon at the snap of a finger. Polish police usually kept order in the railroad stations and on trains. The Ukrainian police patrolled the gentile population in Lviv. Of course, the Germans were above the law, and they ignored both the Polish police and the Ukrainian police. Order in the ghetto was maintained by the Jewish police or by special German units. Gentiles in the city did not pay much attention to the Jewish people because it was hard enough to survive under the German occupation as it was.

One evening, while strolling through town with my friends, I saw about fifty young, apparently healthy Jewish men marching down the street. The two club-wielding Jewish policemen keeping pace alongside were their only real guards because the pair of German soldiers bringing up the rear, rifles casually slung over their shoulders, were too preoccupied in conversation. Slowly and silently the troupe marched on, likely returning to the ghetto after working on some project in the barracks.

I looked at my friends and they returned my gaze. Here we were, standing on packed sidewalks in a narrow street, and none of those young Jewish men dared make a break for it? When it was so obviously easy to do, the guard appearing so lax and the crowd so anonymous?

They could easily have killed those two soldiers and by nightfall have joined the Ukrainian or Polish partisans in the forests.

But on they marched, in good order—ultimately, I'm sure, through the gates of a death camp.

I've often wondered about that response. Was it again that denial I thought I glimpsed in Moshko's eyes, that deep human need to believe this wasn't really happening and couldn't possibly be true, even when you are already falling beneath the shadow of death?

I didn't know then and I still don't know today. But when that shadow passed me by it was only a few feet away.

CHAPTER TEN

Larissa

On February 3, 1943, Radio Berlin finally acknowledged a defeat. That was the day Germany made the official declaration that the Battle of Stalingrad had been lost. The terrific human cost of the defeat it never revealed. But Radio Berlin played solemn music afterwards, some claiming it was the funeral march from Wagner's "Siegfried," others that it was the haunting adagio to Bruckner's Seventh Symphony, still others that it was Beethoven's "Heroica" symphony. Maybe it was all of the above. But a major disaster it had been.

Three months earlier, Winston Churchill had claimed of a similar German defeat at El Alamein that it marked "the end of the beginning." It was easy to turn that around and claim that for us Stalingrad was "the beginning of the end."

At least that confirmed my suspicions that the war would not turn out well for Ukrainians. But if I said that, it was probably in a jocular tone. For I was then fancying myself a young man in love.

While sitting in the office of the Medical Institute in January, waiting for my turn to register for the second semester, I started a conversation with a tall, blonde, and very pretty Ukrainian girl named Larissa. I told her I had never encountered anyone by that name and would like to know how she obtained it. She appeared to be intrigued with our conversation; but in response to my suggestion for a date, she just smiled and said she worked long hours and had little free time.

Then it was my turn to register, and when I had finished, she was gone.

I asked the secretary to find me her name and address. The secretary said no, she couldn't do that. But after some persuasion she came up with a certain Larissa Smola who lived in a distant periphery of Lviv. When I later told Bohdan about my meeting with this Larissa, I prefaced it with the prediction that if he ever met this tall blonde girl, he would know it was *this* Larissa because her smile would make his heart skip a beat.

While sitting with Bohdan in his second-floor apartment that January, we could look out the window and see people being transported in the back of military trucks. This appeared to be another phase in the Nazi liquidation of the Lviv ghetto. Most of the truck beds contained stacks of people lying face down and guarded by a single gun-wielding soldier. Since I didn't see any suitcases or bundles, I assumed these were people being taken to a camp or to an execution site.

I remember especially well that on one day in February a truck passed beneath us carrying only one woman, lying naked in a pool of blood. I hoped she was the one who had supposedly thrown a heavy diamond ring at a Gestapo officer, damaging his eye. At least she was fighting back, if she were the one. Would that more of them did—and we were further heartened when we later heard about the Warsaw Ghetto Uprising of April and May 1943. Around 13,000 Jews were killed in that resistance, a very brave if tragic act of defiance.

One evening the five-year old daughter of Bohdan's landlady came to see us. The little girl told us her mother was in bed with Hans, a German soldier. She described their activity in words we were shocked to hear from a child. Even we did not use such language! We caught a glimpse of Hans from the window when he departed. The soldier's black uniform indicated he was SS, probably one of those responsible for the partial liquidation of the Lviv ghetto. Seeing him engaged in the normal rhythms of daily existence I realized humans can be worse than animals in the way they mix religion, sex, and cruelty every hour of every day without a trace of compunction.

I was surprised I didn't see Larissa at any of the lectures at the university. This indicated she was registered as a student only to obtain an identification card, which protected her from being sent to work in

Germany. But she was intriguing, and I kept an eye peeled for her whenever I was out and about on the street. One sunny day in early spring, I finally encountered her again, not far from the statue of King Sobieski on horseback. She remembered me and smiled when I told her how long I had been searching for her. She was very well dressed, and I playfully asked if she had a date with some lucky man. She replied she had no date; she simply enjoyed wearing nice clothes.

I pressed what little advantage I had. She happened to be on the way to her small shop, I found out, where she sold brown paper bags, always in demand, especially by farmers who used them to bring fruits and vegetables to Lviv's open market. While thus talking and walking we entered Sykstynska Street and a few doors down was the entrance to the shop.

She invited me in and I found myself in a small room that was stacked to the ceiling with various-sized brown paper bags. She introduced me to an old man behind the counter. He was Jewish and came out of the ghetto occasionally to help in the store. Quite likely it had once been his store, but the Germans had deprived him of ownership while allowing him to work there occasionally. After he left, Larissa told me he had taught her how to sell and how to increase the prices of bags during peak demand. During the hour I loitered in there I saw just how efficient a salesgirl she was; she must have sold scores of bags in that time frame. So that's how she could afford the pretty dresses she liked to wear!

When no customers were present, she told me that in 1930 the Poles had killed her father because he had fought against them during the 1919 war. Several years later, her mother married an employee of Maslosojuz, the Lviv-based butter business, and with him her mother had four additional children. Larissa was not very happy at home but lived there because it was much safer to live with a family than by herself. I told her in turn about my life in Tudorkovychi and how much a country upbringing had meant to me.

After an hour of conversation, frequently interrupted by shoppers, I departed—but not before kissing her on the cheek, declaring I always kissed pretty girls at the end of our second meeting. She was so startled she could only say she was afraid to invite me for a third one.

I chanced that third meeting a few days later. Larissa promptly shut the shop by pulling down the corrugated-iron shield over the door. I was pleasantly surprised she was willing to lose a little business to be alone with me.

We began our conversation with the usual banter. It was only when I told her about what I had seen from Bohdan's room, the clearing of Jews from the ghetto, that she turned solemn and looked at me intently. She wanted to see it, too. The Jewish gentleman who helped her in the store had not come to work lately and she was worried about his fate. She was praying he was well and had avoided the evacuation.

We locked the store and went to Bohdan's apartment. His welcome was unusually warm, and we soon found out why: He claimed God must have sent us to him so that he could have some company with which to drink horilka! He had just received some from home. He could not drink horilka by himself, it seemed, because he had heard doing so was the first step in becoming a drunkard.

We didn't see any trucks leaving the ghetto on that day. Bohdan's landlady had anyway told him the Germans would not completely liquidate the ghetto at this time. So we sat around the table, drinking horilka and eating very tasty black rye bread garnished with pieces of smoked pig fat. At that time, Bohdan and I still had our various skulls sitting about and he had arranged several of them on the flower stand. Larissa couldn't help but notice these ghastly ornaments, but she said nothing. Bohdan was telling us he was lucky enough to get two tickets to the opera "Tosca" but, unfortunately, he was unable to go. He offered us the tickets and Larissa agreed to go with me.

So we sat around and drank; and while doing so, I noticed that Larissa was a very sophisticated girl. She recognized Bohdan's weakness: He liked to hear good things said about himself and tended to exaggerate stories about his exploits. She quickly adjusted herself to our company and matched us horilka for horilka. But it was clear she was a novice at the practice; she had not eaten anything and was drinking the stuff like water. After sunset Bohdan and I spent half of the night transporting her home, which was indeed on the periphery of the city.

That meant Bohdan and I had to return after curfew. To avoid arrest, we pretended to be Germans and rode in a streetcar labeled "Nur für Deutsche." Expecting only obedient Germans to be seated there, the police rarely checked the passengers' identification papers. I happened to look very German. But Bohdan, with his olive skin and dark hair parted in the middle and hanging over his ears, looked more like Rasputin. Luckily, we arrived home without any difficulty.

I was now seeing Larissa at least twice a week. Her paper bag business was so successful that she used some of her profits not only on clothes but also on delicious, albeit black-market, food. We liked to get together with my old friends from Cholm, including my old roommate, Mykola, who had an apartment with two other jovial fellows from Cholm Gymnasium. I usually brought the strong drink and Larissa would provide us with good food. She was friendly and likable and soon became accepted as a member of our gang.

Whether we played cards, listened to romantic music, or had the occasional dance party, we frequently missed curfew. Because it was too dangerous to venture outside, our parties would last all night. The alcohol alone usually gave everyone enough energy to keep dancing until about 4:00 a.m. The following hour was when everything degenerated; conversation or dancing-- much less standing straight--was difficult. At 5:00 a.m. the curfew was lifted and the tired boys were still obligated by unwritten rules to accompany the girls safely home.

Meanwhile, during the winter and spring of 1943, I wrote several letters to Tatiana, and even planned to take a train to Cholm to see her, but I never heard back. After passing her Matura in the early spring, though, I heard she came to Lviv; but she did not notify me or make any attempt to see me. Probably some of her friends let her know that I was dating Larissa or, possibly, she had some boyfriend of her own by this time. I was saddened by this development as I had wanted to get to know her better. But Larissa and my schooling kept me distracted.

One day when I visited Larissa in her shop, her mother came in, and after only a few words, I realized she did not like seeing me, a poor medical student, standing there. She was obviously hoping her beautiful daughter would soon marry someone more suitable, someone powerful enough to take care of her during the changes a German defeat in Russia would surely bring.

But it was too late. Larissa and I were in love and we didn't want to be separated. We met frequently in Bohdan's apartment and spent many happy hours there. One Sunday, Pani Lyda and my father invited Larissa to come to our family's house for dinner. They liked her, too, and were impressed by her intelligence and good manners.

Although Larissa was not interested in sports, she went with me to soccer games and we rooted for the Ukrainian team "Ukrania." Remembering those afternoons reminds me of the rumors circulating during the war about a well-regarded Ukrainian team taking on the Germans and defeating them soundly. When a rematch was scheduled, it was said, the Germans told the Ukrainians they had better lose the match if they valued their lives. They didn't lose, and many of the Ukrainian players were said to have been shot without trial.

Perhaps those are the kinds of stories that circulate during wartime. In any event, the story served as the basis of a movie many decades later.

As the spring advanced, I decided to get some experience in hospital work. I applied to a well-known Ukrainian hospital, financed by Metropolitan Andrey Sheptytsky, called "Narodna Lichnycia," housed in several buildings behind Lviv's Cathedral of St. George. I was accepted and set to work in a diagnostic laboratory with an advanced medical student who was the son of the hospital's director, Dr. Burachinsky. Unfortunately, the son of Burachinsky was not very friendly or helpful and I learned very little. So I went back to the father and asked him to transfer me to the surgery department.

The elder Dr. Burachinsky was a tall, thin man who was always in a hurry. He asked me how much I learned in the histological laboratory and not waiting for my answer, he accepted me in the surgery department, where I would work with him and Drs. Fylipchak and Kuzmowich. I was able to spend two mornings a week in the surgery department assisting with operations and the treatment of wounds. At that time, antibiotics were not yet widely available, and in spite of maximum care, wounds frequently became infected. I still remember the putrid smell in rooms where patients with infected wounds were cared for.

Dr. Burachinsky was too old to perform complicated operations, so Dr. Fylipchak, who was considered to be one of the best surgeons in Lviv, undertook them. Fylipchak knew he was a good surgeon and behaved like a spoiled "prima donna" both inside and outside of the hospital. He was a handsome and well-built man with brown skin and his black hair was brushed and adhered to his scalp so closely it looked as if his scalp was painted with India ink. He also smoked only expensive Hungarian cigarettes. In the operating room, however, he often threw temper tantrums, hurling a scalpel to the floor while giving us assistants a hard time.

Despite dealing with him, I liked assisting in the operating room much more than analyzing blood smears under a microscope. I was often asked to anesthetize and keep a patient asleep during an operation by using ether and chloroform, which involved varying the drops of either substance when applying them to the cotton mask covering the patient's nose and mouth. It was tricky to get the right balance so that he didn't come out of it too soon or, worse, never came out of it at all.

Soon I was helping everywhere in the hospital. But when the physicians went to dinner in the hospital's kitchen, I was not invited to join them. When my father heard the hospital did not feed its volunteers, he was very angry. He always took good care of the people who worked for him in the bank and organized a kitchen to feed anyone who was hungry. It was wartime and, in the cities, people had little food and many were hungry. Numerous large businesses were organizing common kitchens and feeding their workers at least once a day. Insensitivity among the higher ranks was not surprising, but it was especially annoying the hungrier we underlings became.

One day while trying to keep up with a quickly paced Dr. Burachinsky as he marched through the narrow and poorly lit corridors of the hospital a young girl stopped me and asked me something I didn't quite catch. As she stood in the half-light, I assumed she was asking me for an early examination, but I told her to be patient and her turn would come soon.

A few weeks later when I was home in Tudorkovychi for a short visit I was told by Didoon Semen that I had been rude and unhelpful to our family. I was stunned. *What?* He reminded me about the incident with the young girl in the half-light of the hospital corridor. It turned she was Sidorko's daughter, Lesia.

Oh, dear! But of course, I didn't recognize her because she had grown up, the light was poor, and I could not have anticipated meeting her in such an unfamiliar setting. It turned out her mother was ill and they had come to the hospital for *my* help. They apparently got treated elsewhere. Nonetheless I felt terrible that I had appeared to be unhelpful to anyone, much less a member of the family.

In May of 1943, while I was volunteering at the hospital, the Ukrainian Central Committee in Krakow announced the German government had agreed to raise a new military unit, a Ukrainian division more formally called the Waffen-SS 14 Grenadier Division but informally known as the "Galician Division" or, in Ukrainian, the "Divizia Halichina." Since it would only be used on the Eastern Front and not against the Western Allies, the members of the Central Committee encouraged young Ukrainians to volunteer. Within two months it was training thousands of new recruits.

A friend of my father's, Dmito Palijiv, the blue-eyed former Posul and newspaper editor who took me to the boy scout camp a decade previously, played an active role in the formation of the Division. A veteran of the elite Sich Riflemen during the First World War, he knew the Germans would provide outstanding military training to Ukrainian youths who, after this one ended, might liberate our land and establish its independence. For once, my father disagreed with him. Volodimir Kochan was against Ukrainians serving in Nazi uniforms. He was convinced the Germans would lose the war and that any "collaborators" would be punished. He thought it was improper for Ukrainians to associate themselves with Nazi Germany.

Palijiv tried to convince Father that it was better to have trained professional soldiers, even ones serving in the German Army, than to rely on undisciplined partisans in the forests. He also knew Germany would lose the war; but these soldiers could then become the nucleus of a Ukrainian National Army.

Bohdan Yourchuk enlisted in the Divizia. I suspect he was ordered to do so by his nationalistic associates. I was hesitant about enlisting. I worked in a hospital, and though I admired the German military genius, I hated the ruthless and arrogant Nazis. Mykola Zerebecky and my friends from Cholm also preferred to continue their studies and stay in Lviv as long as possible. I might have joined them. But in one rash moment of enthusiasm, I up and volunteered and was duly enlisted into the Divizia by a friend of my father's, Stephan Volynetz.

Like other members of the moderate party, Front of National Unity, or FNU, Volynetz worked in the Ukrainian Central Committee and was responsible for the enlistment of men into the Divizia. When I told my father about what I had done, however, he became very upset. He thought I should first finish my medical training and then decide about enlisting in the military. By that point Germany would already have lost the war.

In a few weeks, the first 10,000 volunteers in the Divizia were called to training camps in Germany and Austria. Bohdan and some of my other friends were among them, but I was not. Before they departed, however, the Ukrainian Central Committee organized a big parade as part of a farewell celebration. German and Ukrainian dignitaries crowded the dais and some of them addressed the crowd. Larissa and I were there, listening to speeches permeated with German propaganda and German regard for the "semi-Aryanised" Ukrainian people. Afterwards, Larissa and I went to the railroad station to say goodbye to Bohdan and other departing friends. They were happy to go and there was much laughter and singing both in the station and on the trains that took them to the training camps.

Larissa and I walked back to the University and sat in a nearby park until late in the evening. I now had my doubts about the wisdom of joining the Germans in their fight against the Soviet Union. For one thing, I did not think the army would be able to extricate itself from Hitler's foolishness and so service in it might be tantamount to a death sentence. And for another thing, I was not sure who the enemy was anymore.

It wasn't the SS designation. By now that was just a military and administrative convenience. The Waffen SS was under the operational control of the Wehrmacht and not Himmler's goons. Volunteers from the Reich's ethnic groups, ranging from Serbs to Danes, were slotted into Waffen SS divisions.

No, it was more than that. I told her about rumors I had heard. "When the German panzers rolled across Soviet Ukraine in the summer of 1941, they were welcomed in every village by women holding aloft crucifixes and icons they had long kept hidden. They were welcomed, it seems, as liberators! And they should have been liberating people so they could return to their churches and their God. But then the Germans did something wrong. They mistreated these people or somehow made enemies of the Ukrainians over there. Whatever it was, it was a fatal mistake."

Coincidentally, the Germans had just announced the discovery the previous year of the thousands of slain Polish officers unearthed in the

Katyn Forest outside Minsk. Here was a Soviet atrocity, they claimed. Well, I told Larissa, "I suspect that if you poke around in the dark corners of Ukraine, you'll find many such mass graves, some dating from Stalin's purges but the fresher ones the work of the Germans. It's unnecessary and counterproductive—it's filling the ranks of the Red Army with Ukrainian recruits. Once again, brothers will be fighting brothers on behalf of whichever side believes to be Ukraine's enemies."

I myself thought Communism was the true enemy. "And if I were a full-fledged doctor," I continued, "I would join and go into battle with fellow Ukrainians to dress their wounds and save lives. But I'm only a poor medical student. And I won't fight fellow Ukrainians."

Sitting on that park bench, Larissa and I decided then and there that I should not go when called up to join the Divizia. But how could I get out of it legally? I did not want to ask my father for help because I had volunteered without asking him for his advice. And any such request would place him in a difficult position. In the hospital, however, I revealed to Dr. Burachinsky my change of heart about joining the Divizia. He advised me to "catch" tuberculosis and notify the recruiting office. A physician friend of his is the one who physically examines Divizia volunteers; this friend might confirm my imaginary disease. So I went to the office of the Divizia and notified Mr. Volynetz that I had had an active case of tuberculosis during my childhood. I told him I hadn't admitted to it because I wanted to join the Divizia, but now I thought it better to determine the actual state of my health before appearing in front of the Military Medical Committee. Volynetz said he was sorry to hear about this matter and sent me to the friend of Dr. Burachinsky.

After the x-ray examination, I told the doctor I was a medical student working with Dr. Burachinsky in Narodna Lichnicia Hospital and recently had become hesitant about fighting against fellow Ukrainians in the Soviet Army. He listened carefully to my disclosure and afterwards he wrote a statement to the effect that I had a bad case of tuberculosis and should not be enlisted into the Divizia. I took this certificate to Mr. Volynetz and he made an appointment for me to appear before the Military Medical Committee. The Committee reluctantly annulled my application.

Subsequently, I told my father I decided not to join the Divizia—just in case Mr. Volynetz asked about the progress of my tuberculosis treatment. Anyway, I was more the healer than the fighter. And a sometime smuggler, to boot.

During the summer of 1943, when the titanic tank battle at Kursk was being fought in Russia and the Allies were invading Sicily, my father received a letter from a friend who worked in the dairies of Uhryniv, the old border town a couple of miles southwest of Tudorkovychi. He was offering my father five pounds of butter—if someone could pick it up. At that time, every member of our family was dreaming about a slice of bread spread with the fresh sweet butter made from the milk of Ukrainian cows. Because of the German persecution of "black marketeers," the transporting of butter from Uhryniv to Lviv was a dangerous enterprise and my father was reluctant to ask me to do it. The Germans were constantly checking trains for the unlawful transport of food from villages to towns. A few pounds of butter could land someone in a labor camp or worse. Nevertheless, the temptation was great, and I decided to take a chance and bring butter home to the family.

I took the train from Pidzamche, a smaller train station in Lviv that was watched less closely by the Germans. While waiting in the station, I heard people speaking about Hitler's former friend Rudolph Hess who, two years earlier, had stolen a small plane and flown it to Scotland, where he hoped to strike a peace deal with Great Britain. The longing for peace is already having people talking of rash and reckless schemes, I thought.

When we were allowed to board, I managed to get a window seat and once again enjoyed the view of the fields and forests while riding in comfort. I reached Sokal without any difficulty. No one in Tudorkovychi knew about my trip, so no one was waiting for me at the railroad station to take me home. It was early afternoon, and I knew I could reach the village during daylight. It was only twelve kilometers, or seven miles, and the weather was perfect. I passed the outskirts of Sokal and continued my walk on a dirt path between the fields of standing wheat, close to the paved road.

Much had changed from that time when as a young boy I traveled by these fields. I was no longer a naïve village lad and life in the city had taught me to be careful and quick to find solutions in difficult situations. While attending schools in Sokal, Cholm, and Lviv I had met many people and learned from them the nuances of day-to-day life in times of peace and war. Although I resembled my father physically, I felt I was more by nature like my mother, who was practical and knew how to help herself without "a man in the house." In dealing with people, I first listened carefully to their understanding of life's problems. Then I critically examined their thinking, evaluating it from my point of view. Even when I did not agree, I still listened to what they had to say.

Reflecting upon my relationship with Larissa, I was pleased she loved me and hoped the approaching turmoil of battle and war would not separate us. While pondering such matters, I passed through Voislavychi and shortly afterwards arrived at the house of Didoon Kindrat, where my mother lived.

The next day, I rode my bicycle to Uhryniv and met my father's friend. While accepting his donation of butter I thanked him, adding that it would greatly help our family, which had not had butter for many months. Butter was a staple in the Ukrainian diet, but since the beginning of the war it was unavailable in stores. Instead of butter, people used pig fat, which gave them energy but had little taste.

The dairy director said he was happy to help my father, whom he had earlier helped elect to the Polish Sejm. I received five pounds of butter and he said he would be glad to do so again during my next visit to Tudorkovychi. He did ask me, though, not to reveal his name in case I was caught by the Germans. I thanked him for the butter and promised to keep secret its source.

My mother praised its taste and color. Buttered rye bread with sour milk was my favorite meal for lunch as a young boy. Now my mother did occasionally make butter at home, but it was more and more difficult to save enough of the necessary milk. I also gave some butter to Didoon Semen. He had become old and was struggling with the farm chores. Petro helped him but nevertheless the farm appeared to be sadly neglected. The next day Petro took me to the railroad station in Sokal and I boarded the train to Lviv.

I detrained in Pidzamche hoping the station would be as quiet as it was three days previously. The building was largely empty and not suspecting trouble I opened the exit door—and realized I was very much in trouble. The station was encircled by German and Ukrainian police and crammed with many people. I could not even step back into the station or discard the butter because of the bright daylight.

So, I went over to where several Ukrainian policemen were checking the contents of bags. I quietly told one of them, while pretending to open my package, that I was a medical student and was carrying some butter for my family. I told him I would appreciate his help in letting me pass. He asked me who the dean of the Medical Institute was and after receiving a satisfactory answer, he told me to wait, and he went to his superior for further instructions. When he returned, he told me to open the package. After seeing the remaining three pounds of butter, he instructed me to close the package and walk slowly through the Ukrainian check line and to behave naturally so as not to attract the attention of the German police.

I walked between two Ukrainian policemen to the end of the line and continued walking slowly until I turned at the corner of the street. I arrived home safely, after everybody there had sent their prayers heavenward that I would return in one piece.

That was the only time I received any help from the police. That officer had known that, without his assistance, I would have been caught by the Germans. Brother for brother, not brother against brother—not all Ukrainians were fighting each other.

CHAPTER ELEVEN

What Song the Partisans Sang

Before the Second World War, life in Ukrainian villages was nearly devoid of crime. Yet by 1943, after several years of war, everything had changed.

The first murder in Tudorkovychi was what we now call an ethnic cleansing. A fine young Polish man was a forester and helped administer the estates—which included much of The Forest--of our local magnate, Count Rilsky. Partisans broke into this young Polish man's house, searched his belongings, and—as one would expect from one of his profession—found detailed maps of both forest and village. Our Ukrainian partisans instead concluded he was collecting information for the Polish partisans, the Armia Krajowa. Our boys took the forester into the adjacent woods, questioned him about the maps, then shot him "when he tried to escape."

This incident shocked the villagers. There was neither judge nor jury. Domestic animals were treated with more respect than this. The peace and tranquility of Tudorkovychi had been forever shattered.

Viyt Korolchuk, the equivalent of mayor, notified the German authorities in Sokal about the killing. The next day a group of fifteen soldiers arrived, ostensibly to probe The Forest for the presence of partisans. These guys, however, hardly stepped foot into the woods. They were approaching middle age and didn't want to tangle with ferocious young banditti, as partisans were sometimes called. Nothing was done, or could be done, about the murder. The forester's bereaved family left the village and understandably never returned.

In July 1943 the violence reached epic proportions. In nearby Volhynia Province hundreds of Ukrainians burst out of the swamps and forests and murdered thousands of Polish peasants—men, women, and children. They torched entire villages and burned down barns around the heads of captives. These Volhynian Massacres, as they came to be known, of course provoked an equally savage retaliation from the Poles—and the cycle of tit-for-tat murder and atrocity was well underway.

Rarely had a corner of this planet been subject to more horrifying and blood-soaked years than Eastern Europe in the 1940s. Not only were two ruthless regimes murdering millions of people, but astride and between their enormous armies hundreds of thousands of partisans lurked, from the Carpathian Mountains in the south to the forests and swamps of Belorussia and the Baltics to the north. Not one group trusted another. Chaos ruled.

The last Germans evacuated Kiev in December 1943 and the following month, despite cold, wind, and snow, the Red Army started reclaiming Ukraine. The misery of the Italian soldiers was visible as they marched through Lviv while returning from the front. The Germans had once tried to hide these dilapidated regiments, transporting them in trucks around the towns. Now there was a shortage of trucks, and so on they marched, slowly, column by column, through the streets of Lviv, covered with blankets worn thin on the windy steppes of Ukraine. These men and boys were tired and hungry and had to be dreaming about their sunny and warm homes. They disliked the war and the Fascists who had placed them in such misery. It was obvious to everyone that Germany had lost an ally in the fight against the Red Army.

By contrast, I occasionally saw at various railroad stations the soldiers of the Divizia Halichina. With their good looks, neat uniforms, and excellent armaments they were most impressive. It seemed the Germans had trained and equipped them well to take on the Soviets.

Yet everyone still knew Germany would lose the war. The Red Army's spring offensive, launched in the snows of winter, had in the region south of the Pripet River brought them by mid-April to within fifty miles or so of Lviv. South of that the Russians were even approaching the Carpathians. Rumors of secret weapons and atomic bombs buoyed some spirits but were downplayed by other people.

As the battlefront crept closer and closer to Lviv, many of its Ukrainian citizens undertook a mass exodus to safer havens in the west. My father moved his family to Krynica, a spa town nestled high in the Beskid Range of the Carpathian Mountains. Located about a hundred miles south of Krakow, Krynica was a beautiful place, set in a broad valley and surrounded by forested peaks. It had long been a summer retreat for wealthy families who came to bathe in its hot springs, quaff its medicinal waters, and breathe its pure and invigorating air.

My father was able to rent a large house not far from the center of town. Pani Lyda and my brothers, Roman and Yarko, were joined by her mother, Knish, and her sister, Yarukha Karanovich, with her two daughters, Danusya and Radusya.

Yarukha had just returned from her own odyssey with the partisans. Her husband was a physician in a Volhynian town when one night a group of UPA partisans—Ukrainian Insurgent Army, an even more militant offshoot of the OUN—came to his house and requested that he join them because they needed a doctor. He understandably declined, having a wife and two young daughters, but of course they took him anyway. Dr. Karanovich kissed his loved ones goodbye and went to live and work in a mobile forest hospital. Eventually he fetched his wife and daughters and they all lived with him, deep in the woods, in constant danger of encountering enemy Soviet or Polish partisans. Yarukha told me how much she enjoyed the beauty of the wintry forest and how much she admired the dedication of the UPA warriors who fought for liberation of Ukraine from the Germans, Poles, and Soviets.

After two months of such spartan living, she and her daughters returned home and were now refugees in Krynica, living with Pani Lyda.

Meanwhile, my father and I remained behind in Lviv, at least until the fate of his bank was decided. Living in the old city was becoming more difficult every day. Most of the stores were closed and it was hard to buy food even with authorized food stamps. Father and I ate our dinners at 1:00 p.m. in the common kitchen he had organized for the bank employees. For breakfast and supper, I re-established the routine we followed in Sokal about ten years earlier: I became an expert at making mashed potatoes served with eggs and onions according to Pani Lyda's recipe. Often my father's friend Dr. Shlemkevich joined us for dinner. He was a well-known philosopher and a respected historian of the Ukrainian community. Educated in Vienna, he was a well-traveled man and an unusually interesting storyteller. Like my father, he had sent his family to Krynica and was living by himself in Lviv. He enjoyed visiting with us and, after a few vodka drinks, I liked listening to his adventurous tales and descriptions of strange customs in foreign lands. It made me dream of seeing faraway places, too—should this cruel war ever come to an end.

It must have been early June when two events promised to further complicate our lives. Yarko, who had been attending the Ukrainian Gymnasium in Krynica, up and joined the German Army, enlisting in a Luftwaffe anti-aircraft battalion. I tried to dissuade him from making such a foolish move as fighting for a lost cause. But he had been influenced by physical education teacher at the gymnasium—the same one I had in Cholm—who was urging all the teenage boys and girls to serve in the German armed forces. But you couldn't be heard complaining about that.

The second event was the closure of the Institute of Medicine. The offices were transferred from Lviv to Krakow, and I followed. I said goodbye to the hospital physicians who were also in the process of leaving, then boarded a train for Krakow. My father was lending me his one-room apartment there, and I would volunteer to work in the General Hospital in the old Polish capital.

The apartment was fine, although it shared a common kitchen and bathroom with three other one-room apartments; and I was fed one free meal a day at the General Hospital. The problem was the Poles, or rather the war-within-the-war that fueled their animosity toward Ukrainians.

Partisan violence had reached a new peak of intensity. The term "ethnic cleansing" had not yet been coined, but ethnic cleansing it was, brutal and sadistic. Ukrainian partisans were cleansing Volhynia of Poles, Polish partisans were cleansing Kholmshchina of Ukrainians. The numbers of murdered men, women, and children; of burned houses, barns, and villages; of slain cattle and ruined crops, were appalling and growing worse. And it was all heading to my beloved Halichina.

My Polish language skills had improved dramatically, thanks largely to Mrs. Romanovska and her pretty daughter, Noosia. That helped me in the hospital, where the employees and most of the patients were Polish. And any remaining animosity towards me was muted by the fact that the hospital was under German supervision and the Germans had no tolerance for any of this.

Anyway, I was helped considerably by a new friend, a fellow Ukrainian who was also a medical student in the Krakow hospital. His name was Ivan Volynetz, and he was the nephew of Stepan Volynetz, the man who enrolled me into the Divizia Halichina and then later helped me extract myself. Ivan's family was still in Lviv and his father was a Greek-Catholic priest in one of the villages nearby. His older brothers were in the forests serving with the partisans of the Ukrainian Insurgent Army, a fact we kept well hidden.

In Krakow, Ivan had no place to live so I invited him to stay with me in the one-room apartment that fortunately had two beds. He was a quirky guy with a thin, small frame, a Hitler-type mustache and dark, curly hair. His most distinguishing feature, however, was the eyepatch; as a child he had accidentally blinded himself in one eye with a large sewing needle. Since his brothers were in UPA, Ivan had Banderite inclinations, but I think he sensed that I did not. We avoided that topic altogether. He was much better qualified in culinary matters and prepared various dishes out of simple cream-of-wheat I brought from Lviv, the only edible item remaining after Pani Lyda had left. Since we had no milk, Ivan cooked a carefully measured amount of cereal in water, and then we sweetened the top of the "kasha" with molasses made from sugar beets.

Hospital work left us with little free time, but whenever we could we took a train to Krynica and spent our weekends eating much better food, drinking worse tasting medicinal water that smelled like rotten eggs and supposedly cleaned impurities from the blood and kidneys, and above all roaming around the mountains. Another time we visited Yarko, whose training camp was just outside Krakow. The recruits were housed in nice barracks, but we were puzzled by the song they sang at the end of the day. It was an American military tune to which someone had put Ukrainian words! When the Germans realized this, they forbade it.

While there we had a close call. Visitors were naturally forbidden to spend the night in the barracks. Yet we couldn't stay outside the fence, either. Tensions with the Poles were such that their partisans had recently killed some visitors. This was Polish territory and Ukrainians were not welcome. So Yarko snuck us in. During the night, however, the recruits were called out on field exercises. We hunkered even lower into our top bunks. Sure enough, the guard detail came in to inspect the room. We pretended we were not there, and these soldiers did the same. Yarko snuck us back out before dawn.

Occasionally we had visitors to our one-room apartment. Larissa came and I showed her the city. She loved the many gardens and especially the Sukiennice, Krakow's belt of greenery, and the big old trees called "Planty." Hardly had she left, however, then my father arrived—unexpectedly.

He was in Krakow on bank business and found me sitting at the table with Ivan eating *bryndza*, a sheep's milk cheese made in the Carpathians. I introduced Ivan to him but saw he was very annoyed. When Ivan left the room, my father asked me about my visitors. I told him Ivan was living with me, that I had invited him because he had no place to sleep. Ivan Volynetz—emphasizing the surname—was an honest and good man who worked with me in the city hospital and helped around the house in Krynica. That mollified him somewhat, but his eyes told me he knew about Larissa's visit. A trace of perfume, perhaps?

I told him Ivan and I ate nearly ten pounds of this bryndza cheese because we were so hungry, and I had no money to buy food. My father had not sent me any for several months. He dug around and gave me some bills and from that time on he made sure Ivan and I ate two meals a day, one in the hospital and the other in the Ukrainian Kitchen, which was run by the Ukrainian Relief Organization. Most Ukrainian politicians ate their meals there, too, although many of them hated each other. Nevertheless, the food brought them there randomly and Ivan and I had a good laugh observing these politicians sitting practically next to each other but pretending not to notice the fact.

So, Ivan was a good-natured and pleasant companion, if not as lively as Mykola had been. But Ivan was visiting his father when my next visitor dropped in.

The sleek uniform of an SS officer looked good on Bohdan Yourchuk. Army life had served him well. He lost that long and unruly hair and those languid movements. He also lost much of his fatty posterior and had become fit and trim. I was very happy to see him. He had taken leave to go to Sokal and speed his family's departure before the Russian tidal wave hit. He had also stopped by Tudorkovychi and brought me a gift from my mother: two bottles of homemade horilka and a big piece of smoked ham. We promptly uncorked one of the bottles and, after a few drinks, he told me what I already knew: The Germans were going to lose the war. There was no Wunderwaffe, "Wonder Weapon," being developed in Alpine caves. Or none that would be ready in time. Now that the "Second Front" had opened in Normandy, the British, Canadians, and Americans might be in Germany by the end of the year. His advice was to move up the departure date of myself and my family—and get to Western Europe as fast as possible; get behind the advancing British and American armies.

He also warned me the Soviets on the Ukrainian front showed every sign of renewing their onslaught—any day now.

After Bohdan returned to the Divisia, stationed around a small nondescript frontier town called Brody, I decided there was no reason to hesitate. I knew my family and I had to leave Halichina and go to foreign lands. My father was a prominent anti-Communist, so he and his family would probably be shot by the NKVD or at the least be scattered across Siberia. I was prepared to leave Ukraine for the time being but also hoped I would eventually return to my beautiful Lviv. I still believed the British and Americans would roll back the Bolshevik tide and restore a stable and prosperous Europe, including an independent Ukraine.

So, I asked the hospital supervisor if I might be relieved of my duties for the next week or two. I had to go to Lviv and help evacuate my family. He was polite and did not ask too many questions. To facilitate my travel, he gave me a document stating I was employed in the city hospital of Krakow and my services were needed there.

The trains were still running, and I arrived in Lviv without difficulty. Gloom enshrouded the city. Most of the remaining inhabitants would have to ride it out, come what may. But my father explained his hands were tied until the Germans decided the fate of his bank. That should be any day now. It was already early July. The Soviets had launched a massive offensive to the north in Belorussia in late June. Any day now...

Uncle Miron was in the city, hoping to exchange his nearly worthless Polish zlotys for American money, which would retain its value throughout the uncertain times ahead. One twenty-dollar gold piece was worth about 18,000 Polish zlotys, an amount one could comfortably live on for a year in peacetime. I gave his Polish money to an old classmate of mine who claimed he had a family member who sold twenty-dollar gold coins on the black market. This relative did not want to deal with me directly—this was a dangerous request—so I had to wait for my former classmate to give it to me. Wait, that is, while standing on a corner of Theater Street. For half an hour, he said. Miron was getting impatient as he was taking the train back to Sokal that evening.

I actually waited there for four hours. By that point I thought I had been fleeced. Finally, he turned up with the coin and a tall tale about the delay that I did not believe. I was tempted to knock out some of his teeth. I suspected that all that time he was watching me, hoping I would leave and then he would have some excuse for his troubled conscience. But I *did* wait until he finally overcame the desire to steal from a fellow student.

I learned a lesson that day. Trust people with things only to the point you can afford to repair the loss and not more.

While Miron was in the city he talked of the family. Didoon Semen still had a bad cough and his advanced years had made him very weak. Babunya Marina and Petro were busy, as always, keeping the farm in order. It seemed my Aunt Stefonka and her husband, Mikhalko, and their two daughters, Sarafina and Hania, were doing well. My cousin Mitonko was still working at the public records office in Chorobriv—but, Miron warned, he had become very active with the partisans. That was causing trouble with Mikhalko, his stepfather. Mikhalko had also become rude to my mother and was trying to throw her out of her part of the house, which was given to her by Didoon Kindrat.

This seemed out of character, and was so disturbing to me I decided, despite the obvious danger, to go home and say goodbye, for possibly the last time.

My father tried to discourage me. Partisan activity might disrupt the trains. And when the renewed Soviet offensive began the trains would be commandeered by the military and I could be trapped in Tudorkovychi. I countered by claiming that if the trains were stopped, I'd ride a horse back and forth, which I did as a boy. I only needed three days, I urged, enough time to say "Do Pobachennya" to my mother and other family members. And even if the Germans gave him permission to move the bank right now, I reminded my father, it would take him at least three days to organize the transfer.

I'm stubborn, so I won. The following morning—Friday, July 7, 1944—I boarded the train at the Pidzamche Station and to my surprise I was the only civilian passenger. The car I sat in was occupied by about thirty German soldiers—Wehrmacht and not SS—so they were generally friendly to civilians. On this trip there were three platform cars in front of the engine in case we ran into a bomb or sabotaged tracks. As we passed through one bit of forest the soldiers distributed guns, giving me one, too. They said partisans were now shooting at the trains, and we should be prepared to defend ourselves. When we got close to Sokal, they retrieved the gun and warned me to be careful because this area was considered the front line now, and there were many partisans of different nationalities lurking in the forests and fields.

The railroad station in Sokal was deserted. The streets and sidewalks in the suburb were eerily empty. Once I gained the road toward Tudorkovychi, I heard a blast of gunfire from the direction of the railroad station. Whirling about, I saw a lone airplane flying fast and circling low. I saw a red star on the fuselage as it plowed into a field close to the road. Soldiers from the train raced by in Kübelwagens, the German equivalent of the Jeep. They tore through the wheat and reached the smoking plane. A volley of pistol shots and then the only sound was someone barking orders.

I stood transfixed. This was the real thing. As one of the Kübelwagens returned, the soldier who had given me the gun on the train told me the Soviet pilot must have been checking out the state of the bridge and somehow overlooked the sandbagged machine gun and anti-aircraft positions flanking that span. Oh, and he had emptied his pistol at them before shooting himself. Stalin had ordered Soviet soldiers never to become POWs, my new friend told me. They were supposed to kill themselves instead—with their last bullet.

As I resumed my trek up the road, I was thinking how difficult it must have been to end your life just like that and in just that way. While I wanted to escape from Communism at all costs, he willingly sacrificed his life for it. Might there be something noble about Communism, after all, something never told me by my parents or by German propaganda? And then I remembered the killing of 6,000 Polish POWs in the Katyn Forest, the murder of thousands of innocent Ukrainians in the prisons of Lviv—and my thoughts along this line evaporated.

As I walked between the high wheat fields, the road was empty, as were the fields themselves. The harvest, usually underway by late June, was running late here. The wild red poppies and blue cornflowers intertwined with the wheat and their nodding in the afternoon sun made the very idea of a coming battle unthinkable. As the miles fell behind me, I did see figures in the fields—not partisans, but farmers harvesting the wheat. That sign of apparent normalcy helped me relax.

As I passed through Vislavychi I saw the tall chimney of the mill that had been making flour since I was a child. Next to it stood the cemetery where many members of my family were buried, starting with my great-grandfather, Matvii, my great-grandmother, Hulka, and most recently dear, lovable old Didoon Kindrat.

Finally, I reached my mother's house. Everybody was surprised and happy to see me, but after the customary greetings they wanted news and what's more, reassurance that Communism would never reach Tudorkovychi—and that I could not give them. I told them about the Russian plane snooping around the Sokal bridge; that meant the long-awaited summer offensive would soon be underway. The Soviet Army would occupy the village and their lives would change. Nevertheless, I encouraged them to welcome the Soviet soldiers as they had welcomed the Germans in 1939 and reminded the older ones they had survived nine months of Russian occupation in 1914-15. And their old patterns of life eventually returned.

I also told them I would be leaving Ukraine. I didn't know where I would go or when I'd return, if ever.

My mother suggested that I sleep in the barn, on a platform above the cow stable, where no one would find me. She said that during the night some bad people were roaming the village and it would be better for me to avoid them. She prepared a bed for me on a layer of hay and after a supper of potato soup with pieces of chicken, I went to sleep.

During the night, I awoke and heard, coming from the direction of the burok, someone singing a Ukrainian folksong. The music floated softly across the summer night, down the lanes and across the fields. It was quite beautiful, with lovely intonations and exquisite harmonies, falling like dew, like starlight, over house and barn, meadow and orchard. I had never heard this song, this haunting melody that kept many people awake and listening in our small corner of benighted Europe. And to think it must have been sung by armed partisans wandering through the village!

Many years later I would learn that song by heart, and it would always remain in my memory as the most moving expression of Ukrainian endurance I've ever heard.

In the morning I learned that during the night partisans from Volhynia had indeed visited the village. The border was only three miles away but since there were no bridges over the Variazanka River we had felt isolated from the turmoil in Volhynia at this time. No longer—now the vicious fighting between the partisans of UPA and those of the Polish Armia Krajova might spill over into our fields and forest. Not to mention, in nearby Belorussia, the colossal series of battles historians would come to call simply "The Collapse of Army Group Center" possibly coming this way. Already small firefights between rival factions of Ukrainian partisans were disturbing our local farmers. Like my mother, the villagers were not sure who was a friend and who a foe.

Then there was her more particular worry: Partisans of whatever stripe were increasingly forcing young people into their ranks, and medical students were always prime candidates.

That morning—Saturday the 8th—I crossed the bridge and visited Didoon Semen and Babunya Marina. Of their seven children, only Petro was still home, and he was out harvesting the wheat. Didoon was sitting outside the kitchen cutting small dry branches for kindling. I was saddened to see him reduced to such tasks. I remembered him as being such a strong, energetic, even aggressive man. But I sat with him and after some small talk he turned the conversation to my father. For the first and last time he opened up to me about his eldest son's difficulties. He told me he thought my father's service as a Posol to the Polish parliament had been a mistake for Volodimir. It left him so little time for anything else, especially his family and his finances.

Didoon also thought my mother had not helped the situation—primarily because she had been spoiled by Kindrat. The real reason, in his opinion, that she had left the Kochan household was "too much work." That wasn't for her. Of course, the continuous disagreements between my parents had made life as difficult for the Kochans as for the Kindrats, Yarko, and me. Semen realized my childhood had been shortchanged in important ways—which I tried to protest—but in the end he hoped it would make me a better man. The old cavalryman then looked me in the eye—his were devoid of the tears I was trying to fight back—and told me he was proud to have me grow up in his household.

In the afternoon I rode with Petro to our field close to the Variazanka River. He needed to bring home some clover to feed the animals. On our way we sang songs as we did in the old days. He sang the bass part and I sang tenor. We both knew that this singing would be our last for a very long time.

We passed The Forest and entered the fields close to the river. Villagers were now growing all kinds of crops close to the woods because the wild boars that used to ruin the crops had now ended up on the dinner table. I enjoyed looking at the river that flowed as tranquilly as ever, remembering my happy afternoons with my bamboo fishing pole. We unlimbered the scythes and with long sweeping cuts we harvested the clover and loaded it onto the wagon. The sun was setting, and the birds were busily settling down for the night, continuously chirping as if wishing each other good evening.

Bang! Bang! Birds scattering and air crackling around us!

We threw ourselves into the grass, me thinking how absurd for me to die from a bullet fired by some fucking partisan! We lay there for a seeming infinity, but probably for only fifteen minutes. No further shots. If they wanted us dead, we'd be dead by now. So, we stood up.

Nothing.

The shots were fired either as a warning or, more likely, by a bored partisan simply messing with us. In this lawless time, he could have killed us just for the fun of it and no one would even ask why. We calmed the horses, climbed into the wagon, and made our way home in the twilight, leaving a dark and malevolent forest, now stripped forever of its magical status, behind us. We were both certain this partisan knew at whom he was shooting.

It was probably meant for me. Whether warning or lark, I finally realized how dangerous the situation in the village had become.

Sunday morning was sunny, and the blue sky was lightly painted with thin veils of cottony clouds. The air was refreshingly cool, as if Mother Nature herself was enjoying her own beauty. I went to church to thank God for giving me this last opportunity to visit with my family and friends. The service took place in the newly built if still unfinished church, which was full of villagers wearing their Sunday best. The women were draped in their finest headscarves and embroidered blouses. The men wore tall black leather boots that fit nicely with their gray felt riding britches. The men had furthermore trimmed their beards and combed their hair with generous dollops of brilliantine to hold it in place. Standing throughout the entire two-hour service, people shifted their weight from one foot to the other frequently, even though Father Hardibala and the choir sang the mass most beautifully.

Afterwards, people assembled in the churchyard exchanging rumors about the approaching battlefront. They were rooted to this soil and would remain here come what may. The German crop quota system had broken down by now, being unenforceable in the current military crisis, so the farmers were building up surpluses that, hidden, might keep them going whatever changes the Communists might impose—if they could keep the roving partisans at bay.

I had seen most of my family by this point, but I wanted to greet someone else. I might be in love with Larissa, but I wanted to see Slavka, too.

Looking around, I saw a group of girls and directed my steps towards them. But Mitonko was suddenly in my path, proposing to walk me home. I told him I wanted to speak to Slavka first. But he told me she did not want to speak to me. Perplexed, I walked back to the farm with him.

We sat in the orchard and Mitonko told me Slavka had become a leader among the local partisans, who were closely associated with the Ukrainian Insurgent Army (UPA)—dominated by Banderites. He warned me that ever since Uncle Miron had opposed welcoming the Germans to our village, members of the Kochan family were under suspicion of favoring Communism. If I were to be seen even speaking to Slavka, it might put her in mortal danger.

I sat there stunned. Yet worse was to come. Mitonko informed me that our cousin, Vlodko—Volodimir Levosiuk, the moody boy we once rode with on summer trips to the Variazanka River—was also an important figure in the organization. He had always been sullen and arrogant, but now he had become cruel and untrustworthy as well. Mitonko had had no contact with Vlodko for quite some time, but he was scared by our cousin's unpredictable actions.

Uncle Miron had told me the boys whom we taught in Chitalnya had tried to kill him. I had dismissed that as exaggeration. Now I believed it. Mitonko himself was in danger because of his Melnikite affiliations. Even more perturbing was the news that many villagers were farmers by day and partisans by night—partisans, moreover, who had committed atrocities, having taken part in the killing of innocent people, ethnic Poles who had refused to flee our neighborhood.

I was so upset by these developments I resolved to leave Tudorkovychi the next morning. It was dangerous to stay any longer and I was rather tired of sleeping in the company of cows that digested their food all night long. On Monday, July 10, I left the village that had once been my home but now was changed forever by war. The older people still preserved their dignity and friendliness; but those growing up in these violent and uncertain times had become something else altogether.

Petro was waiting to take me to the railroad station in Sokal as I said farewell to Didoon Semen and Babunya Marina. We gazed at one another and hoped to reunite after the war. We are stoic people; goodbyes are short.

Petro and I then stopped at the church to see my mother one last time as she came out from morning mass. She kissed me goodbye and told me to take care of myself and to grow up to be a good man. She knew I could not stay and live under Communism and that I could not take her with me, the turmoil of war being too unpredictable. I asked her to take care of my gymnasium pictures that I had decided to leave with her. Maybe I subconsciously hoped to convey the message I would come home, or bring her home, as soon as possible—a gesture that might help her endure the difficult and lonely years that lay ahead.

As we trotted down the road to Sokal, Petro and I did not feel like singing. The day was sunny, but we were somber. We knew the war would separate us for a very long time, if not forever. Much wheat had been harvested in the last four days. There was even an autumnal feeling in the air. Over empty fields fluffy seed pods were floating. I wanted desperately to slow this approaching separation from my family and friends and from the village in which I grew up.

I told Petro that neither my father, nor Yarko, nor I would ever become farmers. He should take the farm and consider it his own. At the railroad station in Sokal, we embraced one final time and I asked him to take good care of Semen and Marina. He was very moved and in spite of our pretending to be stoic and tough the tears finally came. I boarded the train realizing I might never see my mother, grandparents, or uncles again. I felt this chapter of my life was over. The simple village of kind and gentle farmers had all but vanished. Its culture and traditions would soon be ground to dust by a Communist heel.

Three days later, on Thursday, July 13, 1944, the Soviets launched their Ukrainian offensive along a 200-mile front.

CHAPTER TWELVE

Trains in the Night

I returned to Lviv without difficulty, and when I arrived at the Centrobank, my father was glad to see me. Now that the Soviet Army was about to move, he expected to receive very soon the required permission to transfer the bank to Yaroslav, a handsome old town on the San River about seventy miles west of the city. He told me Larissa had come to his office during my absence, inquiring about my whereabouts. She was worried that since I was now a medical student the partisans might kidnap me. My father promised to notify her as soon as he heard anything, but now he told me to go see her in person.

Larissa, too, was relieved to see I had returned safely. During my absence she had finalized her plans for escape, volunteering to help transfer military hospitals back to Germany. This would put her out of reach of the Communists, for the time being, and possibly within reach of me, since my family would be heading west, too, aiming for Germany and the protection of the Allied armies. With no fixed addresses, however, we would just have to find each other—somehow, sometime, in the clouded future.

Larissa seemed perplexed about her own family, though. Her mother and her stepfather were planning on leaving their four small children in Lviv in the care of their grandmother! Yet these four children, ages three to ten years—whom Larissa didn't know all that well—were too young to face the horrors of urban warfare and Soviet occupation. Her mother and stepfather were prime examples of people who, under enormous pressure, lose their ability to think clearly. How could they leave their own children behind? Once the Soviet pall had fallen over Lviv, retrieving loved ones would be a very difficult thing to do.

The next day I helped Larissa pack her belongings into two suitcases and a small backpack tied with blue and yellow ribbons. We took a streetcar to the place where she would meet her fellow hospital volunteers. While rocking on the cars, though, two Polish men jeered at those Ukrainian ribbons.

"So Ruthenians are leaving their city to us!" they taunted.

Fools! I wanted to scream. As if the Russians would treat them any better!

I was still angry when we arrived at the stop where the hospital volunteers were gathering. Larissa found the friend she would work alongside, and I was glad she would have a companion on her travels. That relieved me of much anxiety on her behalf. We promised to write to one another as soon as we knew our new addresses and to always to think about each other before going to sleep. We had no doubt we would meet somewhere in Germany and hoped our separation would not be a long one. If she was at all upset at our parting, however, she did not show it.

A day or so later, once the Russians had launched their offensive and the battle around Brody was underway, the Germans finally allowed my father to transfer the bank to Yaroslav. He had long ago given up the apartment on Tarnawsky Street and we were now sleeping in the bank upon comfortable couches. After Soviet planes started bombing sorties we slept in the bank's walk-in vault instead. We weren't afraid of the bombs in there.

The bank had two trucks and one car at its disposal. The problem was finding truck drivers willing to carry employees, their families, and the bank's money and documents that far when there were no assurances, they would have time to make the return trip to their own families before Lviv fell. And none of us passengers knew how to drive.

Eventually, a pair of drivers was found, but only after my father agreed to let them keep the trucks afterwards. We had no other choice. Since we did not find a driver for the car, we tied it to the back of one truck and an employee named Chapelsky agreed to steer it.

A day before the departure, I went to say goodbye to Ivan Volynetz, my friend from the Krakow Hospital. He was not home but I spoke to his father, the priest in a village close to Lviv. When he heard I was leaving he asked me to take Ivan along. He said two of his older sons were with the partisans and could soon be killed by either German or Soviet soldiers. He just wanted to save his third son. I replied to the kindly old man that I would first have to ask permission because we might not have room for Ivan. My father did agree to take Ivan with us and requested that he be at the bank by 6:00 a.m. the next morning. The old priest was very happy and promised to pray for a safe journey.

My father and I arose at 4:00 a.m. on July 16, 1944, and by candlelight we packed our belongings. Some of the bank workers had slept in the bank, too, and were already awake and boxing up money and documents. Those went on the trucks first, followed by the heavy suitcases, arranged to provide seating for the passengers.

Just before 6:00 a.m., my father ordered the bank cleaned. He said those who would occupy Lviv should see that we had employed conscientious workers. Ivan and I were skeptical about that; we argued that we should take some of the expensive furniture because the bank would only be looted of everything valuable. We also wanted to get his permission to cut the blue and red leather out of chairs in his office, leather, at that time, being unavailable at any price. But my father disagreed, and the beautiful leather remained behind—to cushion some Communist's derriere.

After all the rooms and corridors were cleaned, he locked the doors and gave the keys to the maintenance man, also giving him the unenviable task of keeping looters away.

As soon as we were underway, both Ivan and I soon knew the car attached to the first truck by a ten-foot chain wasn't going to work. Mr. Chapelsky could not control the automobile. Each time the truck slowed down and then sped up, there was a sharp jerk that neither the car nor the driver could long endure. Then again, the streets of Lviv were jammed because during the night the Red Army had broken the German line and many military vehicles packed with soldiers were speeding east to patch it up.

Soon we stopped at a small side street and decided to ditch the car and travel without it. Someone suggested taking the automobile's gasoline and completely filling the tanks of the trucks. It seemed like a good idea, but as we began to transfer the fuel a fire started beneath the first vehicle. Perhaps gas was spilled on a still glowing cigarette. Panic-stricken people began pulling their stuff out of the back. Then Ivan shouted to the driver to release the truck's brakes, then told everyone to push the vehicle away from the burning gasoline! We then abandoned the car and continued our journey westward with only the two trucks.

The road to Yaroslav was crowded with every wheeled conveyance imaginable. At one checkpoint, traffic was stopped, and vehicles were being examined by the German military police. They released the cars but kept the trucks, needed for ferrying soldiers to the front line. My father asked Mr. Chapelsky, who spoke fluent German, to present our orders for transferring the bank's assets to Yaroslav. He then urged him to explain that important documents and public moneys of the Generalgouvernement were also on the trucks.

The policemen paid no attention whatsoever to the papers or to Mr. Chapelsky. They ordered him to clear our trucks of people and their possessions. I suggested we try bribing them. At first my father pretended not to understand; but eventually he got out 10,000 marks of public money and asked who among us was willing to bribe the German military police—a deed that was both illegal and very dangerous. Mr. Chapelsky said that, since he had already spoken with one policeman, he would approach him again with money in hand. It was a heroic decision and we all realized the risk he was taking.

Mr. Chapelsky said goodbye to his young wife and walked over to the policeman. The officer promptly pocketed the proffered money and announced no further need for trucks—we should continue on our journey. That money stayed in that pocket. Its loss, considering the crumbling state of affairs, was insignificant.

We finally reached Yaroslav in the early evening. The bank employees there had a good dinner waiting for us. While we were at the table my father thanked Mr. Chapelsky for his act of bravery, the drivers of the trucks for bringing us safely to Yaroslav, and Ivan Volynetz for his quick thinking during the gasoline fire. He also wished a safe return trip to the truck drivers, standing there impatiently waiting to start back to Lviv.

After that busy and exciting day, my father departed to see his family in Krynica while Ivan and I took a train from Yaroslav to Krakow to resume work in the General Hospital—or to flee, each day being its own adventure now. It was Monday, July 17, the day the Red Army crossed the River Buh and Tudorkovychi was lost forever—what was left of it, because later I learned my cousin Vlodko and his band of partisans had torched most of the village, starting with his own family's house.

There was also another battle raging nearby—a colossal one.

The Brody Cauldron, it was called, such was the ferocity of the fighting as it surged back and forth over dozens of square miles around the little town of Brody northeast of Lviv. The jarring concussion of artillery fire, the piercing scream of Katyusha rockets, the relentless grind and clank of approaching Russian T34 tanks, the roar of Soviet torpedo bombers, and everything burning—houses, buildings, barns, human flesh. Because one panzer army had pulled out of line, the Red Army finally encircled half a million German soldiers. It only had to tighten the coils and after two weeks of fighting in July 1944 its prey shuddered violently to death.

In the very midst of all that fury the Divizia Halichina had stood its ground. Of its 13,000 men, however, only 3,500 would escape the anonymity of the mass grave.

A few days later, just after the Soviets had taken Lviv, Ivan and I saw some of those survivors. They had reached Krakow and were filing into the Ukrainian Kitchen to be fed. They sagged in their dirty, dilapidated uniforms and gazed around them with those infamous thousand-yard stares. I was the gentlest of inquisitors, and they told me that, here and there, a few small units of the Divizia, even a dozen here or an individual there, had broken through the encirclement. These guys had reached Lviv and were entrained for Krakow to recuperate and redeploy. Others were rumored to have headed for the Carpathians, where bands of friendly partisans might take them in. That's about all they knew.

I had my sources—my father's friends—in the Ukrainian Relief Committee, from whom I soon found out more information. For one thing, German officers were commending the Divizia for heroic performance throughout the battle. By holding their ground, they allowed other units to escape the pocket, and apparently were only overwhelmed by sheer numbers.

I also learned that Dmytro Paliiv, who helped to form the Divizia, had been killed in the Cauldron. I had seen him only a few weeks earlier, when he visited my father in Lviv. On that occasion, Captain Paliiv knew that shortly the Divizia would be sent to the front and, dressed in the uniform of a Waffen SS officer, he came to say, "Do Pobachennya." As always, he had looked very impressive. His eyes were still as blue as I remembered them from boyhood, from the night I stayed with his family before he took me on the streetcar to meet the train for the boy scout camp. He had been a Sich Rifleman during the First World War and remained a great hero to many Ukrainians. As the three of us stood in the bank, he said goodbye to my father and then shook my hand. I then asked him to watch over my friend, Bohdan Yourchuk. He promised he would do so, if possible.

He had kept that promise. Before the battle, he had ordered Bohdan away from the front line to help better organize the supply of horses and train more soldiers for the Divizia. While whatever remained of Paliiv now rotted away in the blasted earth around Brody, Bohdan still lived, and I was grateful for that.

Meanwhile, it was time to move.

Lviv had barely fallen to the Red Army when Soviet-allied partisans cut railroad and telephone communications between Krakow and Krynica. Now that the Russian steamroller was heading toward Krakow, a nervous Ivan Volynetz was advocating that we move west without delay. I was concerned about my family in Krynica, but now I was unable to establish contact with them. Most other Ukrainian refugees were heading across the Carpathians to Slovakia. The Ukrainian Relief Committee would provide trains to assist them. The office workers there told me the next train would be leaving in a few days.

Ivan was right, it was time we packed our belongings and moved on. We managed to pile them all into four suitcases, though I had a problem with a heavy overcoat that belonged to my father. It was a handsome and very warm coat; but however tightly we rolled it, the coat was still bigger than two of my suitcases. I decided to leave it in the apartment—a decision I'd later regret.

Still no news from Krynica, but it was time to leave Krakow for Slovakia. So, I left a note for my father in the apartment telling him of our plans, such as they were. We cleaned our rooms and loaded our belongings onto a two-wheeled cart provided by Alosha, a friend of Ivan's. Alosha decided to come with us, so early in the morning we rolled the heavy cart to a secondary railroad station, where we would wait for the evacuation train.

We found many people already there, camping and waiting for the train—any train. Among them was a medical student named Mikhaylo Huk, his wife and infant child plus his mother-in-law. They had been waiting two days for the train. We just stacked our suitcases next to theirs and made ourselves comfortable on the hard earth. At noon, an automobile arrived from the Ukrainian Relief Committee, bringing drinking water, several loaves of bread, some butter, and some cheese. The officers assured us the Slovakia-bound train would come the next night. They did not know exactly where in Slovakia our journey would end, but they promised to bring us more food and some milk for Mikhaylo's baby.

That afternoon, however, a train with fifteen boxcars rolled in and we began to climb onto the high platforms. To facilitate loading, some people stayed on the ground and handed the bags to those in the boxcars. The cars were relatively clean and there was enough space to make beds on the floor. We younger people stayed together, dividing our car by hanging bedspreads, women in the front and men in the back. And then we sat there. Before evening, however, two automobiles from the Relief Committee arrived with food and drinks. This time we received some kovbasa, cheese, butter, honey, and many loaves of tasty bread. They even brought hot coffee, milk, soap, and toilet paper. Unfortunately, there were no lavatories and we had to wait until darkness to relieve our swollen bladders and intestines.

We were asleep when the train jerked and started its journey. When we awoke, we were already traversing the Carpathian Mountains. We did not know when we crossed the actual border between the Generalgouvernement and Slovakia but the first place our train stopped was a Slovak town called Zilina. We opened the sliding door and were surprised by the cool fresh air. Zilina was situated in a valley encircled by mountains. Here an officer of the Relief Organization distributed some food for breakfast. Some of the travelers made small fires on the ground between two bricks and boiled water for coffee. This coffee was made of chicory, roasted rye grains, and roots of various flowering plants.

While we were eating our breakfast, another train rolled into the station. It was similar to ours and was filled with refugees from Warsaw. Even though it was morning, it was like trains in the night, one passing another, anonymous, each full of refugees fleeing one fearful life and hoping for another and better one somewhere, who knew where?

Scanning the people crowding the doors of the boxcars making up that train, however, I noticed a pair of shapely legs dangling over the side. I *knew* those legs—and when my gaze snapped to her blue eyes, Tatiana Sawycka was as surprised to see me as I was delighted to see her.

Soon we had piled out of the cars and were beaming at each other, Ivan and I on one side, Tatiana and her sister Natalia on the other, delighted at this chance encounter in the heart of the Carpathians in the midst of the worst war in history. Just as coincidental, the girls and their mother, Adela Sawycka, were traveling on a train organized by the Greek-Orthodox Bishop Mstyslav, whose daughter, Tamara, had been one of my other girlfriends in Cholm.

We all sat on the grass, close to our trains, and caught up on each other's lives. Their train was traveling to the capital of Slovakia, Bratislava. Ours was heading we knew not where, but we promised the girls we would find them in Bratislava and buy each one a big dish of ice cream. They laughed, because there was an ice cream shop in the Zilina station but we had no money. Since our trains stayed parked in Zilina until evening, we had time enough to talk of many things. But Tatiana never mentioned my unanswered letters nor our failure to meet in Cholm or Lviv, and neither did I. She was, however, more friendly and thoughtful than she had been in the past.

I wanted to spend more time with her but that night each of our trains rolled its own different way. Trains in the night. We did not control their directions, their destinations, or even our own futures.

In the morning our train arrived in the pretty city of Trencin. The town was bursting with greenery and colorful flowers. Here we would stay until the Slovakian Government decided what to do with us. We piled into the backs of several trucks and they transported us and our belongings to a nearby school encircled by an apple orchard. Several classrooms would serve as living quarters and the town would provide a daily dinner of meaty soup and bread.

Some religious organizations snooped around, asking why we had abandoned our homes. Their representatives could not understand why we would flee from our Slavic "brothers," the Soviet Communists, who were defeating the ruthless German Nazis. These annoying people did not understand that for those of us who simply want freedom there wasn't much difference between the extremes of Nazism and Communism. Obviously, these Slovaks were sympathizing with the Russians because of a common Slavic bond. Some of them even tried convincing us to return to Ukraine and ask forgiveness for our sins. They said Communism was a humane and forgiving system and surely it would be better for us to live among our own people than to seek our fortunes in foreign lands. I should have replied that our Slavic brethren to the east had deliberately starved millions of my fellow Ukrainians to death. But I didn't.

Whatever the Slovaks' ideas about Communism, the soup we received each day was surprisingly good, spiced with paprika on the surface and rich with meat and vegetables.

After settling down in one of the rooms Ivan, Alosha, and I investigated our new surroundings. We found we were living close to the right bank of the Vah River, a deep and swiftly flowing stream. Its water was clean and cold and held many huge boulders. There were also some hidden beaches beneath cave-like overhangs where we could shelter from the chilly winds that blew each morning from the craggy mountains.

We spent most of our first week on the banks of this river. Alosha, however, was happier with several prostitutes he improbably met on the nearby footpath. He was frequently gone for hours. He was very secretive, and we never knew where he got his money. The only thing we really knew about him was that he was good at swearing in Russian. At swearing, he was perfect; he used language so juicy any Russian would be put to shame. Hence his Russian nickname— "Alosha"— and we never learned his real one. There were some refugees from the Soviet Union in our group and listening to Alosha—well, they were dumfounded. They thought he must have underworld contacts in the Communist world.

Alosha dressed in a semi-military outfit and wore a pair of Polish officer's boots, shining them frequently with a soft brush and his own spit. He had a crush on the older Maika sister, but he was prepared to make any willing female happy.

Eating only once daily and swimming in the strong current of the Vah River trimmed off our fat and built up our muscles. But we needed more calories. And that meant we had to find work to earn some money to buy decent food to supplement our daily meal. First, we applied for work in a tobacco company, but they did not want us because, according to the bureaucrat interviewing us, we were students and hence not used to hard work. On the way home from that disappointment, we asked for work at a construction company that was building offices for the Slovakian government. To our surprise, we got the jobs. Our task was to supply bricklayers with cement and bricks, the heaviest work on the site. We were told we would be paid in good Slovakian crones, enough to buy tasty food, loads of ice cream, and maybe even some clothing.

We started the next morning and to the surprise of our Slovakian coworkers we did quite well. Actually, they were somewhat disappointed because they thought that by noon we would quit, and they would all have a good laugh. We were tired after a few hours of work, but we had no desire to quit. On the contrary, we were thinking about improving the process. We found a new way to deliver bricks to the second and third stories of the building: Instead of pushing a wheelbarrow heavy with bricks to the upper floors, we decided to use a long, wooden board balanced like a teeter-totter as our principal tool. We placed a brick on one end and jumped on the other. This threw the brick up to another worker who caught it in mid-flight. Eventually, we were so good and dexterous at this that people stood on the street and admired our skills.

We worked hard and earned good pay for our efforts. When we received our first paycheck, we even invited our coworkers to an ice cream shop. We told them our dream after coming to Slovakia was to buy large portions of ice cream and to eat it very slowly. We wanted them to share our dream. They still did not understand our fear of Communism, but they were now convinced we were not criminals and did not perform any dirty work for the Germans. Actually, they liked us because we were not afraid of hard work and were similar to them in many ways. We labored on this building site for several weeks and saved enough money to do other, more interesting things.

For one thing, our friend Mikhalo Huk was eager to finish his medical training and persuaded us to accompany him to Bratislava and apply to the medical school there. It seemed like a good idea, and we went to the railroad station to find out how much tickets cost. They were quite expensive, so we asked the attendant if there were any lower fares for refugees who wanted to be students at the University. He laughed and started to make some telephone calls. A few minutes later, this helpful official told us that, due to our special circumstances, his superiors would sell tickets to us for a twenty-five percent discount. We bought the tickets and the next day the three of us—Ivan, Huk, and I—boarded a train to go to the medical school in Bratislava.

Bratislava, the capital of Slovakia, was located on the left bank of the Danube River, close to the border of Austria and not far from Vienna. It was a city resembling a large village with several churches and some fancy stores. Upon our arrival we made an appointment to see the Rector of the University for the next day and afterwards we looked for a place to spend the night.

We found a third-rate hotel with a room for two people, and we convinced the owner to rent it to the three of us for the cost of two. Someone had to sleep on the floor and a lottery decided this man should be Ivan. The room was relatively clean, though the shower and lavatory were shared by everyone sleeping on our floor. The next morning, we put on clean shirts, dressed neatly in our best suits, and polished our shoes. We drank some hot water and crunched on some dry biscuits.

We felt very good about our visit to the University. We met the Rector and told him about our desire to continue our education at the Slovenska Univerzity Bratislave. He was very impressed that three refugees wanted to study despite the war coming closer with each passing day. He immediately ordered his secretaries to issue each of us a "Potvrdenie" certificate. Mine stated that Ivan Kochan expressed a desire to be accepted at the Lekarska Fakulta Bratislava and my application was strongly recommended for approval by the Ministerstvo Skolstva. This happened on September 6, 1944, and we were all pleased with this result.

Afterwards, walking the streets of Bratislava, we met some Ukrainians who told us there was a Ukrainian Committee in town, and we should go there and ask for help. From its director, I discovered my father and his family had also moved to Slovakia and were living nearby. Since the director knew my father and had some matters to discuss with him, he volunteered to drive me over so we could be reunited. Soon enough, I was shaking Volodimir Kochan's hand and hugging Pani Lyda, my brother Roman, Lyda's mother, and Lyda's sister with her two daughters. They were all happy to see me, too, and asked me to stay with them. I did agree eventually I might do that; but first I had to go back to Trencin, collect all my belongings, and say goodbye to my friends.

Back in Bratislava, Ivan, Huk, and I also sought out the Ukrainian community living in exile there. Not a day had passed, in this Slovakian idyll, this welcome break from the war, that I didn't think of Larissa, wondering where she now was and hoping to be reunited soon. But I must admit I often thought of Tatiana, as well; and since Bishop Mstyslav lived in Bratislava, I hoped she and her family were somewhere near him.

I found them without any difficulty and learned Tatiana and her mother were working in a thread factory. Their family occupied one room in a big building that the city government had given to Ukrainian refugees. After my friends and I knocked on their door Tatiana and Natalia came out into the hall to greet us. And there we stayed. No invitation to come into their room. Our entire visit was spent in the corridor. I was very hungry and hoped we might be fed by Tatiana's mother. But my hopes were dashed when the mother called the girls in for supper and pointedly did not invite us. I got the feeling her mother wanted someone more suitable for her very smart and beautiful daughter than a poor medical student.

By nightfall, we were back in Trencin. Since I was not in a particular hurry to rejoin my family in its sleepy Slovakian village I stayed for a few days. I had become friends with several Slovakian boys, and we spent time down by the river. They were teaching Ivan and me to swim in the dangerous cascades where the angry water seethed and foamed. One afternoon, however, when Ivan and I were visiting our previous coworkers, there was a tragic accident. A Ukrainian boy who did not know those treacherous waters jumped into its cascades and was drowned. His body was found about an hour later. We began organizing a choir to sing at his funeral. After about three hours of practice, we were ready to sing the funeral mass. But fate had different plans for us.

The war had returned to our lives.

CHAPTER THIRTEEN

Dust and Ashes

There is a favorite Ukrainian proverb: "A man can be shooting but God directs the bullet." The men doing the shooting this time were Slovakian partisans, who on August 29 had launched the Slovakian Uprising, which by early September had spread so far and wide across the countryside that the Germans, massing in force along the borders, needed to clear us refugees out of the way so they could retaliate. Instead of going to the boy's funeral, we boarded a train that took us to Bratislava, where our train was attached to another one and we all learned that we were going to Austria.

Ivan, Huk, and I wanted to stay in Bratislava, and we showed our Medical School acceptance documents to the German officials. They only laughed and said we would get a better education in Austria. There was something suspicious about that laugh and I told Ivan nothing good would result from this forceful transfer to Austria and we should leave the train. Having a family with him, Huk had to remain, but Ivan and I could disappear. Alosha agreed with me but Ivan, let us say, was slow to make quick decisions.

Suddenly the train was encircled by German soldiers, and nobody was allowed to dismount. The sliding door of each boxcar was shut and locked, and we pulled out of the station. Ivan seemed satisfied we were underway for Austria, but I did not like it. I preferred to be free and decided to escape at the first opportunity.

Because of heavy military traffic on the rails between Bratislava and Vienna, our train moved very slowly. Through a small window in the boxcar, we saw that we crossed the brown, not blue, Danube River. After crossing the bridge, however, we observed our train changed direction and was traveling north instead of west to Vienna. We found this to be worrisome. It was early evening when the train stopped, and we saw through our window a flood-lit enclosure with many wooden barracks. Barbed wire encircled this entire compound, broken by only a single gate, and that was guarded by German soldiers who checked the papers of all who entered or left.

This looked very much like a concentration camp. I felt sure we were in a dangerous situation.

The doors slid open, and voices ordered everyone to get out and to move toward the gate. As we climbed down, I managed to read the name of the camp: "Strasshof." Then we were ordered back onto the cars. There were too many of us to register and place in barracks before nightfall. This sowed chaos and confusion among such a large group of people. Looking all around for some avenue of escape, I saw at my feet a broken wooden dowel that looked similar in size to the sliding iron bar used to lock the doors of the boxcar. Hiding the dowel, I slipped around to the opposite side of the train. Alosha followed me and Ivan stayed with our suitcases.

There were no guards on the far side. Only a large field with scattered hay bales. We turned to the sliding door on the field side of our boxcar, I climbed onto Alosha's shoulders, pulled the iron bar out from the lock, and inserted my broken wooden dowel in its place. Now, we would be able to open the door from the inside at a suitable time to attempt an escape. It would soon be completely dark, and no one would notice the dowel.

We then returned to help Huk with the luggage. After we were back aboard and the doors were locked, we placed most of our possessions in two suitcases and gave them to Huk for safekeeping. With the rest we made three small bundles to take with us.

And then we waited—while I grew feverish. My throat was scratchy and painful. In my youth I had frequent tonsillitis, usually accompanied by a high fever. It usually cleared after three or four days of bed rest and profound sweating. Now I just had to disregard it, and in the dead dark of night we slid the door open, glad the broken dowel made no noise hitting the ground. No soldiers. So we carefully slid to the ground and one by one made our way to the first hay bale in the field. Then we tiptoed from hay bale to hay bale, further and further from the train and Camp Strasshof. When we reached the border of the field my strength gave out and I had to rest. But Alosha and Ivan supported me with their arms, and we continued our escape. After two hours, we reached a small Austrian village and urgently needed a place to hide. We had to get out of the empty streets of the village for fear of police patrols, especially so close to a concentration camp.

My clothes were soaked with sweat, and I was very weak and could hardly stand on my rubbery legs. Close to a streetlight, we saw a nice, small house with a neat garden in front. I felt this was the place to ask for help. We went to its entrance and lightly knocked on the door. We waited for several minutes and finally the door was opened slightly by a man who asked us what we wanted. I noticed that behind the old man was a woman hiding from our sight. They were scared and so were we. In broken German I told the man we had escaped from the train that brought us to Strasshof and we needed a place to spend the night. I told him I had an infection of my tonsils and a high fever. I asked the man to hide us for one night and the next day we would go away.

The old man and his wife invited us inside. They did not want anyone to see them talking to us. Once the door was closed the woman finally emerged from behind her husband and told us they had two sons fighting on the Eastern Front and that she prayed to God every day for their safe return. By helping us, maybe someone would help them. We knew they could be punished for hiding us, or even sent to a camp, so they had to be very careful.

They gave us warm tea and sent us to the woodshed at the back of the house to spend the night. They gave me an aspirin and a blanket because I was shivering and needed to keep warm. The lamplight had been minimal, so we hardly saw their faces. We went to the shed, sat on a pile of chopped wood, kept close to each other for warmth, and tried to sleep. Because of the cold and our hunger, we were awake most of the night. By morning, I was less feverish. Despite our discomfort, we felt satisfied with our achievement: We had managed to escape from German imprisonment. We had found a safe place to hide during the night and we exulted in the feeling of freedom.

Our landlord knocked and asked us what we intended to do. He and his wife decided they could not take us into the house, and we could not stay in the shed for long because their neighbors might see us and report our presence to the police. We assured him we would only stay a short time. As soon as I felt better, we planned to find work in Vienna. Nevertheless, the man was obviously scared and therefore Ivan and Alosha decided to go to Vienna that very day. They asked the landlord to buy them train tickets and since he wanted to facilitate our departure he did so immediately. My friends asked the lady to keep me warm, give me aspirin, and force me to drink a lot of tea. In an hour, Ivan and Alosha were off for Vienna. The hospitable lady invited me into the house, put me to bed, and took good care of her patient. I was feverish, slept much, and remembered very little.

On the third day, Ivan and Alosha came back and happily announced they had found jobs for each of us. We would be working in an ambulance service, the Rettungsdienst, located on Radetzky Strasse 1, in the very center of Vienna.

Everybody was happy. The next day my temperature was normal, so we thanked our landlords for their help and sincerely hoped their sons would return safely home. At the railroad station, nobody paid any attention to us. We bought tickets with the money Ivan and Alosha received as advance on their pay, boarded the train, and traveled the eighteen miles to Vienna as free men.

We noticed the Austrians at this time were not particularly scared or nervous about the outcome of the war. Perhaps they put their trust in new "wonder weapons." Or maybe they relied on their traditional cosmopolitanism; their tendency, dating back to Habsburg days, was to live more amicably than their cousins to the north with heterogeneous and polyglot peoples, Czechs, Slovaks, Poles, Hungarians, Slovenes, Croats, Ukrainians, and Jews. Yes, many Austrians were Nazis; but when I arrived in Vienna that fervor seemed to have subsided. Their cosmopolitanism might indeed see them through whatever challenges the oncoming war might bring.

Vienna was certainly a city close to the heart of many Ukrainians. Before the First World War, many Ukrainians from Halichina considered the relatively democratic Austro-Hungarian Empire their country and Emperor Franz Joseph their monarch. Many young Ukrainians studied in Vienna; one of them wrote the famous and popular song, "Vienna, Vienna nur du allein." Ukrainians even elected representatives to the Austrian Parliament. Empress Maria Theresa built many public buildings in Ukraine, especially in Lviv. Among them was the railroad station with the motto above its entry: "Leopolis Semper Fidelis" or "Lviv Always Faithful."

The Viennese ambulance service was the oldest medical organization in Europe. A century earlier it transported sick people to hospital by horse-drawn wagons. When I became a Rettungsman in 1944, the Rettungsdienst had three separate stations in Vienna, each one outfitted with five to eight motorized ambulances, all equipped with two beds. Ivan, Alosha, and I went to work in the main station on Radetzky Strasse, close to Stephansdom and the world-famous amusement park called the Prater.

We wore handsome navy-blue uniforms with the emblems of Aesculapius on both sides of a high collar. Our working day lasted for twenty-four hours, then we had twenty-four hours free. Day or night, three teams of people were at the station on-call for service. Each team consisted of a driver, two sanitary men, and a physician. The aim of the team was to bring the sick or injured person to the proper hospital as quickly as possible. Alosha disliked all this regimentation and after a few days, he terminated his employment without permission, and we did not see him again.

While at work, we were fed mostly soup with some meat in it but usually it was turnips. Turnips did not agree with me. They stimulated anaerobic bacteria in my intestines, which produced large quantities of poisonously smelly gas. This gas extended my abdomen and disturbed me and the people around me. Naturally my coworker riding alongside opened all the windows for fresh air. Unfortunately, there was nothing else to eat and my digestive problem caused me much discomfort during work. Eventually I got used to turnips and to other strange dishes put before us during our workdays. When not at work, however, Ivan and I would go to restaurants and eat tasty, well-prepared meals. Austrians liked to eat well and there were some very good restaurants in Vienna even during the last days of the war.

The work was exciting. Sometimes we were called to the woods of Prater to pick up people who were injured during a duel or by gangsters. Other times we received calls for help from the very rich houses in which I saw beautiful furniture and ornamental gardens, but we also went to bordellos and observed the scum of this big city. The citizens of Vienna respected the workers of Rettungsdienst and frequently we received generous tips, which we divided at the end of the workday. We also received generous pay and I accumulated many German marks in my suitcase. Ivan and I led a simple life—one large, rented room served as an apartment for both of us—and we did not have many opportunities to spend the money.

Some of it, I admit, went for expensive cigarettes that I smoked too frequently. Ivan did not smoke and drank alcohol only on special occasions. In smoking and drinking, Mykola Zerebecky in Cholm and Bohdan Yourchuk in Lviv were much more entertaining than Ivan. They both enjoyed good cigarettes and strong alcohol and we had much more fun than I had with Ivan Volynetz in Vienna.

One Sunday in late September, after we were settled down in the Rettungsstelle, as our quarters were called, I went to the old Austro-Hungarian era Ukrainian church standing near the Stephansdom. After mass, while standing outside on the porch, I saw two people I was very happy to encounter.

One was my father. And the other was Larissa.

We celebrated this wonderful occasion by eating lunch in a nice restaurant. My father, after the Slovakian Uprising broke out, had left the little village near Bratislava and moved his family to Melk, the small town with the famous abbey perched above the Danube about forty miles west of Vienna. There he rented a big house that comfortably accommodated the families of Pani Lyda and her sister Yarukha. He went there on weekends, working the other days in a refugee office in Vienna, where he kept a small apartment. His job was helping Ukrainians to establish themselves and organize their lives. This weekend he had remained in the city rather than going to Melk, helping with another tidal wave of refugees fleeing the Red Army.

Larissa had indeed gone to Germany and then followed the refugee trail through Slovakia to Vienna, where she had encountered my father, and they both set out looking for me, since I was not on the rolls of the Strasshof Refugee Camp. I told them about my escape from the gates of Strasshof, then described the work of the Rettungsdienst. Larissa was now working in one of the city's military hospitals.

After lunch, she and I went to a small park, found an empty bench, and gazed deep into one another's eyes. We were very happy to find each other again, despite the chaos of war and the mass movement of millions of refugees. Since the park was nearly deserted, we had ample opportunities to embrace and kiss.

Larissa lived in one room of a large house in Grinzing, the grape-growing suburb of Vienna. I went out there with her that afternoon, meeting her landlady, an older woman who was also a French teacher. She told me how much she enjoyed having Larissa in her home. She even volunteered to help me to improve my French, but I insisted on paying her five marks for each hour of instruction. At that time, my father thought we all might end our wanderings in France.

Grinzing had as many fine restaurants as vineyards, and wine drinking was very popular there. Larissa and I went to one of them, and I regaled her with tales of drunken patients I had picked up in the ambulance. There were no worse patients anywhere; they vomited in the vehicle and behaved obnoxiously. If an intoxicated patient was not seriously hurt, I usually dropped them at the nearest police station.

At one restaurant, however, we could not get meaty dishes because we did not have enough food stamps. I had enough money; but in Austria, as in Germany, there was no black market and money did not help if one did not have food stamps. After a meager supper and several glasses of good wine, I escorted Larissa to her apartment and took a streetcar safely back to the Rettungstelle. It had been one very lucky day.

The autumn of 1944 was sunny and dry. In the middle of October, several squadrons of American heavy bombers flew high over Vienna, probably raiding the refineries around Budapest. The bombers began flying daily and we had a good show standing outside the Rettungsstelle and observing the exploding shells of anti-aircraft flak around the planes. The anti-aircraft never seemed to reach the bombers that were flying, and I couldn't understand why such a well-defended city as Vienna, second only to Berlin as the leading city of the Reich, did not have better anti-aircraft crews.

Eventually, however, the Germans adjusted their aim and the Americans started paying a price for flying this route. It cost them two or three planes each day, yet it now took a long time before the planes changed course. For us on the ground, it was a pretty sight. The bombers were silver against a blue sky and their formation resembled that of storks or cranes flying to Africa. At the same time, one could see black puffs of exploding shells around the planes, courtesy of the Viennese anti-aircraft defense system. The sight of a hundred or more bombers flying against the background of a brilliant blue sky, not to mention their earth-shaking roar, was so impressive that even now, seventy years later, I can imagine them in the blue sky of California and tremble hearing their earth-shaking thunder.

In early November, the Americans started to bomb Vienna itself. The wailing sirens warned people of the approaching enemy planes, and everybody rushed to cellars or bomb shelters. Designated civilians with white armbands directed traffic to the shelters. Soon traffic was halted, the streets became empty, and there was a strange silence in this usually noisy city.

When the anti-aircraft alarm wailed the Rettungsstelle, like everything else in town, shut down. If I were on duty at such a time, I'd be sent to Stephansdom and directed to the underground passages some thirty feet below the surface of the street. These passages dated back to 1529 and the Siege of Vienna by the Ottoman Empire. The walls of the tunnels were solid rock, but they were lined with benches and the passages were illuminated with electric light. On both sides of the passages were rooms recently hollowed out of the rock and housing telephones, large maps, radio communications, and similar military equipment. The doors to those rooms were usually closed but occasionally I could peek inside and spy the generals at work defending the city. One time, however, they noticed me and asked me to leave. They were polite because I was dressed in the Rettungsstelle uniform, which always garnered respect.

Sitting in those tunnels, one could hardly hear the bombardment taking place in the streets above. We could soon determine how far away the bombs were falling, though, by watching the electric lights. The closer to the cathedral the explosions, the dimmer the lamps flickered. One time the lights all went out. This was the time a bomb fell on the Rettungsstelle building and hit our apartment. The blast destroyed the structure and all our belongings.

I lost most of the things I had brought from home, including my embroidered shirts and memorabilia from my mother and Tudorkovychi. Fortunately, I had all my documents with me and hoped I would recover the things I had given to Huk for safekeeping. We spent much of our free time looking for our lost possessions. We moved bricks and lumber from the rubble, but never found anything resembling our belongings. The bomb ignited fires in stores that were directly beneath our apartment. Everything was destroyed. A beautiful and noble city was being gradually reduced, building by building, to dust and ashes.

One day the warning wailed when I was on my way to the new apartment we received after the destruction of the previous one. The streetcar I was riding stopped and I had no other choice but to go into an unknown shelter that did not impress me as being solid and reliable. Many people were crowded inside but I found a place to sit close to some German soldiers who were coming home from the Western Front for a visit. Watching the light of the electric bulbs flicker and dim suggested that the bombing was creeping closer to this shelter.

Closer and closer came the explosions and I grew all the more fearful our shelter was directly in the flight path. Would the bombs fall to each side of the shelter or directly into the building beneath which I was cowering? There was a terrible crash, all the lights went off, and the air was filled with acrid smoke. I could not move and found that I was now lying under the bench on which I had been sitting before the blast. How I got under the bench I'll never know. The bomb did hit the building dead-on, but the explosion did not seal off the shelter's exit. After this close call people were relieved, greeting one another with the giddy, adrenaline-fueled high of the survivor. The soldiers told me they preferred the front line rather than this city shelter because if one is not killed outright here, one could be buried alive—and that might be much more unpleasant than instantaneous death.

Near our new apartment Ivan and I discovered a small cemetery located on a hill from which we could see most of Vienna. During our duty-free days, we liked to go to the cemetery and enjoy its tranquil beauty and the charming neighborhood surrounding it. We were sorry Alosha was not with us. But he just never liked regimentation or dealing with old and sick people. I think the work in the Rettungsstelle interfered with his other activities, whatever they were. Although strange in his behavior, he was a good and interesting companion and we even got used to his juicy language. We paid little attention to what came out of his mouth during his bouts of uncontrolled swearing.

After my terrifying experience with the American bomb, Ivan and I decided to avoid the common shelters and during bombardments to hide in the peaceful cemetery on the hill. From there, we could observe the war up close and eye-level—a unique perspective indeed.

We observed planes lowering their altitude and dropping their deadly loads over designated parts of the city. These explosions collapsed buildings, cratered streets and avenues, and generated shock waves hitting us with considerable force even at ten or more kilometers away. We also saw planes hit by anti-aircraft shells. Some of them tumbled aimlessly, exploding with much force among the buildings. Others tried to avoid the burning city and crashed in the surrounding woods. There were no German planes in the air—by that time, Goering, head of the Luftwaffe, probably had no planes to spare, the remaining ones being lost on the Eastern Front.

After perhaps three hours of continuous bombardment, the planes would leave the burning city and the sirens would announce it was safe for people to return to the streets and offices. It was astonishing how quickly those streets were repaired. Restaurants and retail businesses reopened and tables returned to sidewalk cafes. It took about two hours and the city then resumed to semi-normal life.

After a bombardment, however, we employees of the Rettungstelle were kept very busy. Many injured people obviously needed to get to the hospital. Matters worsened considerably when in December the Americans started using delay-action bombs that did not immediately explode upon contact. Instead, they exploded some designated period of time later. Nothing was so harrowing or disruptive to rescue or salvage teams. These "time-bombs" were intended to paralyze life in the city.

Such devices were very dangerous for the Rettungsmen. On one journey we nearly ran over one of them lying in a small crater a few feet from our ambulance. On another occasion a time-bomb exploded behind the window of a room from which I had just removed a patient. The room was destroyed. Soviet POWs cleared many a time-bomb before it could detonate because the Germans had promised them that for every removal of ten bombs to the city outskirts, they would let a POW go free.

Since Ivan and I lost everything when our apartment was destroyed, we were entitled to go to a warehouse and request needed items of clothing; one of these was down on Radetzky Street. We went there and received two used shirts and underwear but no suits we could wear when we wanted to change from our Rettungsstelle uniforms into civilian clothing. Though this was of little help, I did admire the efficiency of the organization that facilitated life in a city of a few million people in spite of the ruthless daily bombardments.

Eventually, many streets were closed because the rubble had become impassable, amounting to mountains of cement and twisted metal wires. In one case our ambulance had difficulty reaching someone in the cellar of a destroyed house. In such places the Rettungsman had to carry a patient for quite some distance through the debris to even reach the vehicle. It was especially bad for sick people. The hospitals were so overcrowded with patients that the admission of new ones was sometimes impossible. After three months of bombardments, not only were all the rooms full but also all the corridors in the hospitals were filled with beds—each bed holding at least one patient.

One day while working amid all this fury and destruction, I had a premonition. While taking patients to a hospital, I had a feeling Yarko was nearby and that I might see him. I scanned the faces of soldiers I drove past and although I didn't spot my brother the feeling persisted. Sure enough, that same day, Yarko showed up at my father's office in Hietzing Platz.

Although he was wearing a handsome uniform, he had one very big problem on his hands. He had deserted after exposure to combat on the Eastern Front made him realize the folly of enlisting with the Nazis. Just where he deserted, how he had managed to outsmart the German military police patrolling the roads, even how he acquired a pistol that was not standard issue to new recruits—I didn't want to know.

Yet if caught he faced the death penalty. The bodies of deserters could be seen hanging from telephone poles lining the roads. We first needed to get Yarko out of uniform and into civilian clothes, which meant some of the used stuff I could obtain. With Yarko newly outfitted, he and I snuck out that night to one of the bridges spanning the Danube Canal. We had packed his uniform and that pistol into a military duffel, and we promptly dropped it into those waters, hoping it would quickly sink out of sight. It didn't—the bag was impregnated with water-repellant substances. We could do nothing but walk quickly away.

Then we had to get him new papers. That's where my father's wealth of connections paid off. We put him on the train to Linz, a major town on the rail line west of Melk, where my father's friend Dmytro Kuzyk had a construction business. He agreed to employ Yarko and provide him with a certificate to that effect. This was an important step in the re-establishment of his legal status.

I've often wondered about that premonition, how it was I foresaw Yarko's presence in Vienna and his dire need for assistance. It seems humans have a sixth sense, stronger in some of us than in others, something not unlike Jung's notion of synchronicity. We suddenly know something, above and beyond the usual cognitive channels. This has happened not infrequently throughout my life.

When we weren't dodging American air raids, we were watching with increasing unease the oncoming tide of the Soviet armies. By October 1944 they had won back most of the Baltic Republics and, though paused on the banks of the Vistula to let the Germans take care of the Warsaw Uprising, they had taken most of Western Ukraine and only stopped east of Krakow because, once again, they had outrun their supply lines. They had stormed through Rumania and were already in eastern Hungary, forcing the Germans to withdraw from Greece and Yugoslavia. The approaching winter would slow their momentum, but only for a few months.

In the West, the Anglo-Americans had broken out of Normandy and were racing for the Rhine. Who would get to Austria first?

During my off hours I was usually with Larissa, but one weekend I took the train to Melk to see my father's family. The Americans never bothered bombing it because it had no industrial facilities, and its beautiful abbey was world famous. Nevertheless, the city had built strong shelters in the nearby hillsides and Pani Lyda, terrified of bombardments, was at one of every morning at 11:00 a.m., when it opened.

When I arrived, I was fed like a king. I was craving Ukrainian food and ate several helpings of borscht, many varenyky with skvarky and sour cream, and nalysnyky filled with sweet cottage cheese. It was good to relax with all these excellent dishes around and then play with Roman and his cousins Danusia and Radusia. Yarukha, Pani Lyda's sister, was still hopeful that her husband was alive in those forest hospitals in Volhynia. She didn't want to go much farther away from him. She was a very pretty and cheerful woman and I hoped for the best outcome for her and her daughters.

Another Sunday I had to go see Huk, who still had some of my things I left when escaping the train at the gate of Strasshof, which I now realized was not a concentration camp per se but rather was being used to house thousands of Ukrainian refugees. I was dressed in my uniform so I easily passed the entrance, the guards not even bothering to check me out. Huk and his family were glad to see me and returned the suitcase that they had kept for me.

I enjoyed my visit and was both surprised and delighted when Huk told me Tatiana and her family were also in the camp. Like me, they and every other Ukrainian in Slovakia had been taken here after the Uprising broke out. Bishop Mstyslav had been released because of his prominence, but most of the others were stuck here, all of them suffering from bed bugs that infested the barracks. Huk told me Tatiana's father was an officer in the Divizya Halichina and he, too, was trying to get them out.

Two weeks later I learned Tatiana and her family had been let out and were now also living in Vienna.

Tatiana wasn't hard to find. One day I invited her to supper in a very fancy restaurant called "Emperial," located next to the Votivkirche, and in my eyes once the prettiest of all churches in Vienna. Even after bombing had destroyed its stained-glass windows and caused extensive damage elsewhere, its twin steeples were still standing.

At the restaurant we had a nice meal, but when walking out she stopped, and then approached a tall, handsome, bald man in a SS uniform who was sitting alone at a table.

He was her father. Petro Sawycky stood up, genuinely happy to see his daughter, and after she introduced me, he invited us to sit and join him. He was very courteous, and apart from a clipped mustache he had not a hair on his head. Tatiana later explained he had lost all his hair after a bout with scarlet fever as a teenager. He was a naturalist, she told me, with a doctorate from the University of Prague, and had taught in Warsaw's agricultural institute, the Major School of Rural Economy. A staunch Ukrainian patriot, he had served in the First World War and had volunteered for the Divizia Halichina in this one, believing it would become the nucleus of the future armed forces of an independent Ukraine.

After saying goodbye to him, Tatiana and I strolled through the rubble-heaped streets. We walked in companionable silence, both of us reflecting on our parents' broken marriages. Beneath us all was dust and ashes; above us the gleaming white steeples of the Votivkirche punctured the sky, tracing paths that stars might follow.

CHAPTER FOURTEEN

The Cossack's Gift

Christmas in refugee-crowded Vienna was a glum affair. It was cold, and the Americans and British, we had heard, had been stopped in the Ardennes of Belgium during the famous Battle of the Bulge. The Russians had encircled Budapest and would soon be at the gates of this city. The German Reich was contracting in upon itself. There would soon be no place to hide.

Ivan, Larissa, and I had decided to make a break for it anyway. Our remaining questions were how? And when?

We celebrated Christmas Day with our fellow employees. They asked me to invite Larissa and the music was provided by an old Austrian who played the zither. The kitchen served fairly good food and we ended the evening by singing carols. Larissa, Ivan, and I sang two Ukrainian ones, and everyone chimed in for that loveliest of hymns, "Stille Nacht, Heilige Nacht."

Leaving work without permission was punishable by death so we couldn't just walk away. We just had to keep our eyes open to any possibility of escape. The Red Army was already on the move. It finally took what was left of Warsaw on January 17, 1945, and beautiful Krakow fell two days later. By February they were on the banks of the Oder. Berlin lay only fifty miles away.

The Germans were getting desperate. Old men were being mustered into service as the "Volkssturm," all folk and no storm when you are fifty or sixty years old. Other civilians were building anti-tank ditches out-side of Vienna. In the second week of February the besieged garrison in Budapest tried to break out—and was annihilated. That city fell. Vienna, after Berlin the second city of the Reich, would be next.

At the Rettungsstelle we were even busier than before. Daily bombardments only increased the number of people needing our help. Despite the time-bombs scattered over the city and the streets closed by debris, we managed to get most patients to the hospital.

By March despair and desperation were increasingly evident in every face. One group of desperate people, however, we Rettungsmen did not like helping, or even collecting. These were high-ranking Nazis who, terrified of falling into Soviet hands, opted for suicide instead. Generals usually shot themselves in restaurant bathrooms after a good supper and much drinking. We disliked dealing with them because it was messy work. The floor was usually covered with blood and excrement that had seeped out from their trousers, so it was very slippery. We usually pronounced them dead and left them where we found them. Party officials were more inclined to jump from high buildings and at least this did not make such a mess. I remember one party member, however, who jumped into an elevator shaft and was impaled by the metal scrollwork that embellished the decorative elevator gate. His ribs were all entangled with the bronze flower petals, and we were called to remove him. We never took dead people into the ambulance and scolded the caller for wasting our time when there were hundreds of injured people waiting for our services.

But woe betides the would-be suicide who somehow managed to survive the attempt. They then had the temerity to demand we take them to a hospital! That made us quite angry. Children and oldsters were being sent to the front to fight the Soviet Army and these pigs drank themselves nearly unconscious, mangled their suicide, and then demanded to have priority!

Most desperate people took to their heels. The roads leading west from Vienna were packed with them, carrying their belongings by hand or pulling them on small wagons they had prepared for such an eventuality. Without any such conveyance, it would be difficult for Larissa, Ivan, and me to leave Vienna on the roads. Nor could we as a trio travel by rail because at this time ordinary civilians were not allowed to take up valuable space on trains needed for the transport of soldiers and equipment. But to allow ourselves to get caught in the chaos of an impending invasion was unthinkable, too. Then Larissa developed a urinary tract infection, and at a time when there were no antibiotics, she was not well enough to travel. Every day we discussed how best to escape from our difficult situation in this disintegrating city.

One day toward the end of March, while sitting on the remnants of our apartment and contemplating our fate, Ivan and I saw a colorfully garbed figure entering the building in which the Vlasov Army was headquartered. A curved and shining scabbard could be seen swinging beneath his red-lined black mantle or cape. On his head he wore a Cossack hat, made from the black fleece of a new-born lamb, called a "krimka," a name derived from Crimean sheep. He strode in knee-high black leather riding boots as he mounted the steps into the building.

His was a memorable passage when seen against the background of ruin and destruction all around us. Then, in a flash, we both knew how to legitimately leave work and escape from Vienna in style. We would join the Vlasov Army.

Vlasov's Army was named for a promising Soviet general who had been captured near Leningrad and once in German hands had promptly turned his coat. He seems to have been genuinely anti-Bolshevik, but it took several years to convince Hitler that he could raise a division, even a corps, of anti-Bolshevik Russian troops from the ranks of POWs alone. His only stipulation was that the troops would only be used against the Red Army. In these desperate days, it was now being pressed into service.

We expected volunteering for military service would have precedence over working in Rettungsstelle. We also suspected that after enlisting we would be sent to a training camp somewhere—somewhere far away from the imminent battlefront. That was our gamble: We would be *sent* there, but we had no intention of *arriving* there.

The next day we marched up the steps into the headquarters building. Since Ivan had lived in Lviv after its 1939 annexation under the Nazi-Soviet Pact, he knew the Russian language better than I did. He would do the speaking and I would restrict myself only to the necessary "da" and "nyet." We entered a large entry hall with a big desk in the center and behind the desk sat a huge man, dressed in a similarly exotic uniform. He had a long Cossack mustache that hung down to his chest. His shiny scalp was cleanly shaved. And he paid us not the slightest bit of attention.

After finishing his paperwork, he finally looked up and asked us in Russian with a tired but still vibrant voice what we wanted? Ivan told him we wanted to volunteer for the Vlasov Army. The man was so surprised that for a moment he did not know what to say. All kinds of thoughts appeared to pass over his face, the predominant one being, "Who in their right mind would volunteer to join an army that was losing the war?" His piercing gaze took us in, a tall youth with blond curly hair; a short one with dark hair and a rakish-looking eyepatch. Finally, his eyes brightened when he thought he knew the answer.

He asked us some questions and when we told him we were Ukrainians, he knew his guess was correct. He knew no Ukrainian man would willingly join a Russian Army. He suspected we had to leave our work in Vienna and joining the Vlasov Army was the only way to do it without risking arrest or worse. It seemed to me that he smiled under his mustache. Playing the game to the end, he asked how many of us there were, and I replied before Ivan could open his mouth, that there were four of us.

When he finished preparing the military documents, he said having four strong Ukrainian boys would strengthen the Army, but first they had to learn how to fight. Therefore, he was sending us to a training camp in the Austrian Alps. He then gave us the papers stating our status, our destination, and a request that all authorities should help us in our travels. We thanked him and everyone knew that there were thoughts left unsaid, but we understood one another. He was saving two Ukrainian boys from probable death. Although we were of different nationalities, hatred of Communism had united us. He knew that if we were to survive, we would remember him and his benevolent act. He also knew he would probably die soon, but wanted to give us a chance to survive and continue the fight against an ideology that had ruined so many lives.

He also knew that Vlasov's Army was already posted on the Oder River in Germany, where it would have to fight in the upcoming Battle of Berlin. Vlasov's Army had no training camps in the Austrian Alps. But the Cossacks did. The Cossack Corps had fought in Russia alongside the

Germans, and when the German tide finally ebbed many of the Kuban Cossacks retreated west across the steppes with their women and children and horses. They were now quartered in the Drau River Valley on the Italian border south of Salzburg. Its cavalry was fighting Communist partisans in Slovenia. Its uniform closely resembled that of Vlasov's Army. And like the Galician Division it, too, was fighting alongside the Germans not to promote Nazism but rather to defeat Communism. Like Ukrainians, the Cossacks sought an independence not afforded to them in Russia.

So, our savior might have been a Cossack and not a Russian. His great-grandfather might even have ridden in the Zaporizhian Host. How appropriate would that be, as Ukrainians have no tighter bonds with any other people.

The men in the Rettungsstelle were sorry to hear we were leaving but agreed that joining the army was more important. Since we had little clothing, they told us to take our Rettungsstelle uniforms with us. They would prove a godsend.

I felt terribly guilty leaving a still-ailing Larissa. But she thought she could get out when the military hospital evacuated its patients and nurses. I gave her most of my money and told her to buy as much food as possible because if she were still here when the Red Army did arrive there would be shortages and hunger. In a time of so much death and loss that we became insensitive to it, neither of us could know whether we would live, die, or even see one another again. I promised her after the war I *would* find her. I was heading toward Salzburg, that's all I knew now. Salzburg might be the first place for us to look for each other.

Before my departure she made a delicious supper for the three of us. We drank wine and wished each other the strength to survive the war. I stayed with Larissa that night and the next morning we said our sad and poignant goodbyes, hoping it ensured we would meet again.

Then I left to pack my things and that same day, Ivan and I left Vienna by train to Salzburg, first stage on our way to the "training camp."

While still at the railroad station, we went into the soldiers' cafeteria and received a daily ration of food, cigarettes, and schnapps enough for four soldiers. While clattering west, we slaked our hunger and thirst. Because of frequent bomb alerts and overloaded railroad traffic, it took us two days to get to Salzburg, generally a half-day train ride. The first night we passed Melk and I thought of my father. Close to Linz the track was destroyed, and we had to walk several kilometers to the station. Once there, I decided to check in on Yarko and see what his plans were. I found him in the construction company barrack living with several other boys who also worked for Dmytro Kuzyk.

It turned out he'd rather travel with us—but I thought it was much safer for him to stay hidden in the outskirts of Linz. What identification documents he had wouldn't pass muster with the military police stalking the trains. What's more, since Ivan and I weren't going to the "training camp" and were hoping instead to wait out the war somewhere in western Austria, it wouldn't be good for him to be caught with us. His desertion from the Luftwaffe was a far more serious matter.

We pushed on to Salzburg, where Allied bombing had been equally severe. After a day poking around the refugee-crowded town we decided to seek a more remote haven. Here was the moment of decision. According to our papers, we were now to go south through the mountains to the "training camp" near Italy. Instead, we decided to go west through more mountains to Innsbruck, in part because the Soviets had now launched their attack on Vienna and Innsbruck was that much closer to the Swiss border.

That otherwise short journey also took all day. Fortunately, our uniforms ensured only a cursory glance at our papers. We arrived at night in a town so blasted by aerial attacks—four railroad lines converged here—it was surprising there was any train service still running. We then faced another problem. The military police were in the station closely examining the papers of all the arrivals. People whose travel documents were as sketchy as ours now were –well, we could see others like us avoiding the station and filing down side streets. We followed.

After walking several kilometers, we arrived at the entrance to a huge system of tunnels, the air raid shelters slave labor had carved into the surrounding mountains a year or so earlier. These tunnels were as wide as streets and branched off into many large rooms that had electric lights and benches. In one empty room, Ivan and I made beds by putting two benches together and using our baggage as pillows.

Soon we were asleep, but not for long. Around 2:00 a.m. a pair of prostitutes woke us up. Their solicitation was simple: Come with us and sleep much more comfortably in their soft beds. We declined the invitation but offered them a late supper of bread, kovbasa, and some horilka. They accepted and we had a good time entertaining them. Before departing, however, they told us that at 5:00 a.m. all the exits would be blocked by the military police. It would be better for us to leave now if we did not possess good documents.

That was only an hour or two away; but Ivan, despite my protest, as usual hesitated. He stubbornly refused to leave the shelter, claiming the whores had been lying in a last-ditch attempt to seduce us and get our money. I told him if he wanted to survive this war, he was going to have to trust somebody at some point. I was quite upset with him and decided to part ways with him the next day. He was too stubborn and the thought of my father trying to flee Melk with five women and no help was beginning to trouble me. Before going back to sleep I decided I would go back to Linz, pick up Yarko, and then go to Melk and help my father transfer the family to a safer place.

At 5:00 a.m., I snapped awake: Loud noises reverberated outside our room. People mustering in the corridor said the military police had ordered everyone to leave the underground passages. They had closed the exits and would check documents before releasing anyone.

Ivan pretended not to hear this commotion and waited for me to wake him up. I kicked his bench and told him the time had come to pay for our play. Policemen were already impatiently waiting for us. Ivan got up, collected his belongings, and without saying a word went out. I followed him.

There were hundreds of people pushing and trying to get to the exit as quickly as possible. They reminded me of wild animals that suddenly found themselves trapped in a cage. We were in no hurry to meet the police but inevitably it was our turn. Ivan showed them his military order for our travel to the "training camp." The policeman saw immediately that we were not going in the right direction. Innsbruck was not on the way to our proper destination. The policeman pointed to the room behind him—the room in which he was collecting people with questionable documents. We entered, wondering how we would get out of this one.

The policeman was working alone, checking documents while blocking the doorway to our room. I noticed that occasionally he would step out to reach for papers or speak to people. I motioned to Ivan to stay close and follow my every move. I was waiting for someone with questionable documents to panic and run. Then this happened! The policeman stepped away from the door to stop an escapee and, at that very moment, bags in hand, we stepped out of the room behind him and walked slowly toward the exit without looking backwards. I fully expected to hear shouting or even the firing of a pistol. But I heard nothing.

Our trick had worked. Or rather the chaotic situation had worked on our behalf. Too many people and too few policemen. At a safe distance from the shelters, I told Ivan I had decided to go back to Linz and Melk and help my father move the family westwards. He thought I was crazy, that Vienna had probably fallen, and even now the Soviet Army might be occupying Melk. He was not going to risk the gulag. We found an unoccupied bench in a nearby park, divided our food supply, shook hands, and each went his own way.

The Red Army was now fighting in the streets of Vienna. I prayed Larissa had escaped by now.

I still had my identification and my Rettungstelle uniform provided me with some security from the police and more respect from the Austrian people. So I strode directly into the Bahnhof at Innsbruck and bought a ticket to Linz. Only a fool, a brave man, or a medical orderly would be traveling east, into the maelstrom—so I quit worrying about papers and documents.

I arrived at Linz despite the train being attacked by two American planes. Fortunately, we stopped in a tunnel between Innsbruck and Salzburg and waited there until the planes were gone. In Linz I had to trudge out to the barrack where Yarko lived—only to find he was gone. His roommates told me he left a day or so earlier with a friend and the friend's family, but no one knew the destination. Yarko had only said that I should look for him through the Ukrainian Center in Munich.

Recent bombing had torn up the tracks to the east, so Yarko's friends invited me to stay in their barrack while repairs were made. In a nearby forest, they showed me some damaged planes left by the Luftwaffe and I spent one afternoon learning how to "operate" them. In the evening

I even went to a movie theater that was still open and spoke to several German girls while waiting in line for a ticket. They were obviously lonely because the German men were all away fighting. Brief encounters in the night that could never have a future. The war was always closing things off.

The next afternoon I finally found a train to Melk, even though I had to walk a long way in order to reach it. A moonless night wrapped all in darkness when I arrived—all except the eastern sky, which reflected the reddish hue of Vienna burning, for the battle in the city was now reaching its climax. Looking for my father's house, I followed some people who had a flashlight and were heading in the same direction. When they turned aside, I was in complete darkness. I had to light my way with matches, but I finally found it.

Although it was late, I knocked on the door. No answer. I began tapping on windows. Still no answer. Finally, a thin voice from inside asked me what I wanted? It was Yarukha, Pani Lyda's sister. I said I was Ivan and asked about my father. Letting me in, she told me that the previous morning he and his family had left for the railroad station to flee west. From what I knew about the few civilian trains still running I suspected they were still at the station and would be when the sun rose. She told me that she, her children, and her mother had decided not to travel any farther west.

I slept in my father's old room. Before doing so I peeked out from behind the blackout curtain and took one last look at that glowing surreal eastern sky. Vienna fell on April 14, 1945. This must have been the very same night.

I arose early the next morning, wished Yarukha luck in finding her husband, and set off for the station. At one point, I had to hide behind some bushes. What looked like prisoners from a nearby camp were walking up the road, several soldiers serving as escorts. My wandering around at this hour might look suspicious. I didn't want to take any more unnecessary chances.

In the dim half-light I could see, in the yard of the railroad station, three long trains composed of twenty to thirty cars each, a combination of passenger cars and cattle cars. The compartments and corridors of the passenger cars were obviously packed with civilians. So must be the

cattle cars, I reasoned. The railroad men told me that no train with civilians had left the station in the past twenty-four hours. This indicated to
me that my family must be in one of these three trains.

I gave the railroad men some cigarettes and vodka. As a result, they
became friendly and pointed out to me the train that would be the first
to travel west. They also promised to help me transfer my family to that
train if I were to find them. My Rettungstelle uniform was still working
its charm.

How was I to find my family? I did not want to go around the trains
shouting my father's name. Such a disturbance might attract railroad
police. Then I had an idea. I knew Pani Lyda would recognize a tune that
Yarko and I used to whistle. If I walked along the line of each train whistling that tune, she might recognize it, if she were not asleep. With no
other choice at hand, I started walking and whistling. After about fifteen
minutes of this, a voice from one of the cars sang out my name. It was
Pani Lyda! Not only did she recognize the tune; she had also recognized
the whistler—because I was never very good at whistling.

I called my railroad "friends" and not only did they transfer my
family—with their suitcases, bundles, and packages—to the first train
designated to leave the station; they also found an empty cattle car for
us, a relatively clean one, with enough room to walk around in. Later
that morning I found two more Ukrainian families, surnames Triska
and Korbutiak, and we transferred them to our car as well.

Hours passed, perhaps even another day or so. But finally, our train
started to roll. I was reminded of the German propaganda slogan, "Roder
sollen rollen für den Sieg," which meant, "Wheels of trains must roll for
victory," laughing at the grim irony now that we were heading west on
German wheels. West—but where in the west we did not know. We did
follow a roundabout route because we avoided the damaged tracks at
Linz. Westward we crept at an agonizingly slow pace. Mr. Korbutiak
had a map and after nightfall we stopped briefly in the border town of
Braunau, where Hitler was born, and then crossed the Inn River into
Bavaria. By early morning we had decided not to go as far as Munich,
another large target for bombers, and studying the map, preferred to get
off in a smaller town just up the track, one we had never heard of but just
jabbed at with our fingers, Vilsbiburg.

We arrived in Vilsbiburg toward the latter part of April 1945. It was early in the morning when we unloaded our suitcases and bundles and stepped onto the platform. The train departed and we sat on the bundles discussing what to do. The stationmaster finally emerged and asked us who we were? We said we were Ukrainian refugees fleeing the Communists. He apparently thought that was a sensible enough reply and suggested we see the Bürgermeister. It took a long time to find the house of Herr Bürgermeister; but when we did, he gave us the name of a local farmer in whose house there was an empty room that would accommodate us.

The farm was about three miles from town, so a municipal truck took us there. We just handed Miss Meiser, who administered the farm for her brother, the official papers prepared by the Bürgermeister requiring her to accommodate us in a large room with kitchen privileges. It was a spacious old farmhouse, and Miss Meiser duly showed us an empty room with four tall windows. Six people would have to live in it: Mr. and Mrs. Triska, distant relatives of Pani Lyda from Sokal; my father, Pani Lyda, Roman, and me.

We needed straw to make up beds, which Miss Meiser seemed reluctant to supply. But since she couldn't determine the importance of my uniform, she finally showed me some straw bundles but charged me ten marks for them. To make a bed from straw was not an easy job, especially on a cement floor with no frame to hold it in place. But at least it provided some insulation from the cold. It was still April, and the nights were occasionally frosty.

I requisitioned a table from the kitchen, placed it in a corner before two built-in wooden benches, and this became our dining area. Pani Lyda went to the kitchen and boiled water for tea. We ate stale bread and cookies we brought from Melk, drank hot tea, and thanked God for the roof over our heads. It had been a long journey. We had been on the move for at least forty-eight tense hours and now we finally had a place to sleep, if not comfortably at least peacefully.

Vilsbiburg was a place out of time, a handsome Bavarian town of about 5,000 people that showed no trace of war. It had one main street, paved with square cobblestones, and in the heart of town a sixteenth-century

Tower Gate opened onto a market square with an old Catholic Church. Since we weren't the first Ukrainian refugees to come here, we were happy to discover we could use that church for mass every Sunday at 11:00 a.m. Our fellow Ukrainians had even organized a choir, and many Roman Catholic Bavarians enjoyed listening to the melodies of our church songs.

The River Vils flowed through the town, a restaurant and several stores lining its banks. The road leading north to the Meiser farm eventually went to Landshut, a much bigger town. It took about an hour to go from the farm to Landshut and that road was lined on both sides with apple trees.

Miss Meiser and her sister administered the farm in the absence of their brother, who had been called to defend the Vaterland. They were uneducated women who spent weekdays working in the fields and weekends with their Hungarian men, enforced laborers sent to work in German farms and factories. No amount of screaming from the Misses Meisers could make them work any harder than they wanted to—because the sisters spent every Saturday night drinking with these handsome rogues and either making love to them or arguing with them. When they made "love," it was quiet in the house, and we could sleep. But when they fought, they banged doors and screamed curses. Those were sleepless nights.

The farm buildings were arranged in a square, the house in front, stables along the sides, and the barn in the back. In the middle of the square was a manure pile, and behind the barn stretched fields and a distant forest. It resembled the farmlands of home. But we knew we were in Western Europe because even the roads out here were paved with asphalt.

Yet without a radio or newspapers we lived in complete isolation. We had no idea what might be happening in the war. We saw no soldiers and no policemen. Friendly German neighbors who had a radio said that all they ever heard were lies issued by the failing government. The rumor mill was hard at work, though. One rumor had the Russians fighting in the streets of Berlin; another suggested they'd be in Salzburg soon and then would take Bavaria.

We didn't want to be "liberated" by the Soviets. We prayed the American Army reached us first. Speculations about our future filled our hungry days waiting for this war to end. If the Russians arrived here first, we were prepared to leave all our meager possessions behind and walk to the American lines. We had not given up so much, or come so far, to still fall beneath the ruthless rule of the Soviet Union.

Every day we looked hopefully to the north and fearfully to the east.

CHAPTER FIFTEEN

The Displaced Ones

The first soldiers came from the north; but when I initially glimpsed them through my binoculars the two military trucks were coming up the road from Vilsbiburg. It was a tense moment until I saw the stars painted on their sides where white and not red. Americans. I turned around and announced to everyone that the Americans had arrived!

But if they came as liberators, they acted like Russians.

Within an hour, American soldiers and their vehicles filled the yard. Our friend the Bürgermeister must have sent them here because it was the most spacious farm close to town. We were happy to have them; but despite declaring we were Ukrainian refugees and not Germans their commanding officer ordered us out of our room and to take our things with us. We placed our possessions in the basement and moved our bedding to the hay-covered loft in the stable above the cows. There was also enough room there for a newly arrived Polish woman with her two young daughters.

During the evening the American soldiers made a large fire in the middle of the yard and sang songs to the accompaniment of a guitar. I admired their nifty little jeeps and the speed and precision with which they drove them. They ate food mostly from cans and continuously smoked cigarettes or chewed gum. The chewing of gum was new to Europe; people occasionally chewed tobacco but only in the privacy of their homes. Public chewing was not a polite, socially acceptable activity.

Americans seemed a little different. They seemed careless about their armaments, for instance. They left guns on the ground while throwing a small ball and catching it with a large glove. This was baseball, identical to the game I played in Sokal that we called palanta. They also seemed sexually overcharged. I understand how young men coming off weeks or months of campaigning might look for a woman. But these guys were already asking about the availability of "fräulein" and were willing to pay with nylon stockings, chocolate, or cigarettes for their favors. Later there would be strict rules about "fraternization"—rules widely ignored and unenforceable with Americans. With some bitterness and irony the older German men said that what their soldiers were unable to accomplish on the battlefield, the German whores did in the beds of the bordellos.

Sadly, I had first-hand experience of this shortcoming. One night when the Americans were camped at the farm, I was awoken by the two daughters of the Polish woman also sleeping in our hayloft. They were asking me for protection. I assured them nothing bad would happen to them and asked why were they scared? Then cold steel pressed against my head. It was a gun.

I tried to grab it but my hand was stopped and someone whispered in English: "Keep quiet or I'll kill you."

I backed down. If the mother had cried or shouted, I would have called for help. But there were no signs of struggle. I'd stay with the girls to ensure they remained unmolested but felt there was little else I could do.

The next morning, I saw soldiers looking at the woman and smirking. It appeared that tales of recent performances had already made the rounds. I went to an officer and told him, in broken English, that some of his soldiers raped that woman and intimidated us into silence. He promised to investigate and punish the perpetrators.

Within an hour, without any shouting or commotion, the officer and his unit disappeared from the house and yard. They were probably scared I would speak about the rape to other Americans and opted to leave it all behind them.

Returning to our room with the three windows, we found the GIs had left it a pig sty. It was the first time in my life I had seen condoms and they were scattered all over the floor. It took us the whole afternoon to clean up their mess. I was upset to find that the soldiers had also rifled through our belongings in the basement and taken my binoculars, which

I had bought in Vienna with the money I earned in the Rettungsstelle.

All that commotion must have taken place on the last day in April or the first two days of May 1945. By then other rumors were reaching us: Hitler had shot himself; Berlin had fallen; and a week or so later, not rumor but fact: On May 8, 1945, Germany had surrendered. The war in Europe was over.

Wreckage stood where once had been the leading continent on the globe. Hardly a major city remained between Moscow and the Rhine that had not been at least partially destroyed. Vast areas were largely depopulated, for strewn across Western Europe, like sea-wrack piled high on a beach by a storm from the East, was what one journalist was calling "this new kind of debris of modern war, the displaced ones."

The official term was Displaced Person, or DP for short. There were around eleven million of us in May 1945—eight million in Germany alone, three-quarters of whom were the imported workers, some "volunteers," but mostly enforced laborers from Eastern Europe, like those Hungarian men who quickly disappeared. The roads were soon packed with them tramping homewards, the younger ones looting as they went, the only payback for years of wasted life. Then there were sizable numbers of prisoners of war and concentration camp survivors still in Germany. Those who could still walk soon dispersed to their homes as well. Outside of ex-Nazis and their collaborators on the run, the remaining refugees were all civilians who had fled the Red Army.

Of course, we didn't know such statistics at the time. Our first priority in May was to determine which of the rumored zones of occupation we were living in. If it was to be a Soviet sphere, we had to move. A second and closely related priority was to find Yarko and reunite the family. He had left word with me to check first in Munich. A third priority, for me, was my promise to find Larissa.

The first was solved quickly enough. We knew American forces had secured Wurttemberg, Bavaria, and nearby parts of Austria, including Salzburg, Innsbruck, and Linz. The British had swept through northern Italy, crossed the Brenner Pass, and occupied much of southern and alpine Austria. They were also in northwestern Germany. The Soviets had everything to the east, including Lviv, all of Ukraine, Poland, Berlin, and Vienna.

By the terms of the Yalta Agreement of February 1945, of which we then knew very little, we had indeed fallen into the American zone. When Austria was likewise partitioned, it, too, was divided along the lines the respective armies had reached.

We felt safe for the moment. Now to find Yarko. I had started on that quest before the U.S. soldiers had even left the farm. I had spied the Meiser sisters' bicycle and occasionally they allowed me to use it. With such a convenient vehicle, I went to visit other Ukrainian refugees who either lived in our pretty Bavarian town or on one of the farms surrounding it. I remember in particular a Mr. Sahan who had traveled with his family all the way from Ukraine to Vilsbiburg in a wagon pulled by two horses, through several countries, during wartime. What an accomplishment!

Bicycling to Munich to find Yarko would not be so ambitious, even if the roads were now full of military trucks and carts of refugees. It was our only viable mode of transport, so my father found a local young man who volunteered to bike with me to the city. His name was Roman, only a few years older than me, and he had a nice bicycle. I needed to find one for myself since the Meiser sisters, afraid the Americans would confiscate it, refused to lend me theirs. Or, they refused until my father persuaded them—with money.

We took off for Munich, about sixty miles to the southwest, about a week or so after the Americans had left. We departed early in the morning, when the road was nearly empty, the sun was rising, and the birds were singing. We passed small towns and beautiful landscapes showing no sign of war and destruction. But close to Dorfen, about halfway there, we were stopped by the American military police. It was 10:00 a.m. and the policemen had been sleeping in their station but must have decided it was time to wake up and do some work. Why not stop some traffic? In broken English we tried to explain we were not Germans but Ukrainians who were traveling to Munich to find missing family members. It seemed they did not hear us, because they ordered us to put our bicycles in a ditch near the road and then to sit down and wait. After this we were of no further interest to them. We sat and observed young men who wore their trousers so tight they showed every muscle of their well-fed bodies.

After an hour they drove away. We decided it was high time we continued our ride into Munich. We pulled our bicycles out of the ditch and a few miles down the road encountered another soldier. This one, however, was friendly and asked if we were hungry, pointing to a mess tent pitched in the field nearby. His company must have cooked too much breakfast, so we said yes and he invited us in.

There we were served the best food we had ever eaten. For the first time I enjoyed bacon, grapefruit, and peanut butter. There were so many bread choices and fruit jams we didn't wonder why Americans had such fatty bottoms. The black man who served us this excellent food was a revelation, too. We had never seen a Negro before. He in turn enjoyed our display of appreciation, especially since it was mostly in Ukrainian, as our poor English wasn't up to the task.

We thanked the friendly soldier for inviting us to share his food. In turn, he gave us two packages of American cigarettes—a boon for black market times—and said, "Yak sia mayesh"—which astonished us, because that is Ukrainian for "How are you?" He explained he was the son of Ukrainian immigrants who had settled in Pennsylvania after the First World War. He was proud he knew a few words in Ukrainian.

While riding away we wondered how a child of Ukrainian immigrants could not speak their language? Many years later, having lived in the United States, I no longer wonder!

We arrived in Munich in the early afternoon. The closer we came to the outskirts and then into the center of the city, the more destruction we saw. It was worst near the railroad station, most of the nearby houses totally destroyed and some streets impassable. Nearly half the population had fled the relentless bombing. But in general, Munich showed less destruction than Vienna.

Eventually we found our way to Dachauer Strasse, where we found the Ukrainian Refugee Office in full operation even though it was located in a partially destroyed house. The director reassured us that Bavaria would be in the American zone under an American administration. He also confirmed Yarko had indeed spoken with him before the end of the war and had given him both the name of the people with whom he moved from Linz and the name of the village where he could be found. Since that village was about a dozen miles from Munich and on our way back to Vilsbiburg, we decided to return that way and spend the night there.

It was evening when we arrived. Since we knew only the name of the Ukrainian family, we had some difficulty locating them. We needed the name of the German farmer in whose house they lived. Eventually we found a man that knew a refugee family with two boys, and he gave us detailed instructions on where to find them.

Yarko was delighted to see me because he was having difficulties living with his "adopted" family. So, after spending the night there, all three of us decided to say, "Do pobachennya" to the family and ride toward Vilsbiburg. That meant Yarko and I would share my bicycle, one of us either riding on the top tube of the frame, between handlebars and seat, or jogging behind. Sitting on the tube could be somewhat painful, but the road was smooth, and we managed to make good time.

We were home before sunset. Everyone was glad to see the family back together again and my father was happily reassured that we were indeed in the American Zone. In the short time he was with us, I introduced Yarko to the town, its surroundings, and to the Ukrainian connections I had made. We did not have much to eat, even though Pani Lyda was exchanging the last of her fancy dresses for food from neighboring farms. But she wanted to honor the return of the prodigal son, appropriately enough, with a feast.

So Pani Lyda made a deal with a German farmer that should have provided meat enough for our family for a month. She exchanged my father's chinchilla-lined winter coat for a sheep carcass, some bread, and some eggs. I borrowed a wagon from one of my new friends and with Yarko drove about five miles to pick it all up. Pani Lyda decided to preserve the meat by hanging it in the chimney of the kitchen to smoke. She marinated the carcass in a garlic sauce and we hooked it in place over the embers. Yarko and I went into town for another errand, hoping to return to a good dinner. A tired Pani Lyda became so absorbed in a good book that she completely forgot about the sheep.

When she finally checked it, the meat had so shriveled and charred in the heat that it was inedible. We never even saw what a charred sheep looked like. She was so mortified she buried the remnants in the ground. There was some shouting and much crying but mostly we laughed. It was such a bitter disappointment that all one could do *was* laugh—even when you had to go to bed hungry.

My father shouldn't have yelled at her. Pani Lyda was a good-natured, trusting person and I suspected the German housewives were taking advantage of her so that she always came up on short end of her barters. At least she was trying—my father would never have stooped to such matters; in reality, he wouldn't have even known how to barter. Yet that was the one ability needed to survive in the black-market world of immediate post-war Germany.

When a cash economy completely collapses, the underground black market becomes the main economic arena. You couldn't live without participating in it, and that meant you had to have something to trade. The most stable commodity was cigarettes, and desperation became such that people picked up cigarette butts off the sidewalks—cigarettes being filterless back then—in order to retrieve the minute bits of tobacco left in them. Pick up enough and you could make several handmade cigarettes for trade.

The Americans banned the black market, of course, but their MPs were too overwhelmed with other tasks, and the Occupation authorities had enough work clearing rubble from streets and railways and canals, with rebuilding an electrical grid and transportation networks, that they often turned a blind eye to it.

Furthermore, many U.S. soldiers were getting rich, for the PX and quartermaster depots were the principal source of exchangeable goods, like cigarettes. That's why, shortly after he came to live with us, Yarko found work up in Landshut helping in the kitchen that prepared food for American GIs. For compensation he was fed very well and received American cigarettes—as good as gold on the black market.

I was good at bartering and did so whenever possible but my principal task that summer was to learn as much English as fast as I could. We had decided France would not be a good fit for us and that our best chance for a viable future together was in North America. While trying to contact my father's brother, Uncle Harry, who had migrated to Canada before I was born, someone had to be the point person for talking to American MPs, officials, and immigration authorities; someone who could write letters and fill out interminable forms in English; someone who could make deals in the Anglo-Saxon vernacular. That person was to be me.

I spent upwards of five hours a day memorizing English words, using a battered German-English dictionary. English is a Germanic language, but I was surprised to find that many of its words have their roots in Latin, which I studied in high school. So a rudimentary vocabulary and grammar came quickly enough. Then I tried it out on American soldiers and discovered the challenge was not in the vocabulary but in the *pronunciation* of English. The Ukrainian language is phonetic; once one learns the sound of each of thirty-three letters there is no question about pronouncing words. In English I could not understand how one letter could have so many different sounds even in two similar or identical words. To speak English well, one has to learn the sound of every word and not merely the sound of letters. No wonder American children study the English language in elementary school, middle school, high school, and then in college and still they make errors in spelling and cannot write a well-structured sentence.

Whenever not studying English, I was chopping kindling for the kitchen stove or bicycling around the neighboring farms collecting what tidbits of news I could find. Soon my new English vocabulary contained one word I disliked very much: "Repatriation."

One of the greatest sins of the British and Americans at the Yalta Conference, outside of giving Stalin half of Europe, was agreeing with his demand that following the close of hostilities all war refugees should be repatriated, "regardless of their individual wishes," to their nations of citizenship as of 1939. That this edict would be forcefully applied was all too obvious when we heard, in the summer of 1945, about the fate of the Cossacks.

Bands of fiercely anti-Communist Cossacks, perhaps 30,000 to 50,000 in all, had come west with the retreating German Armies in 1943 and been settled in the sparsely populated mountain valleys of Axis Italy and Austria. In late May 1945, about half of them surrendered to the British in Lienz, Austria, a small town on the Italian border. Here the fierce warriors were paraded and feted and promised asylum in the West—given, in fact, the British "word of honor." But 1,500 to 2,000 of its leading officers were then trucked not west but east, to Judenburg, on the border of the Soviet Zone of Austria. With bayonet and club, they were then forced across the bridge over the Mur River and pushed into Russian hands. All day long, witnesses on the British side of the river heard machine-gun fire from the Russian side: The Soviets were executing the "traitors."

Similar rumors abounded. Some Cossacks reportedly killed themselves in the Lienz town square after being rounded up for repatriation. Tens of thousands of remaining Cossacks, including women and children, were trucked by the British to Graz, where they were turned over to the Soviets, to be killed or scattered throughout the Gulag Archipelago.

Was the Cossack, if Cossack he was, who signed our passes to freedom, among them?

This murky sequence of events would be endlessly debated for decades after the war, even in high government circles. But to any refugee who heard these rumors in the summer of 1945, only one word sprang to mind, which in my newly acquired English was "betrayal."

Such faraway events had a direct impact on us. Stalin wanted all Eastern Europeans—Russians, Ukrainians, Poles, Balts, Czechs, Hungarians, Rumanians, various Balkan peoples—back behind his front lines. He based his claim on two foundations. One was the huge losses, some twenty million people, the Soviet Union had suffered during the war. This had created a severe labor and agricultural shortage. The other was more insidious: He wanted them back in order to control any and all propaganda about Communism. And all Eastern European war refugees were all, down to each individual man and woman, anti-Communist.

Would the Allies betray millions of refugees from Eastern Europe to the unmerciful claims of the Communists? It looked frighteningly possible when for months on end Soviet teams were allowed access to refugee camps in Western Europe, hunting exiles to repatriate—or grabbing anybody they wanted, regardless of origin. Thus one of the biggest items in demand on the black market was "false papers," forged new identities.

By the beginning of July 1945, more than a million Soviet citizens had been returned to the Soviet Union, many of them against their wishes. How was this possible? The Soviet hunting squads had assistance from two well-intentioned but mistaken organizations, the Supreme Headquarters Allied Expeditionary Force (SHAEF) and the United Nations Relief and Rehabilitation Administration (UNRRA), created in 1943 as the first international organization designed to deal with refugee issues.

UNRRA provided food, lodging, and medical care to DPs and took care of administrative issues. SHAEF was in effect General Eisenhower's army, the Occupation force, the American soldiers and their military police. The trouble was the latter had orders to obey: Yalta and subsequent agreements allowed the Soviets to enter the UNRRA camps and forcibly take their citizens to the Soviet Union. The U.S. and Britain had agreed "Soviet citizens" meant people who had resided in the Soviet Union at the outbreak of war on September 1, 1939. The Russians had access to the name lists of everyone UNRRA or SHAEF had registered. They found the Slavic names and went after them, regardless of their true citizenship.

If someone refused to go, as most of them did, the American soldiers helped the Soviet agents load them forcefully onto the trucks taking them to the Soviet zone. If a refugee fought back, the Soviet NKVD or SMERSH officers would beat him, assisted by the American soldiers. It was not uncommon for women to lay themselves in the path of the trucks so as to prevent their departure. They were dragged away. We felt such actions were as much a betrayal as what the Cossacks faced.

The Soviets also exploited the fact many refugees had destroyed their IDs or waved false identification papers in officials' faces. They claimed all such people were war criminals or Nazi collaborators and hauled them away. Nor did the average GI or UNRRA employee understand the complex nationality puzzle that was Eastern Europe. This meant we Ukrainians in particular—who believed we were "occupied" by Poland but in Western eyes held Polish citizenship in 1939 and in Russian eyes were now Soviet citizens, thanks to wartime annexation—felt that we were in a double bind. Poland could claim the Kochans; the Soviets could now claim Pani Lyda from Sokal and Larissa Smola from Lviv—if they hadn't repatriated her already.

So, we lived in dread of one day seeing trucks stopping at the farm and military personnel climbing out, led by a figure in a trench coat and a cap emblazoned with a red star.

There was little we could do about it. In part to relieve our anxieties and in part to dispel boredom, Mr. Triska, my father, and I played chess. That soon brought its own level of stress, which started when my father lost several games to me. He did not like losing. I had had more recent practice at chess than he and more opportunity to match wits with very good players at school and in Slovakia. I was surprised at his being upset, thinking it should have pleased him to lose to his son. So, I quit playing, which upset him even more.

By the end of September 1945, SHAEF had helped deliver more than two million "Soviet citizens" from Germany, Austria, and Czechoslovakia to the darkening East. Then came a ray of hope emanating from President Harry S. Truman. "Give 'Em Hell" Harry, in office since April, had apparently had his fill of Stalin. In October he told General Eisenhower to quit assisting Soviet attempts at forced repatriation. That was a relief to both the soldiers, who hated having to do it, and to us.

That left about 1.2 million displaced persons in Germany and Austria who refused to return home. Nearly a quarter of them were Ukrainians from old Galicia. The rest were Poles and Balts with a smattering of Czechs, Russians, and Hungarians. UNRRA personnel, composed mostly of American military people and English speakers from Allied nations, now started moving all the refugees into Displaced Person Camps, organized by nationality, a big step to getting everyone some-place else to start their lives anew.

By the late autumn of 1945, the refugees around Vilsbiburg were or-dered by UNRRA officers to move into a DP camp established on the outskirts of town. Yarko and I went to examine the site. It was locat-ed two kilometers, a little over a mile, from the town square, close to a small river and bordered with a forest and some farms. The barracks had been built to house foreign farm workers during the war. They were rather dirty and needed some cleaning inside and out. But each barrack could house two families; each family would have a kitchen and two small rooms. There were ten barracks, enough for twenty families, all Ukrainians, all anti-Communist, and all planning to emigrate to the United States, Canada, Argentina, or Australia.

We then went to the UNRRA office on the town square to reserve a place for our family. We received an apartment in Barrack Number Two. It took us several days to clean the floors and paint the walls. Each family kitchen possessed a small wood-burning stove, so I spent many an autumn afternoon in the nearby forest cutting, splitting, and stacking birchwood for the coming winter—only to find that UNRRA teams with axes and saws would later take care of the wood supply. According to the number of family members, UNRRA also provided food staples from which the refugees cooked their meals.

It was snug but it was home. There were hundreds if not thousands of these UNRRA camps strewn across the landscape of south-central Germany and western Austria. They were found in old barracks, like ours; in old factories; in old scouting or summer camps; even in former concentration camps. Those camps found in big cities held many refugees and had common kitchens where hired cooks provided the meals. Others resembled small towns, with department-store style shops, barbers, cobblers, lawyers, even newspapers. All held, in the autumn of 1945, what were called the "last million" war refugees who refused to be repatriated, mostly Poles, Latvians, Lithuanians, Estonians, and Ukrainians, all of whom were here because they had fled Communism.

There were many young people in the camp and Yarko and I made some friends. The three Sochan brothers were our most frequent companions in the acquisition of firewood and the playing of volleyball. I remembered Oleh Sochan from the Academic Gymnasium in Lviv where he had played the violin during various school festivities. His playing had improved significantly since then, and we spent long hours singing Ukrainian songs to his accompaniment. Oleh, like me, was a medical student and we had many common interests.

In town we met a young Jew called Moshe who had a restaurant on the main square. We enjoyed going there to dance and drink beer. He hired Oleh and Vlodko Sochan to play dance music on Saturday nights. Oleh played the violin and Vlodko tried to play the drums. He also hired Dushku Nedilsky to play piano and wanted me to sing, but I didn't think I had a suitable voice and declined.

Moshe—or Moshko, as we called him—had been in a concentration camp until the end of the war. He was one of the few lucky ones. He did tell us about a time when he was led with twenty other prisoners to another camp by two German soldiers. Before they arrived, the two soldiers ordered the prisoners to lie down on the forest floor and cover their heads with their coats. Then the soldiers shot them in the base of the skull. Moshko found a depression in the ground for his head and put his hands under his coat in such a way as to imitate the shape of his head. The soldier shot him, but instead of losing his life, Moshko lost only the middle finger of his right hand.

Knowing that we might eventually immigrate to Canada, I thought I should learn to drive an automobile. When a driving school in Vilsbiburg finally opened its doors, I became a student. I passed the examination and received a driving "Ausweis" permitting me to drive a car in Germany.

For older people, life in the DP camp was edgy but somewhat boring. They finally were on fairly good rations but had no work and no communication with the outside world. Many people played chess and wrote letters to families in America asking for papers that would help them emigrate. Some became interested in politics and there was no end to the heated discussions between Banderites and Melnikites.

At the end of 1945, bus and railroad transportation between Landshut and Munich was partially repaired and I traveled there to enroll, if possible, in the Medical School of the University. That didn't take long. After bribing the registrar with a pack of American cigarettes, I was accepted. I still had to pass several examinations before being admitted to clinical courses and hospital training. I had to find better than makeshift accommodations.

Since the war destroyed so many apartment houses in Munich, a room was difficult to find. Then I learned that, as a refugee student, one could get housing by enrolling in the new International UNRRA University being established in the building of the old Deutsches Museum that stood like a ship on an island in the Isar River. So, I became a biology student there as well, and asked the administration to find an apartment for me in Munich.

I was directed to go to Balan Strasse 5, located about a mile or two southeast and just the other side of the Rosienplatz. There a family named Semmelman could provide me with a room in which I could live and study. The family consisted of a seventy-year-old "Opa," or grandfather, his forty-five-year-old daughter, and a sixteen-year-old granddaughter named Burgel. The four-story house belonged to Mr. Semmelman, but his family occupied only one apartment on the second floor consisting of a kitchen, three rooms, and a large balcony.

The Semmelmans were very pleased and enthusiastic to have a student living with them. I felt at home from the very first day. Mrs. Semmelman cared for me as if I were her son. Every morning before I arose, she had polished my shoes; and after I was dressed, she served me breakfast on the balcony from which, on a clear day, I could see the Alps. Each evening she made my bed that during the day was covered with ornamental pillows. Dinner and supper I ate in the public restaurant that occupied the ground floor of the building. Occasionally, on a major church feast, I went with the Semmelman family to the nearby Catholic Church.

The winter of 1946 was difficult for everyone in the shattered cities of Europe. In Germany there was no food and no wood or coal to cook it with anyway, nor was there fuel for domestic heating. My room was furnished with a bed, a large table, a grandfather clock, a piano, and a free-standing heater that was never used during my stay with the Semmelmans because there was never fuel to feed it. I was dreadfully cold and had difficulty studying, huddled as I was in a goose-down comforter. Some evenings, thankfully, the Semmelmans invited me to sit with them in the kitchen, the only room heated by a cook stove.

Each Thursday, Opa went down to the restaurant that was on the ground floor and drank beer, usually Löwenbräu, with his buddies until 3:00 a.m. After that, he did not sleep well because he had to run to the bathroom frequently on his wobbly legs. Before the war, the restaurant belonged to him, and then it served as a home base for the soccer team called Bavaria. When he sold the restaurant, it was with the provision that Bavaria would continue to have their headquarters there. While enjoying an occasional beer there, I met several Bavaria players and appreciated their open and gregarious nature.

Mr. Semmelman was an outgoing man who liked a good joke and teased his granddaughter, who reciprocated with the same zest. Burgel was a nice and pleasant girl with a good figure but a bad complexion. She played the piano well, though, her fingers floating over the keyboard and bringing to life the songs from Franz Lehar's operetta, "Immer nur Lachen," or in English, "Who Always Laughs." I eventually learned the whole operetta by heart.

The Semmelman family had little food but on occasion they invited me to share it with them. In return, I brought some UNRRA provisions from Vilsbiburg to share in return. Whenever I could I visited my family that winter, in part to enjoy the warmth of their small apartment in the DP camp. They heated their rooms with the birchwood I had cut and split the previous summer. The UNRRA camp was more festive than Munich, the young people preparing performances and organizing dance parties. I had a lively dancing partner named Darka who was from the Carpathian Mountains. Even my father's spirits had lifted. With the help of friends, he was now publishing a Ukrainian newspaper, "Na Chuzyni," or "In a Foreign Land." It was popular among our DPs because it expressed balanced opinions on topics like Ukrainian immigration, prospects in Germany, and the future of Ukrainians in various foreign countries.

What's more, he was elected a director of the Ukrainian Coordinating Committee in Munich and was communicating with Isaak Mazepa, the scion of the noble Ukrainian family I had been so enraptured with as a boy. This Mazepa had been the chief executive of the independent Ukrainian People's Republic of 1919-1920. He was now the Foreign Minister of the exiled government of the Ukrainian Democratic Republic, and the plans he and Volodimir Kochan were formulating would soon lead to the formation of Centralna Rada, the shadow parliament of the UDR. My father was back in his element.

There was good reason for this renewed burst of energy and optimism. In January and February 1946, the Third Committee of the new United Nations Assembly, meeting in London, stated—to thunderous Soviet denunciations—that "no refugees or displaced persons…shall be compelled to return to their countries of origin."

Except for a few isolated and clandestine incidents, forced repatriation had come to an end.

CHAPTER SIXTEEN

Only That and Nothing More

The year 1946 began and ended with no sign of Larissa. UNRRA had no record of her, at least as far as it could tell in ever-changing circumstances. Perhaps she didn't escape the Russian zone was my glum conclusion. Perhaps she had long ago been repatriated to a Lviv now held captive by the Soviet Union.

Otherwise, it was a year dominated by medical studies and freezing weather, the immediate post-war years in Europe bringing with them some of the coldest winters on record. The one ray of sunshine was an unexpected visit from my cousin Mitonko, who came with a friend from a DP camp outside Munich.

The last letter I had received from him was posted in Krakow after it fell to the Red Army. In it he had written that the Volhynian police had helped him escape from the Banderite partisans outside Tudorkovychi. He had then fallen into the hands of the Germans and was thrown into Auschwitz, the work camp part and not the infamous death camp section. Even so, he nearly died of starvation and was still terribly thin when he arrived in Munich. He brought me an Eisenhower jacket and a black French beret, which I enjoyed wearing for years.

Mitonko then moved to Munich and married a girl named Irena Dibko. To have my cousin living nearby was a great pleasure to me, not only because I enjoyed visiting them in their one-room apartment but also because he introduced me to the Melnikites headquartered in

Rosenheimer Platz, almost next door to the Semmelmans. These friends of Mitonko had established a kitchen to feed Ukrainians once a day. For a small payment, I ate my dinners there and met many of my fellow countrymen living in the city. Behind that building was a black market where you could buy items ranging from American cigarettes to gold coins.

Around Christmastime Mitonko asked me to accompany him on a visit to Salzburg to visit Bohdan Yourchuk. Of course, I agreed because I hadn't seen Bohdan since his visit to Krakow. As a soldier in the Divizia Halichina—which had renamed itself the Ukrainian National Army before surrendering in May 1945—he had been interned with his comrades in Rimini, Italy. The Russians wanted them, of course, but the Pope intervened on their behalf and they were classified not as "POWs" but rather as "surrendered enemy personnel." With the war over and the internees lightly guarded, Bohdan just walked away one night, crossed the Alps to Austria, and was now married and living in a DP camp in Salzburg.

We went by train to Freilassing, a small town on the border between Germany and Austria. Mitonko and three of his Melnikite friends didn't want to risk the American checkpoint on the bridge so we had to walk along the bank of the Saalach River until we could find a ford to wade across. At one place the current was simply too strong, so we had to plod another mile or so until we saw a small shack used by railroad workers. We knocked and the man answering said there was another ford a little further up. We found it and crossed into Austria without any further difficulty. We poured the water out of our boots and continued towards Salzburg.

On the edge of a forest, before crossing the paved road beyond which were empty snow-covered fields, Mitonko told us to lie down in the snow. He knew that every hour a patrol car passed, and that hour was now approaching. Sure enough, a jeep came up the road and its two American soldiers flashed a lamp into the woods flanking the road. I thought the railroad guy in the shack must have notified them. But the Americans didn't want to muddy their boots and they continued on their rounds. An hour later we reached the sleeping town of Salzburg.

We spent the remainder of that night in a DP camp barrack that served as a hangout for Melnikites. The following morning someone mentioned a lady from Warsaw lived in the adjoining apartment, and she had two very pretty daughters. That perked me up and after I tentatively knocked on the door Tatiana Sawycka opened it.

This was another coincidence in our wandering lives. She appeared as glad to see me as I was to see her. Yes, they had indeed escaped Vienna before the Red Army arrived. She was now working as a secretary to Averda Lerrigo, a high-ranking American lady in the International Refugee Organization. She was also attending the University of Salzburg and studying philosophy. She had even taken part in a seminar organized by the famous American anthropologist, Margaret Mead.

While I was there, I bowed to Adela, her mother, as unfriendly to me as ever; and met Tatiana's grandmother, Elizabetha Ginejko. I nodded affectionately to Natalia, her sister, whom everyone called Lala because as a child she had a mop of blonde hair but was now a beautiful brunette. I asked about Tatiana's father, but he was still interned with the Divizia in Rimini.

Since Tatiana had a well-placed job, her family was abundantly supplied with food and they could have invited me to dinner—but they did not. During the war it must have been very difficult to survive as a family of four women alone. I understood Adela's protectiveness but nonetheless I left their room rather disappointed and I did not see Tatiana again during the rest of my stay in Austria.

That afternoon I visited the other Ukrainian DP camp in Salzburg to see Bohdan.

He was very glad to see me, too. Soon we were sitting at the table with a bottle of Russian Vodka and a coil of kovbasa. When I asked him about his wife and where she was because I was anxious to meet her, he replied oh so casually that she was in Vienna with Larissa selling American cigarettes and nylon stockings on the black market.

I was thunderstruck. *Larissa?*

Oh, yes, she and Irma, Bohdan's wife, were great friends. They were an efficient team and making good money. He expected them tomorrow on the train.

I was both hurt and puzzled that she had not contacted me. Then, after a glass of vodka, I thought one reason for my visit may have been her desire to reunite us, even though that didn't make sense. It did make me feel better. So, Bohdan and I made the most of the one day we had to drink and speak about our lives during and after the war.

And we did drink and drink. Sometimes we laughed until our stomach muscles hurt and then we cried remembering friends who were killed in the fighting. Those were the painful days of our youth. At one point Bohdan asked me to hit him hard in the nose for the lousy things he did to me regarding the political and private life of my father. I did just that! I hit him hard and with much pleasure. I had been itching to hit him for a long time. Also, I told him his sympathy for the Banderite movement stunk. At that point he was probably so drunk he did not feel my punch at all. The blood was flowing from his nose and colored the vodka in his glass. He did not see the red color in his glass but said his drink tasted like blood. "You probably hit me," he said and we laughed and laughed and eventually fell asleep.

The next morning, we woke up with piercing headaches. I washed all over with ice-cold water and rubbed dry with a hand towel as I did when I lived with my father. Bohdan made compresses he placed on his swollen nose. He did not believe in my Spartan regimen and used cold water only on his aching face and head. We drank coffee while Bohdan complained that I hit him too hard and that we would have some explaining to do to Irma about his nose. Later we went to the barbershop to be shaved and spruced up enough to meet Irma and Larissa at the railroad station.

The train was late but finally arrived with much sizzling and puffing as if saying, oh what a long road to travel. All late trains were like that: The locomotives pretended this was the best they could have done and their hissing demonstrated they had accomplished an unusual task in arriving at all. Then we saw them, Irma and Larissa unloading suitcases filled with items they planned to sell in Salzburg for a profit. They must have been bribing the Russians, whose zone they had just traversed. Bribing somebody to get away with suitcases of black-market stuff. And then Larissa and I were embracing and we were oblivious to time and place. "It is good we found each other again," she kept repeating. We stayed that way for so long that Bohdan finally interrupted, saying, "Enough of that slobbering, get to work!" So, we grabbed the suitcases and carried them to his DP camp.

Bohdan had a full two rooms in his barrack, a luxury for a married couple in a DP camp. He must have had some influence with the Banderites in charge here. It also meant Larissa and I would have one room to ourselves throughout our stay. I thanked Bohdan for his hospitality, and I did prefer staying with him rather than with Mitonko and his longwinded friends in the Melnikite's DP Camp.

Irma and Bohdan were good hosts, and we all had a great time visiting together. She had been the fiancée of a friend in the Divizia who had been resettled in England. Many of my friends did not approve of Bohdan's marriage with the fiancée of his friend. But I thought if there had been true love between Irma and her boyfriend, she would not have married Bohdan.

After two days in Salzburg, Larissa and I took the train to visit her mother. They were not in a DP camp—one reason I couldn't find Larissa—but had settled instead in a mountain village not far from town. Her mother had not changed.

She was as unpleasant to me as she had been at our meetings in Lviv. Our three-day visit passed very quickly. Larissa and I took frequent walks and admired the beauty of the Austrian Alps while her mother was at work in a local hospital. As we had foreseen, her mother could never go back to Lviv and collect her children. They would have to live in the Soviet Union with their grandmother.

While speaking about our future on the return to Salzburg, I learned Larissa had an Austrian boyfriend—but she insisted he was a friend only and their relationship would remain on that level. She said she wanted to come to Munich and be with me.

We would soon be married, I thought.

Months passed before she could make the move. The main problem was the border crossing. Although the Americans occupied both sides of it, they were sticklers about papers, identifications, and proper documentation. Larissa's sketchy paperwork would not pass muster. Mitonko eventually solved the problem. He spoke to the Melnikite leaders, and they found a way to send Larissa on a train to Munich using connections they had developed with the American authorities.

It was nearly summer when she stepped off the train in the station. It was 1947, but she still saw a city in ruins, especially around the Bahnhof. I borrowed a small wagon to help her transport her baggage to the one-room apartment I found for her only a short distance from mine in the Semmelman's home.

A few days later, during my summer break, we took a bus to Vilsbiburg and spent about two weeks with my family. At the same time, Ivan Volynetz came over for a visit. Since we last parted ways on that bench in Innsbruck, he had gone even further west and now lived in the French Zone. The two rooms that accommodated my father, Pani Lyda, Yarko, Roman, and I were already filled to the brim without the addition of Larissa and Ivan. Fortunately, the second room had two bunkbeds for the four boys. Although cramped, we all had a good time. We often played volleyball with the Sochans in the courtyard of the camp or wandered in the forest looking for mushrooms and blackberries.

My father proposed that Larissa stay with the family in Vilsbiburg while I attended the university in Munich. Living in a DP camp could help her obtain a Displaced Person status and hence help from UNRRA and better documentation. Unfortunately, Larissa categorically rejected that offer. She said she wanted to stay with me. I tried to convince her the offer would help us. But I could not change her mind.

This was distressing to me. She and I had very little money, and if she was not registered with UNRRA as a Displaced Person she could not receive food stamps because she wasn't even a German citizen. Without the help of UNRRA and with no food stamps our lives would be very expensive. I had some money from selling American cigarettes. Since this was not enough to feed two people, I found some office work in a DP camp outside Munich registering people who arrived on their way to foreign countries. My work supervisor, Mr. Zanko, knew my father and tried to give me time at work to study for the medical examinations that I needed to pass to be admitted to the clinical courses. I eventually passed them but not without difficulty. The exams were oral and my knowledge of the German language was still too weak. I failed my first examination in Chemistry, but a few months later finally passed it.

Studying and working left little time for Larissa. She further complicated the situation by deciding to study Philosophy on the University's main campus. This required additional money to pay for her tuition and our main problem was still food. We did not have enough money to buy food on the black market and the food I received from UNRRA was not enough for two people. Biweekly I took the train to Landshut, where my family now lived after the Vilsbiburg camp shut down, to obtain my share of food. Sometimes there was not much left for me to take back to Munich. Larissa still refused to register in any DP camp; she was evasive as to why but once suggested that belonging to a camp was beneath her dignity. Her attitude was disappointing, and I did not know how to solve this dilemma. I hoped eventually she would try to help me and if not registering with UNRRA at least get German citizenship or somehow legalize her living in Bavaria.

One sunny and beautiful morning I asked Larissa and Yarko to go with me to see the Herrenchiemsee, a replica of Versailles built by the Bavarian King Ludwig II, more famous for the castle called Neuschwanstein. The Herrenchiemsee was fifty miles from Munich and we arrived in the early morning by bus. The only way to reach the chateau, located on an island in the middle of the Chiemsee, Bavaria's largest lake, was by boat—a boat propelled by strong arms and oars. Learning how to row the oars, held in oarlocks, took some time and patience. Our travels were rewarded with seeing the artful construction of the castle and well-maintained orchard surrounding it. Inside we saw many tastefully decorated rooms with interesting artistic objects.

In the afternoon, while rowing back, the water of the lake looked very attractive. To refresh myself I jumped into it and immediately regretted the impulse. It was a very cold and deep lake and I had difficulty floating due to the absence of salt in the water. In addition, my emaciated body had no fat to help me swim or tread water. When I had jumped in the water, I had also inadvertently pushed the boat away, thus I called Yarko to bring it back to me. My request induced only laughter. Larissa and Yarko knew I swam well and must have thought my cry for help was a joke. Only when I began to swim towards the distant shore did they come to my rescue. Did they really not realize I was panicking? I thought Larissa especially was enjoying my moment of weakness. Many years later I still dislike that memory.

One day in late summer I walked over to Larissa's apartment but she wasn't there. Her landlady, Lina, then took me aside and told me she had noticed a young man accompanying Larissa home on the weekends while I was in Landshut—working at the DP camp there to buy food for our life together in Munich! Needless to say, that news was very disturbing. Being direct and forthright by nature I asked Larissa about her companion. She replied occasionally she volunteered to work with fellow students who were repairing a bombed-out building. After work, one of them would see her home.

Fair enough, I thought. But the ogre jealousy was gnawing at my entrails. The next weekend I pretended to go to Landshut but stayed in Munich. That Saturday evening found me loitering in the shadows near Larissa's apartment. It must have been a long day at the building site because she was late coming home. Finally, she appeared—and she was indeed accompanied by a young man. They kissed, not companionably but a little too friendly for my liking. Then she went inside by herself and he sauntered away.

I was shocked. Stunned. Rooted to the spot. I stood there for the longest time. I knew what I saw but my brain did not believe it. After pondering and pondering I concluded there must be some mistake.

Early the next morning I was admitted to her apartment. Larissa was surprised to see me, believing me to be in Landshut. I was blunt. I asked her why she had kissed this man on the street the night before.

There was a long silence. Those blue eyes then fixed upon mine. There was a frankness in them I had never seen before. Then she replied, "I plan to marry him."

"Marry him? I thought that *we* had planned to marry!"

For almost four years we had been together. The war had torn us apart geographically, but I never thought emotionally. Only in the last few months had we been having difficulties.

I tried to reason with her, promising to help her find a job or assist her in going back and living with her mother until I finished my studies. She should not sing about marrying an unknown German who probably just wants to use her. She should marry me!

She had averted her gaze. But I could tell from the set of her jaw that she did not agree with me. I wasn't going to remain there and be humiliated. I stood up as straight and tall as my heartbroken self could muster, put five dollars in her picture album—all the money I had in the world.

Before turning to leave I said, "I love you, Larissa. Please think seriously about this decision."

Then I walked out the door.

I waited. But no letter arrived. No tearful knocks on my door. I finally had to admit it was over. I had loved her and lost her. I recalled with anguish the joyful and carefree life we shared in Lviv, the wine we sipped in the autumnal Vienna Woods, the gaze which left me with so many happy memories. Yet for weeks I went nowhere near her apartment. And when I finally did so, Lina, the landlady, told me Larissa was gone, had married a German by the name Novacky. She knew nothing more.

It was a difficult time for me. I searched my memory for any clues that might help explain her departure. She had always been evasive, for one thing. From the moment I met her, she had been evasive about identity cards, as if she needed to hide behind papers. What was she running from? *Who* was she running from? She had lived in Lviv throughout the first Soviet occupation. It would be hard to believe a girl like that did not catch the eye of a Russian officer. Then again, why did she avoid registering as a DP after the war? I asked such questions time and time again. But I could never resolve her paradoxes.

As the last of the leaves blew off the trees toward the end of 1947, I quit looking for explanations. I decided to shoulder the blame. After all, I had left her in Vienna when escaping from the Soviets and I did not marry her when she came to Munich to be with me. And when in Munich, I was always either studying or working to make money, which involved spending most weekends in Landshut. She was often left alone.

She had deep needs I couldn't meet. Eventually she turned elsewhere. Only that and nothing more.

I never saw her again. Or—maybe once, in an American movie theater in the mid-1960s, when Julie Christie appeared on screen as Lara in *Dr. Zhivago*. I was gazing at Larissa one final time.

CHAPTER SEVENTEEN

Somewhere in America

In 1947, UNRRA was trying to wrap up its activities and push the remaining refugees—the last 100,000—into permanent homes elsewhere. The first countries that were willing to accept immigrants were Australia, Brazil, Argentina, and some other small countries of South America. In North America, both Canada and the United States accepted refugees who had relatives willing to sponsor them. Otherwise, they weren't welcoming us with open arms.

Canada was accepting young people who would sign a contract to work in the forests for two years. They were provided with a place to live, good food, and fairly good pay. After two years, they were free to move anywhere they wanted to in that country, find work there, and establish a normal life. Many of my friends went to work in the Canadian forests. There they lost some of the body fat accumulated while sitting around in UNRRA camps.

By 1947, the Kochan family had been waiting for two years to get into Canada. Hardly had the shooting ended when my father was writing his brother, Harry, asking him to send us sponsoring papers. Once we received those, we applied to the government of the American Zone for permission to emigrate to Canada. Each member of our family was closely examined for his or her politics, for any collaboration with the Nazis, and for what we planned to do in Canada. We were also subjected to thorough medical examinations. People with tuberculosis or trachoma, for instance, were not acceptable candidates for immigration.

We passed all of the above. But since the immigration wheels turned very slowly indeed. We were still waiting.

By late 1947, however, people were on the move. That's what the DP transit camp outside Munich where I worked was established for; it was a transit camp for refugees heading for the Atlantic ports and the waiting ocean liners. Elsewhere in Europe, though, the movements weren't so hopeful. Mitonko, now married and living near me in Munich, told me some unhappy news. The Communist regime in the new Poland, tired of fighting Ukrainian partisans in the forests and swamps of old Galicia, were erasing their bases of support, the villages. They were uprooting ethnic Ukrainians and moving them wholesale to lands newly acquired from defeated Germany. This was the infamous "Wisla Program" or Operation Vistula enforced by the Polish Army. The soldiers occupied Tudorkovychi and ripped Didoon Semen, Marina, and Petro from their own farm and soil and transported them to Dźwierzuty, a small village near Szczytno, in former East Prussia, a desolate place of sandy moraines and pine trees and an unremittingly cold wind off the Baltic Sea. My mother and Mitonko's mother lost their house, Alexandra opting to live nearby, but in the Soviet Union, in a place on the outskirts of Buchach called Nahirianka. There she had a small house with a large garden and a plum orchard—from which she used to make some locally famous if illegal plum brandy.

Then we heard that my cousin, Ivan, the one who was nearly frostbitten when as a truant schoolboy I took him to find fox dens in the forest, had been fighting the Communists as a member of the Ukrainian Insurgent Army. He was captured by the Poles, thrown into the jail at Hrubieszow, and severely beaten every day. Uncle Miron tried to bribe the authorities to release him, but to no avail. Ivan developed tuberculosis and died in prison. His mother, Kaska, would die of a broken heart a year later, and Uncle Hilarko buried them both in Hrubieszow.

And then there was Slavka. I learned much later about her tragic fate. Once the Communists took over Poland and arrived in Tudorkovychi, the Banderites forced Slavka to spy for them. She would cozy up to the Communist officers and pry out valuable information, tidbits about how they planned to suppress the partisans. During the 1947 Wisla campaign, however, when the Ukrainians in the Sokal region were resettled in East Prussia, the local partisans, deprived of village support, went with them.

But they did not want Slavka to follow. She knew too much—she knew about the murders of Poles and unsympathetic Ukrainians, for instance. The Banderites decided she had been spying for the Poles, too, so she could not be trusted and must be killed. Claiming that she was a traitor, they tortured her to extract a false confession. She proved too tough for them and didn't give in. They then raped her and shot her one night outside the village. They covered her body with the manure used to fertilize the fields in springtime.

All these developments saddened and depressed me. Decades later I would write a newspaper article about Slavka in relation to the release of the book, *Beyond the Eastern Horizon*, by UPA leader Danilo Shumuk. In one passage Shumuk described how Slavka helped him cross the Buh River in 1945, thereby saving that important partisan leader's life. She was not only a beautiful girl, but a brave and resourceful one, too.

Eventually much of the blame for Slavka's death would fall on my cousin, Volodimir Levosiuk—Vlodko—who also burned parts of the village, including my family's house and his own. As if that would slow the advance of the Red Army! In 1947 he was awaiting trial for his partisan activities and for burning our village. He eventually would be found guilty and would languish in prison until the year 1958.

Larissa was gone and now my lost world of Tudorkovychi was truly lost, as well.

By late March 1948 the recent Communist coup in Czechoslovakia had brought the Iron Curtain within eighty miles of Munich and less than that to Landshut. And still no word from Canada, although increasing numbers of refugees were already embarking for distant lands.

One such family was just then arriving in the DP transit camp outside Munich. Soon a note addressed to me at the Semmelmans brought the welcome news that Tatiana Sawycka wanted to say goodbye.

I was thrilled to get her note and was at the nearby streetcar stop to greet her. When she stepped off the tram with those long legs and that dimpled smile, I thought she can't really be saying goodbye! I took her to supper in a restaurant known to serve good Bavarian food. While ordering entrees, I realized that without the government-issued food stamps we could only order the "ein Topf Gericht," which meant the soup of the day. It was a heavy vegetable soup. With turnips. I remembered that turnips used to transform my stomach into a gas-filled balloon. Tatiana made several jokes about my forgetfulness and tried to turn my embarrassment into laughter. So effortlessly could she put people at ease.

She told me her news. Her friend and former employer, Averda Lerrigo of the International Refugee Organization, had persuaded the town of Claremont, California, to adopt the Sawycka family and accept them as neighbors. The Church World Service was bringing them from the Salzburg DP camp to the U.S. via Bremerhaven, where they would board an ocean liner in three weeks. In the meantime, they were staying at the transit camp, waiting for the remaining Ukrainian passengers to arrive and a train to be assembled.

That was great news! I said, despite feeling a pang of loss. Claremont was in sunny California, she said, just outside of Los Angeles and not that far from Hollywood. It sounded like a dream come true.

After supper, I walked Tatiana back to the streetcar stop. Before our parting, I invited her for supper the next night and promised to bring the correct food stamps. She smiled and accepted.

And so began the three-week whirlwind that finally turned our topsy-turvy lives right-side up.

Sometimes Tatiana came into town. Other times I'd go out to the camp. The streetcar track became our shared lifeline. Once, when I was visiting the family, Adela complained about the DP camp food and wondered whether I could obtain some butter from the farmers around Landshut? Since I was still smarting from the inhospitable treatment she gave me and my friends in Bratislava I indulged in a shameful little lie. I said that farmers around Landshut had no cows. She saw right through it but realized I was repaying her in kind.

The next night, while sitting in our restaurant, Tatiana explained the motivations behind her mother's actions. Adela had been born in 1901 in Kiev, where her upper-class family owned a wire-making factory. She had been brought up amid the opulence of the late Tsarist years in Russia, but her experience of it would prove all too short. When she was sixteen her father and older sister were taken away in the middle of the night and sent to Siberia. Then came the Russian Revolution and the terrifying wars between the Whites and the Reds that forced Adela and Tatiana's grandmother to flee Kyiv for Prague, literally walking the entire way and carrying nothing more than the clothes on their backs. Somehow, they persevered, and Adela finished her schooling and eventually received a Ph.D. in Mineralogy from the University of Prague. She met and married Peter Sawycky in that city and there it was that Tatiana was born.

Of course, as I had long known, the marriage had collapsed, leaving four women—Adela, her mother, and her two daughters—to fend for themselves, an even more difficult feat in wartime. Adela was just fiercely protective of her daughters, Tatiana explained; she was watchful as a mother falcon.

I thought maybe I'd have to find some butter, after all.

We usually visited in the evening, after my day at school was done. Now that it was April, I could show her the city in the lengthening twilight. Or rather show her a ghost city—the streetcars might rattle down spanking clean boulevards around Karlsplatz. Moviegoers, like us sometimes, might queue on immaculate sidewalks waiting to see the latest Hollywood film. But the background of central Munich was always a panorama of ruins. Gaunt, grim, sightless, roofless buildings gaped everywhere. Piles of rubble like massive debris fields were banked off the crowded sidewalks. Great twisted cables and heaps of rusted metal looked like modernist sculptures. The towers of the famous Frauenkirche still dominated both the Marienplatz and the city skyline, but the ancient roof had been bombed to cinders.

We'd stroll around this maze of ruins like lovers would in Rome, the spectral scene being sometimes the only witness to a few stolen kisses.

Something as yet unspoken was growing between us. That something was analogous to the ring of hammers and whine of saws coming off the scaffolding starting to rise amid the ruins. Life was returning, and something else with it. We sensed it most powerfully, though, on the weekends, when I abandoned the trips to Landshut to stroll with Tatiana around the Englischer Garten. Those trees not bombed to splinters or fallen to the woodchoppers were just budding out, just starting to leaf. I was a country boy, and the sight always moved me deeply. She was a city girl but had a rare appreciation for the beauties of nature.

At such times she talked of her father. He was not a practical man, she said. Although a qualified academic, there were times in the 1930s when he either could not or would not hold a job. During the years that Petro Sawycky didn't work he spent much of his time with Tatiana. Because he was a naturalist with degrees in botany and geology, they would hike together in the forests outside Prague hunting for mushrooms. She loved those excursions above anything else; and when her father finally left after many confrontations with Adela for not working, she was devastated. She was angry with her mother for having chased him away and angry with her father for leaving.

I said nothing but held her all the more tightly as we strolled beneath the budding trees.

Sitting in the sun on a park bench I told her some of my tales of Tudorkovychi. She listened with genuine interest. She had a down-to-earth streak in her, I was glad to see. She turned to Canada, and soon had me laughing about the time, during the 1939 Battle of Warsaw, that she spent a month with her family in the basement, out of the firing lines— and she passed the hours reading the Canadian novel, *Anne of Green Gables*—in English. When it came to war stories, she had an amusing bagful. Being four women alone they were constantly scrutinized and harassed. In response, you just had to be strong and confident. Adela exemplified that every day.

When I asked her to elaborate, Tatiana replied her mother always admired the American soldiers because they would help her and her daughters onto crowded trains, sometimes by pulling them through the windows. They helped place their luggage and always had chocolate to share with them. They were gentlemen. The Germans? Well, they were not as friendly but were still polite to her and her daughters. But the Russians! If an opportunity existed a Russian would rape them all and probably worse. The Reds made that quite clear to her mother. Once Adela did have to rescue a very young Natalia from the grips of a soldier near their apartment.

I had a story from the other side of a broken marriage. I grew up in a house with six uncles and when I was very young, I watched my grandmother serve all these men at the dinner table. She, and later my mother, were always so busy they rarely sat down and never ate. At least that is what I thought. I actually asked my Didoon one time, "Why was it women do not have to eat like us men?"

We laughed and laughed. I liked being with Tatiana. She was exceptionally interesting, a good sport, had similar interests, and also came from a broken family. We bonded on that and I knew I could trust her. She also had those lovely long legs.

Too soon came the weekend when the Sawyckas would depart for Bremerhaven. That Friday evening, I accompanied Tatiana back to the transit camp. The rest of the family was inside their temporary barrack so in the darkening April twilight I took her aside. I promised to see her off in the morning. But now—I was so tense, so fearful that she would leave and it would mean forever— I just took her aside and blurted it out: "Tatiana…Tatiana, I've fallen in love with you." And then, a moment later, I added, "I think I've always been in love with you."

A shadow hid her face. Then in a voice laden with emotion she replied, "I think I love you, too."

A long pause. "But—but we might never see each other again."

Then she was up the stair and behind the closed door of the barrack.

The next morning, I was back. I was wearing my best suit and my polished riding boots. The train was making up and the passengers were lined in the field beside it, their suitcases and trunks and baggage stacked beside them and ready for loading. We had a little time yet before departure, so Tatiana and I walked far out into the field. The April grass was still short and everywhere the wild clover was growing, each white flower nodding in the breeze, living for the day. I spread out a blanket and we sat down.

She seemed almost overcome with emotion. So, I took her hands, gazed into her eyes, and said with urgency, "Let's get married, Tatiana. Not here, but in America. In Canada, when I get there. Or in California. Or someplace in between. But let's get married somewhere in America! I don't have an engagement ring. But I can get one over there."

She cast her eyes down toward the grass and the clover. She seemed… hesitant. My heart sank. Then she lifted up her gaze, looked straight at me, and said matter-of-factly, "Long ago I vowed never to marry."

My heart now plunged.

"Grandmother, you see, warned me against it," she was saying. "She didn't mean to, but when I was little, she taught me to sew and said I should be very good at darning. Men's socks need constant attention because of the daily wear and tear. So, when you marry, darning will be your evening chore."

She sat back and looked at me. "Sewing I could do. But darning stinky socks every night sounded like a prison sentence!"

Now she leaned forward, intent with purpose. "But if I have to darn, I only want to darn your socks, not those of any other man."

This was such a relief I threw my head back and laughed. The steam locomotive echoed it, wheezing and sighing, whining about endless journeying. When my gaze returned to hers, she was looking at me with those blue eyes.

"Yes, Ivan, let's get married. Let's get married somewhere in America."

And so she left me. They sailed on April 19, 1948, and were in Claremont by May 14. Soon she had a job at nearby Pomona College and thrilled at the prospect of living in the States. Everyone had been so nice to them!

I would read her letters and write mine in return still in Munich, still in Landshut. The Berlin Airlift was getting underway when in the summer we finally received permission to leave Germany and travel to Canada. My father, Pani Lyda, Roman, Yarko, and me would board a ship in Genoa that would take us to Halifax, Nova Scotia. The Trans-Canada Railway would speed us the rest of the way to Fort William, Ontario, Uncle Harry's home and shortly to be ours as well.

We had hardly reached Munich from Landshut when we were told the train would stay in the station until morning. Yarko and I were not going to spend the night on the train when my room at the Semmelman's home was only a few blocks away. We notified the UNRRA supervisor, and she promised the train would not leave without us as long as we were back before 9:00 a.m. in the morning.

The Semmelmans were happy to see us. As in the past, Mrs. Semmelman prepared two basins with warm water for our tired feet and, while we soaked in them, we told everyone about our upcoming trip to Canada. They were happy our hard and hungry times would soon be coming to an end and wished us all the best for our future. We drank hot tea and I thanked them for accepting me into their family and for treating me so well.

In the morning, we found our polished boots at the side of our beds. Mrs. Semmelman always fulfilled her role as a Hausfrau with love and dutiful dedication. When we parted, it was difficult to find words to express my feelings to these good people. With tears in our eyes, we hugged each other for a long time and promised to write letters. Then we ran down the winding staircase, three steps at a time, and sprinted to the railroad station as if that would relieve the pain of parting.

Our train was where we left it the day before. We notified the supervisor of our return and soon we were on our way through Austria to Italy. Salzburg and Innsbruck as we passed were still heaped with rubble. As we crossed the Brenner Pass my father looked solemnly to the southeast, craning for a view of the Dolomites, those mountains encircled by the battlefields of the First World War. There he had been wounded as a young soldier in the Austro-Hungarian Army.

After passing the rugged snowbanks of the Alps we entered warm and level Lombardy. I had never been this far south and I thought the dark, triangular cypress trees silhouetted against the setting sun looked like so many strange warriors guarding the entrance to this picturesque land. During the late evening, we passed Milan, a city I associated with the lives of many famous tenors; and that night our train stopped in Turin because of a general strike of the railroad workers. This was a response to the attempted assassination of Palmiro Togliatti, the head of the Italian Communist party. Italy had nearly gone Communist. Even France had nearly gone Communist. We just had to leave! Because of this strike, though, we were placed in tents at an UNRRA camp for two more weeks.

It wasn't so bad, after all, because we liked Turin. The air in that region was warm and felt smooth and silky as it entered our lungs. I was avoiding Yarko because he was singing Italian songs too loudly, songs which he had learned while attending a voice school in Munich. There was a period in Yarko's life in which he seriously considered becoming a professional singer. He had a good voice; but there was something lacking in it, to me it was a feeling for the song. Since most well-known singers came from Italy, Yarko thought he needed the Italian air for the development of good vocal cords, and he exposed them continually to that air. I am certain the Italians were wondering what was wrong with this strange foreigner who shouts their songs!

When the strike was over, we traveled by train to Genoa and boarded the Greek ship, *Nea Hellas*, on July 16, 1948. Our cabins were somewhere at the bottom of the ship but I chose not to go there. It was better to be outside and enjoying the Mediterranean Sea. Traversing the Strait of Gibraltar we gazed at "The Rock" on the right hand and the low, undulating coast of Morocco on the left. In Lisbon we were not allowed to leave the ship, but we saw the abundance of food for sale alongside the quay. Staying neutral during the war had made them prosperous. The ship was then loaded with some agricultural machines that *Nea Hellas* had to deliver to Canada. That evening we weighed anchor and entered the broad Atlantic Ocean.

The trip to Halifax took nine days. About a third of the way over we encountered a storm that shook the ship from stem to stern. The continuous rocking made many people sick and copious amounts of vomit were hurled overboard. Fewer and fewer people came to the dining rooms and most of the tasty Greek food remained untouched. Yarko and I joined some of our friends and found a place in the bow sheltered from the cold strong wind. Here we enjoyed watching the big waves that reared up before us. Usually, we had several bottles of wine from the dining room to give us cheer. While drinking we watched the dolphins riding the bow wave and swimming as fast or faster than the ship itself. They leaped and frolicked and seemed to enjoy this swimming competition. We leaned over the railings, and it appeared they were watching us and doubling their efforts to display how dexterous and fast they could be. We had never seen dolphins before and were fascinated by their behavior. We drank more wine and nobody in our group became seasick so maybe alcohol has a palliative effect, after all.

Pani Lyda, however, was very ill. Her seasickness, the stormy weather, and having to care for my six-year-old half-brother upset my father and he directed his anger at Yarko and me. We stayed away from their cabin.

I can understand his frustration. We left Germany about one month before the official establishment of Nacionalna Rada, the National Council or parliament of the democratic Ukrainian government-in-exile. He had been one of its principal initiators and he disliked missing the opportunity to participate in its important meetings.

Another factor that disturbed our relationship with our father was money. Yarko and I knew our father had some American dollars that he was using to purchase some products in the ship's store. We were interested in tasting Coca-Cola or some other American products but had no money. We were disappointed he did not offer us even a few dollars and we were too proud to ask him for any. We finally decided we were satisfied just drinking wine on the front deck of *Nea Hellas*.

Several days before arriving at Halifax, the ocean quieted, and the sailors of the ship organized a show for the enjoyment of the passengers. They dressed in the national Greek costume, white hose and short blouses over embroidered shirts. They danced in groups, lined up and holding each other by the shoulders, changing direction frequently. We in turn showed them some Ukrainian dances. A thousand years ago there had been close contact between Ukrainians and Greeks. Christianity came to us in 988 from the Greek-speaking Byzantine Empire—long before it came to the so-called "Great Russians," still worshiping their heathen idols in the dank forests to the north.

It was a nice evening and on the ninth day of our trip, we saw high-speed boats jumping over the ocean waves and knew we were close to our destination.

We arrived in Halifax on July 27, 1948, transferred our suitcases from the ship to the Canadian Pacific Railroad, and registered with the Canadian Mounted Police. They were dressed in their fancy red uniforms and their attitude toward us was indifferent, neither hostile nor friendly; but they did give us twenty-five dollars to buy food in town to eat during our two-day trip to Fort William.

The inside of the train was dirty, the benches were made of hardwood, and there were no places to sleep. We shared our car with some Canadian passengers and observed them with interest. Most of the time, they were loud and spoke about money and the lack of jobs. They were dressed plainly and their shoes had not seen polish for a long time.

From Halifax we traveled west into the French-speaking Province of Quebec, following the St. Lawrence River and stopping briefly in its beautiful capital with the famous red-brick fortress on the Plains of Abraham. Montreal sped past the windows, and we entered Ontario. At each station, some of the immigrants left the train and were met by relatives whom they had never seen before. Slowly the train scattered the passengers of the *Nea Hellas* throughout Canadian towns, villages, and wilderness settlements. The life that would follow would be completely different from that which they had known in Europe. In some places, our train did not stop and mail packages were thrown to carriers from the moving cars.

In one place, the train stopped deep in the "bush" to unload a husband, wife, and three small children whom I had known from the DP camp in Landshut. There was no building and no sign of human habitation. There was nobody waiting to meet them and after removing their baggage from the train, they stood motionless, looking back at us. I could see the despair and fear in the eyes of the man who had brought his family to build a new life in the woods. As the train left, I leaned from the platform watching the family grow smaller and smaller, still looking at us as if our train was the last link connecting them to the only life they had known. I can still see them, that lonely family displaced by the war and left to make a new life in an unimaginable wilderness.

On the third day, after passing the shore of Lake Superior, we arrived in Fort William. Uncle Harry and his friend Yatso Roback, who was a distant relative of my mother's, met us at the station. My uncle had immigrated to Canada just before I was born and here, nearly a quarter century later, he and my father were reunited. Harry was a friendly man with a ready smile and looked similar to all his brothers: The same light complexion and reddish-blond hair. We piled into two automobiles and were taken to 331 Cameron Street, my uncle's tall, narrow house.

The house had a basement, a first and second floor and an attic suitable for sleeping during warm summer months. Uncle Harry with his wife, Marika, had two teenage daughters, Vera and Natalia. He worked for the city of Fort William as a truck driver and since he did not earn much money, they rented out the two rooms on the second floor. The money to pay for our trip Harry borrowed from Yatso, who as a single man and a store owner had managed to save some. After we started working, we repaid Yatso all we owed him. As a welcome gift, Yatso even gave me twenty dollars.

Fort William was a city of grain elevators, office blocks, department stores, and endless miles of cozy suburban houses. No piles of rubble anywhere. The city crest featured an Indian and a French Voyageur standing over a Latin motto: *A posse ad esse*—from a possibility to an actuality.

Uncle Harry and Aunt Marika were very hospitable hosts. She was an excellent cook and fed us so very well we soon regained our strength and began to look for work. There were too many of us in the small house, so I decided to leave. I had already observed that Canadians may have felt some prejudice towards the immigrants daily arriving. I understood the feeling of having strangers occupy your home, but that didn't make it any easier.

I found work in nearby Port Arthur, where the Catholic nuns of St. Joseph's Hospital employed poor immigrants to do the dirty work around the place. Although I assisted in the surgical department, helping patients before and after operations, Sister Monica used me for all kinds of chores, like washing instruments, floors, or windows. She was a middle-aged Irish woman in her forties with a superior attitude stemming from either an excess of piety or of sadism.

Once she even sent me to wash the outside windows of the surgical rooms—on the sixth floor, standing on an eighteen-inch cement ledge without any protection whatsoever. The other nurses in the department saw this, but pretended not to notice. I had come this far, I thought grimly, survived bombings and Nazis and partisan gunfire, only to fall to my death so close to my goal of marriage and children! People on the street had stopped and were gazing up at me, perhaps admiring my circus-like performance. But I needed the money—a hundred dollars per month and a room to sleep in—and had to take some chances.

The room I shared with two Polish men who were several years older than me. One of them had served in the "Anders Army" of Polish exiles and had fought in the battle of Monte Cassino. He wanted to save some money and to return to Poland. The other man still had a wife and a child there and he was hoping to bring them to Canada. He had attracted the sexual ardors of a sixty-year-old woman and for each performance he was paid twenty dollars. With that money he would bring his family to Canada!

The other Pole and I joked about this guy because we knew he was spending more money than he received from the old lady on whores pimped out by a fellow worker with whom he washed floors. Were we wrong! With the help of his older *amour* he was indeed able to bring his wife and daughter from Poland—and all of them lived together in her house!

I saved the money I earned in the hospital to pay for Tatiana's trip to Canada. She and I exchanged letters frequently, making plans on how and where to get married. The best option for us would have been to live in California with the rest of Tatiana's family. But the quota restrictions did not permit me to enter the United States because I was born in Poland and was reckoned a Pole, and the Polish quotas were always filled up. Therefore, we decided I should apply to bring Tatiana to Canada. At that time, Canada only had seventeen million people, so I thought the Canadian Department of Immigration would be happy to acquire a few young couples to help populate such a vast country. Was I wrong!

After several visits to the immigration office in Fort William, I was finally and grudgingly granted an interview. A pompous official did agree to let Tatiana come to Canada for a visit, but only if I would sign a statement that I would not marry her. This jerk thought he could control the desire of immigrants to marry! But I suppressed my anger, put my signature on the paper, and began to prepare for Tatiana's trip. Her letters indicated she liked California and the friendliness of the people in Claremont who cared for her family. I disliked taking her away from such a nice place to start our lives together in Canada, where both the people and the climate were cold and unfriendly. Californians, it seemed, were always happy and welcoming to everybody.

She would come in late December, spending Christmas with her family and the remainder of the holidays with me and mine.

When she finally arrived at the Canadian border, about seventy miles from Fort William, everything was covered in deep snow and the temperature did not rise above -10 degrees Fahrenheit. Uncle Harry and I were preparing to pick her up in the Fort William bus terminal when she telephoned me. In a voice edging on tears, she told me she had been denied entrance at the border crossing. Apparently, the Immigration Office in Fort William had not sent the required papers to the passport control station.

Cold fury gripped me. I told her to go back to Grand Portage, Minnesota, about six miles from the border, and check into a hotel while I tried to fix the situation. Naturally, it was the nasty Immigration office that did not do its job! Although it was Christmastime, I telephoned that office and somehow got through to someone who understood our dilemma and promised to dispatch the documents immediately. I then telephoned the hotel in Grand Portage and the clerk agreed to help Tatiana contact the passport control station the next day.

I was distressed that Tatiana, after all our well-formed plans, could not get across the border. I desperately hoped she would not be upset with me and decide it was just too scary to be married in this cold and inhospitable land. She had been so hurt when her father left her and her family during her youth and I didn't want to be a man who let her down, too. Her mother had never been my champion but had accepted that I might make something of myself and so decided to entrust me with her oldest daughter. Although her own marriage had failed, she never failed her girls! As a highly educated woman alone during the war she did whatever it took—styling and coloring ladies' hair, taking in sewing, working odd jobs—to provide opportunities and education for her children. I promised myself I would do likewise. And I further promised God above that I would never let Tatiana feel abandoned again.

I was so desperate that she not be alone I wanted to drive down to Grand Portage then and there. But Uncle Harry said no. I had no experience driving in deep snow and ice and in terrible weather like this he said to leave the driving to the professionals. I could do nothing but toss and turn all night.

The following afternoon Tatiana telephoned from the hotel with the happy news that the correct documents had arrived! Since it was too late for the twice-daily bus to Fort William, I asked her to stay one more night and take the first bus in the morning.

By the time she climbed aboard the bus I had been up for hours, dressed like a Ukrainian gentleman should be, in an embroidered shirt and tie with a jacket and riding breeches and polished leather riding boots. I had a little bouquet and when I climbed into the automobile with Uncle Harry, I found myself getting very nervous. As we drove through the snowy streets everything was still decked out with Christmas festivity, Christmas trees, wreathes, Santas, sleigh bells, reindeer. The world had paid a huge price for the war in Europe. These North Americans had done their part in winning it, no doubt, as their military cemeteries in Western Europe amply proved. But Tatiana and I had nearly lost everything. We were lucky to be here now and to have the freedom to begin a new life together in a new country.

The nervousness drained away. I had that sixth-sense feeling again. I suddenly *knew* we would end up in California. I *knew* we would be blessed with children and grandchildren. I was now feeling elated. Yes, Didoon Semen, I have finally arrived in the land where the sun sleeps, the Far West, the New World, and it bears the face of Tatiana!

As I stepped through the door of the bus terminal, though, I nearly dropped the bouquet. There she stood beside her two suitcases, looking radiant. That dimpled smile, those eyes as blue as the deep sea or the starry night—to be together again after such long distances and from such different places seemed like a miracle but one that was meant to be! And the poor thing was wearing a flowery summer dress and a coat too thin for this place, and she was *shivering*, was cold to the bone. I stepped forward and embraced her and I knew it was an embrace that would never end. Tomorrow would be the beginning of a new life for us. *A posse ad esse*—from possibility to actuality, at last!

The Daughter's Tale

— PART TWO —

That's where Ivan's European memoir ends—closing with a new beginning. My parents were married two weeks after reuniting in that bus station. It was a quiet ceremony in a Ukrainian Church among friends and family. Everyone adjourned to a Fort William hotel for a wedding supper.

Not long thereafter, most of the Kochan clan resettled in Winnipeg, capital of Manitoba and a drive of several hours west of Fort William. There my father enrolled in the University of Manitoba to continue his education and improve his English language skills. Since he was, practically speaking, starting higher education all over again, it soon became apparent that medical school was now out of reach. He chose medical research instead, graduating from the University with both a bachelor's and a master's degree.

Ivan and Tatiana made a good team. While Ivan studied, Tatiana worked administrative positions in various hospitals. Both were resolute workers and saved every penny they could. They enjoyed the outdoors, camping with friends and having memorable encounters with bears and other wild animals. They made new friends easily and welcomed an old one enthusiastically when Petro Voroby from Starhorod, the village on the Buh outside of Tudorkovychi, arrived in town. The young man with the big head on a small body who had attended the University of Berlin came to Canada clutching yet another advanced degree, this one a Ph.D. from the famed University of Göttingen. He would have a very illustrious career as an economist at the University of Regina in Saskatchewan, and he and my parents always remained close, Ivan and Tatiana becoming godparents to his eldest daughter. When Petro died in 2002, one obituary described him as a "true gentleman, with a keen intellect and a tender and gentle heart," a tribute which could equally apply to my father.

During their Winnipeg years my two brothers were born. When they were still toddlers, however, a letter Ivan wrote to a distinguished professor, Sidney Rafael, at Stanford University in Palo Alto led to his being offered a position as a graduate assistant in the Department of Microbiology and Immunology at that institution. Immigrating to sunny California was what they both dreamed of for their family. As my father was wrapping up his Ph.D. in Immunology at Stanford, I was born, their third and last child and only daughter.

Then began our nomadic academic life, first at Baylor University and the Wadley Research Institute in Texas; then, almost a decade later, at Miami University in Ohio. His passion was the study of Nutritional Immunology and the role iron played with infectious bacteria, and his research was widely published in medical textbooks and periodicals. He participated in scientific meetings all over the world and his work was funded by the National Institutes of Health, the National Research Foundation, and the American Cancer Society. After retiring he wrote an immunology textbook in his native language that is now used at the University of Lviv.

It was after publishing this book that he struck up, improbably enough, a correspondence with Darka Tkachuk, the girl from Belz whose grandparents had the old church on their property. She did marry the older teacher and had three children. But after a few years Ivan never heard from her again. Eventually he heard she had died—of heart failure. Others in this story closed their earthly pilgrimages years earlier. Didoon Semen died in 1950 while in exile in old East Prussia. Babunya Marina then went to live with her son Hilarko in Hrubieszow, a town about thirty kilometers from Tudorkovychi, where she died in 1963.

Petro eventually married and returned to Ukraine to live out his days. Miron, the one with the radio and the leather shop, also eventually came to Winnipeg, where he worked as a printer at the Ukrainian newspaper "New Path." From exposure to the lead used in the printing process, however, he developed a fatal cancer of the esophagus.

Family was the most important thing to my father, and he was always saddened by such inevitabilities. One death that shouldn't have been inevitable, however, was that of Lesia, his Uncle Sidorko's daughter. They ended up living in Soviet Ukraine, and in 1965 she was poisoned by Communist bureaucrats who discovered she knew about their graft and corruption in relation to a sugar-producing factory. Sidorko and Evhenia were left to care for her two daughters.

And what of Ivan's parents? I remember Volodimir Kochan, my grandfather, but mostly from photographs. He had moved to Winnipeg in 1948 where, unsurprisingly, he became "a tireless and prominent civic leader," according to one newspaper article. He was especially active in the Ukrainian Canadian Committee, an umbrella organization representing the interests of an estimated half-million Ukrainians in the country. One Monday in June 1966, however, he was working so hard on an upcoming World Congress of Free Ukrainians to be held in New York that he had a heart attack and died on the way to the hospital. When Pani Lyda was informed a few hours later, she collapsed on the spot and also died. They had a joint funeral a few days later, an appropriate enough ending.

And Alexandra? My father had built a wing on our Texas home and in the early 1960s he made arrangements for her to come to the United States. She spoke no English and I was somewhat frightened by her unusual customs. She was a small round woman with skinny legs—now recognizable from my father's description of his own Babunya Maria. And, yes, she did have a special touch with all living things, as did my father. Our family pets included rabbits, pigeons, and guinea pigs from his laboratory. He spoke to the birds, lizards, and snakes in the garden, just like Didoon Kindrat, Alexandra's father. His soothing words and gentle touch with a frightened rabbit was a tender sight. He inspired us to be the same. Once my brothers and I decided to incubate chicken eggs in a box with blankets and a warm light. Most of our dreams of baby chicks didn't develop but finally a chick hatched. Though I selfishly wanted to keep the chick to myself it had already imprinted on my Baba Alexandra and followed her everywhere.

Later, in Ohio, she had her own apartment two blocks from the Catholic Church but came over to our house to visit with our dog and work in the garden. While I was learning to drive, it was my job to shuttle her back and forth. She insisted that we cross ourselves three times, like in the traditional Greek Catholic Church, before I shifted into drive.

After she died, Ivan kept her ashes in a small urn. In the early 1990s, after the breakup of the Soviet Union, he carried that urn back to Ukraine and buried them next to the church she had so loved.

Ivan and Tatiana traveled extensively, and I remember well one trip to Munich I took with my mother because it was the one and only time I met her father, my grandfather, Petro Sawycky, who had a position at the university there. But even more than travel my parents loved home and family and friends. We all adored his cousin Mitonko, who had washed up in New Jersey and then Florida. He was a sweet, funny, wonderful man and we regularly visited with him and his family. We also frequently visited with Tatiana's mother and Lala and her family. And after my father retired, he and Tatiana moved back to California to be closer to me and my family. Good Ukrainians, all!

I also enjoyed Ivan Volynetz, my father's friend in the Rettungsdienst and the man who accompanied him on the escape from Vienna. He immigrated, married, and was a doctor in Chicago with two pretty daughters, ultimately retiring to Florida. He was nice, on the quiet side, but a quirky guy with a funny shuffling gait in his later years and he always wore that eyepatch. The third musketeer, Bohdan Yourchuk, disappeared from view. We last met him in Salzburg, so we assume he settled in Western Europe, and hope he lived a long and happy life. His name always brought a smile to my father's face.

One other character of some importance to this story had also gone before Ivan and I undertook this memoir. My mother left us all too soon, the victim of a stroke in her brainstem that left her in a state of suspension somewhere between life and death. It was an illness that washed away everything she knew and felt, so my father and I lost her long before she actually departed. My father cared for Tatiana as only a lover of fifty years could. It was a difficult thing to watch, Ivan continuing to care and feed my mother after her will to live had vanished.

My mother did know just how nurturing Ivan could be. Tatiana witnessed how he cared for her mother, Adela, before she died in her nineties. To the nurses' dismay, Ivan would visit her care home with his large black dog, Hector, while smuggling some good bread, stinky smoked fish, and horilka in there to share. The old animosity had long ago evaporated, and he provided her some comfort to ease the ending of her final years. He had done the same for his own mother only the previous year. The rituals of the old country stayed with him, the lesson to honor these passages.

After my mother's death, Ivan married Stella Jean, and they lived happily in Grass Valley, California, for almost twenty years. Ivan continued his woodcarving and they traveled together to Ukraine. He subscribed to Ukrainian newspapers and occasionally wrote letters that were published in these various periodicals. Living in California brought Ivan closer to Roman Kochan, his youngest brother, and they visited and enjoyed each other's company. Yarko remained in Canada, and as of this writing, is still hale and hearty though past the age of ninety-five! There were many family reunions that included their children, grandchildren, and even some great-grandchildren. Ivan made a good life for himself and his family, and he lived in the United States almost seventy years after his adventures in Ukraine.

Writing the memoirs was a shared ritual for Ivan and me, a safe haven with well-defined roles for us both. Sometimes the daily rhythm changed due to his other needs. Since Ivan no longer drove himself to the barber, every six weeks I needed to cut his hair. He didn't have a lot remaining, but the fringes that remained were prodigious. Holding his head in my hands, turning it this way and that, studying the shape and the slight lean to the left of his neck, was an intimate role reversal. Draping him in old, softened sheets, I was careful with the buzzer to clean his neck without nicking the skin and to blow away small hairs from around his collar. I trimmed the strays in his ears and eyebrows to help him look like the doctor and professor he knew himself to be. He would often sing while I worked, or recite poetry. I would join him when I knew the words.

Ivan was lucky. He continued to live well into his nineties and still enjoyed walking his dog, a good drink of horilka, and the company of an attractive woman. Besides losing the sight in one eye, his health was relatively good, considering that in his youth he sometimes only had bread dipped in vinegar to eat. Yet I sensed a loneliness within him for the people that he had known and loved. He would often lament to me, "Oh, Christya, there is no one left who knew me when I was young!"

In the end, Ivan became the best version of himself. I am sorry my mother didn't get to know this new version of an older Ivan. She would have appreciated the wiser and softer side of the man she had known for almost sixty years.

The memoirs that traveled so long in Ivan's heart were finished weeks before his death. They were written as a testament to how, once upon a time, life was lived and what happened to ordinary human beings who lived in extraordinary times. He and his family adapted to the upheaval and displacement of war as millions of people did in much of Europe after World War Two. The Americas, both North and South, absorbed many Ukrainian refugees and these new citizens became the best patriots for their newly adopted countries. They gave greatly in return, as immigrants often do.

The last eight days of Ivan's life he spent in the hospital. I visited him every day. He was happy sometimes and struggled others. One day he wouldn't look at me, he was angry. Another day he wanted and needed a shave. After shaving his prickly cheeks and chin I rubbed baby lotion on his face as he gently smiled, his eyelids heavy. His confidence waned and his breathing became a gurgle. He turned inward. In the end we knew he would not see the coming spring. The nurse in hospice told me that exiting the world is as difficult as entering it. Ivan was on yet another journey. He was finally going to see "where the sun sleeps at night." We spoke sometimes, but mostly I was just there, telling him I loved him and holding his hand. Forgiving and being forgiven was all I could hope for.

The struggles—mental and physical—around the war had taught him many things but mostly that war, simply put, is not good for any living thing. No political cause is worth the collateral damage. Writing these memoirs and reliving and telling the story was his therapy and his gift to us. He reconciled with himself that he had done the best he could. At his funeral I wanted to say what an interesting man he was, how fine a father, how truly a renaissance man—but I could not. I was overwrought and was only able to recite a poem that Ivan loved. He had recited it to me often and the author was an immunologist, like Ivan, credited with finding a vaccine for typhus. He was the famous Hans Zinsser (1878-1940), author of the celebrated *Rats, Lice, and History*. But he was also quite a good poet. And the poem we so loved was about Zinsser's own approaching death and how he wanted to be remembered by the people he loved:

> Now is death merciful. He calls me hence
> Gently, with friendly soothing of my fears
> Of ugly age and feeble impotence
> And cruel disintegration of slow years.
> Nor does he leap upon me unaware
> Like some wild beast that hungers for its prey,
> But gives me kindly warning to prepare:
> Before I go, to kiss your tears away.
> How sweet the summer! And the autumn shone
> Late warmth within our hearts as in the sky,
> Ripening rich harvests that our love has sown.
> How good that ere the winter comes, I die!
> Then, ageless, in your heart I'll come to rest
> Serene and proud, as when you loved me best.

Afterwards, my daughter Larissa claimed the poem was sad; but I saw it as an embodiment of Ivan's grace and spirit, lovingly letting go of life after living it so well. My mother's gift to me of my father proves more important as the years pass, not just for the understanding of the man himself, but for understanding myself and my culture.

As for our journey, Ivan's and mine, I hope it reflects how the simple act of spending time in a mutual pursuit, with no expectations, can create a powerful bond, heal past wounds, and reaffirm the strength of the love between a father and his daughter.

Family Photos

Volodimir Kochan 1930s

Pani Lyda 1930s

Ivan Kochan 1942

Tatiana Sawycka 1942

Yarko Kochan, Ivan's brother

Mitonko, Ivan's cousin

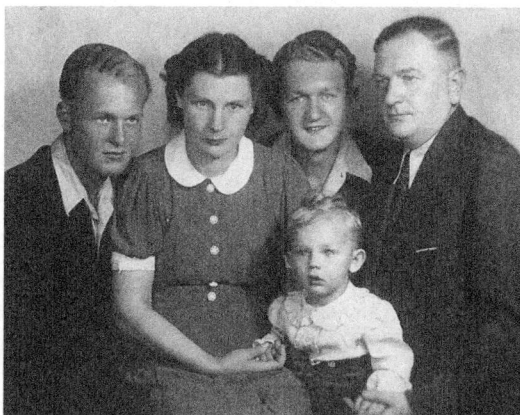

Kochan family 1948, left to right; Ivan, Pani Lyda,
Yarko, Volodimir and Roman in front

Sawycka family 1948, left to right: Tatiana, Natalia, Adela and Elizabeta Ginejko

Ivan and Tatiana's engagement 1948 Munich

Tatiana after coming to California 1948

Acknowledgements

Finishing my father's memoirs has proven to be a fulfilling yet time-consuming venture. Thanks to my very patient husband Don Joy, for his support and belief in my ability to finish the book even when I had my doubts. My children have also listened to me and given technical advice at various stages and I appreciate their confidence in me. I am particularly happy that each of them, Daniel, Peter, and Larissa had a good relationship with their "Dido" Ivan and can now appreciate this man for the many things he endured and overcame. Thanks also to my dear friend Ann Perry who encouraged my writing and believed in the historical significance of my father's story, not to mention her very careful proofreading skills. The history in the book was significantly bolstered by historian and editor Mark Collins Jenkins. My father's memory was excellent but Mark contributed weight, poetry and accuracy to his words. I need to thank him for encouraging me as well to write from my heart.

As the child of immigrants, I now recognize the intergenerational trauma that is carried in all our family histories and probably in our DNA. It is now easier for me to understand the struggle of oppressed peoples; of native and indigenous peoples, of black Americans and, yes, Ukrainians; all having decades and more often generations of ancestors who have fought not only for their families' rights, but their very right to exist. I hope we never forget how to stand up for that right and maybe someday we won't have to.

Slava Ukraina!

Printed in Great Britain
by Amazon